Natural Law Ethics

Recent Titles in
Contributions in Philosophy

Understanding Confucian Philosophy: Classical and Sung-Ming
Sue-hsien Liu

Myths of Freedom: Equality, Modern Thought, and Philosophical Radicalism
Stephen L. Gardner

Platonic Errors: Plato, a Kind of Poet
Gene Fendt and David Rozema

Asian and Jungian Views of Ethics
Carl B. Becker, editor

The Last Choice: Preemptive Suicide in Advanced Age, Second Edition
C. G. Prado

Self-Construction and the Formation of Human Values: Truth, Language, and Desire
Teodros Kiros

Diogenes of Sinope: The Man in the Tub
Luis E. Navia

Simone de Beauvoir Writing the Self: Philosophy Becomes Autobiography
Jo-Ann Pilardi

Stalking Nietzsche
Raymond Angelo Belliotti

The Transient and the Absolute: An Interpretation of the Human Condition and of Human Endeavor
Mordecai Roshwald

The Adventure of Philosophy
Luis E. Navia

Intentionalist Interpretation: A Philosophical Explanation and Defense
William Irwin

Natural Law Ethics

Philip E. Devine

Contributions in Philosophy, Number 72

GREENWOOD PRESS
Westport, Connecticut • London

Library of Congress Cataloging-in-Publication Data

Devine, Philip E., 1944–
Natural law ethics / Philip E. Devine.
p. cm.—(Contributions in philosophy, ISSN 0084–926X ; no. 72)
Includes bibliographical references and index.
ISBN 0–313–30702–4 (alk. paper)
1. Ethics. 2. Natural law. I. Title. II. Series.
BJ1012.D455 2000
171′.2—dc21 99–25006

British Library Cataloguing in Publication Data is available.

Library of Congress Catalog Card Number: 99–25006
ISBN: 0–313–30702–4
ISSN: 0084–926X

First published in 2000

Greenwood Press, 88 Post Road West, Westport, CT 06881
An imprint of Greenwood Publishing Group, Inc.
www.greenwood.com

Printed in the United States of America

The paper used in this book complies with the Permanent Paper Standard issued by the National Information Standards Organization (Z39.48–1984).

10 9 8 7 6 5 4 3 2 1

For Celia

Seek the welfare of the city where I have sent you into exile.

—Jeremiah 29:7 (RSV)

Contents

Preface

This is a book about grounding ethics and morality in human nature. In my view, Aristotle and St. Thomas Aquinas are right about the core issues, though I do not commit myself to following their judgments in detail.

One of the most persistent issues in ethical theory is to what extent we can expect to resolve moral issues by reason, and to what extent emotions, and the contingencies of an individual's moral formation, are decisive. Even the most determined rationalists admit persistent obstacles to moral rationality, and sophisticated emotivists concede that our attempts to sort out our feelings at least mimic reasoning. In my own view, moral judgments are like judgments about controversial historical events, and about the character of historical actors (including the way in which they would have behaved had circumstances been different). One's position reflects the sort of person one is, but reasons can be given for our positions, and we have no reason to deny the existence of truth.

Another much discussed issue concerns the mutual relations of goods, virtues, duties, and rights. Traditionally, the first three of these concepts were closely linked. Rights can also be fit into this frame, though their political ramifications place them further from the center of ethics proper than goods, obligations, and virtues.

I also discuss selected moral issues—lying, suicide, sexual questions including homosexuality, and the claims of nonhuman nature—selecting them, not merely for their inherent interest, but for their strategic position, without, however, claiming to be able to deduce concrete moral positions from principles of ethical theory. Issues of social justice must await an attempt to apply the theory developed here to political and jurisprudential questions.

Morality makes sense only as part of a larger understanding of human nature, and, at least by implication, of all that there is. The attempt to probe fully the question of natural law will, moreover, lead us into theological territory, including a glance at the doctrine of hell. As George Marsden has pointed out, it is absurd to ask Christians or other believers to stay in the closet when intellectual and cultural issues are debated; Christianity also forms part of the shared cultural tradition on which all philosophers, whatever their personal persuasion, need to reflect.

Like nearly all writers on natural law, I write under the influence of the Roman Catholic tradition, though at the initial stages of this project this influence was remote and indirect. This book remains, in any case, a work of moral philosophy, not of moral theology, and it is not appropriate for a philosopher to treat revelation or communal authority as a substitute for his proper inquiries. Revealed norms might go beyond what can be established by natural reason, or support positions less plausible to the unaided mind than their denials, but there are ill-defined limits on how far this sort of tension can go without destroying the credibility of the supposed revelation. Philosophers are, however, no better than workers in liquor stores in their ability to see that cult leaders do not speak for God when they counsel self-castration and suicide, or call upon their followers to feed cyanide to their children. Neither grace and nature, nor general revelation and the outcome of unaided reasoning, can be distinguished by inspection.

The most challenging opponents of the natural law tradition are thus Calvinists, who claim that truth (including truth about human nature) is inaccessible to the reprobate mind, and hence that ethics requires special revelation. The implication, that moral discourse is possible only among the redeemed, is echoed in practice by the secular relativism prevailing in much elite culture; and the result is covertly allied to libertinism, which argues that, since virtue is impossible, we might as well make peace with our vices.

This book is the fourth of a series. *The Ethics of Homicide* (1978) attempts a systematic discussion of a family of moral issues turning on what human beings owe one another just as such. *Relativism, Nihilism, and God* (1990) is concerned about upholding the concept of truth (and indeed of Truth) against relativists and the nihilists they engender. *Human Diversity and the Culture Wars* (1996) argues that, precisely in view of the diversity of human beings, there is a need to look for a common human nature.

This work has had a long prehistory. A year (1980–81) as a Liberal Arts Fellow at the Harvard Law School confirmed for me the necessity of addressing core issues in moral theory, and the need for natural law perspective on jurisprudence; further stimulus was provided by a number of seminars and institutes sponsored by the National Endowment for the Humanities, especially those held under

Ralph McInerny (1985) and Norman Daniels (1988). Special thanks are due to the late Father Lockary, C.S.C., for providing me with access to the excellent computer at Stonehill College, on which I wrote an ancestor of this book while I was Professor in Residence there, and to Dr. Ray Pepin for continuing my account. The final work was done while on sabbatical from Providence College, and I am grateful to the College for its support.

The comments of an anonymous reader, and conversations with friends and colleagues—including Myron Anderson, Peter Garber, Jim Gordley, David Jacobosky, James Hanink, James Nelson, George Rutherglen, and Patrick Walker—shaped the argument of this book in its early phases, at points too numerous to list in detail. Thanks are also due to Gary Culpepper, Pawel Ozdowski, Robert Rafalko, the Rev. Ronald Tacelli, S.J., Michael Tori, John Wagner, and Michael Wreen for reading parts of the final version in draft, to Robert Pontbriand for useful conversations, and to Stanley Hauerwas for illuminating correspondence. Thanks also to Patrick for proofreading, and to Joseph Ryshpan for preparing a camera ready version of the manuscript. My debt, both personal and intellectual, to Celia Wolf-Devine is as always incalculable: I have abandoned the attempt to specify the many places in which her insights have enriched my argument. Portions of chapter 12 appeared as "A Fallacious Argument against Moral Absolutes," *Argumentation* 9, no. 4 (November 1995), pp.611–16, and are reprinted with kind permission from Kluwer Academic Publishers.

Disliking loyalty oaths, I use "he" as a common gender pronoun, except when specifically referring to a male individual, or when it is specially important to emphasize that the class in question includes females as well as males. I use the capitalized "He" for God, without implying anything about God's gender. I have consulted the original of all Latin philosophical texts quoted, and used the existing translations eclectically. For ecclesiastical documents I have made do with translations.

Introduction: The Need for Natural Law

The natural law tradition, though frequently debunked, reappears whenever the dangers of moral chaos become evident to all observers.[1] Thomas Aquinas is the paradigmatic figure for the tradition, writing under favorable conditions of religious homogeneity. But after the breakup of united Christendom, natural law writers attempted to derive a moral code from premises available to unaided reason, in order to replace the code promulgated by the medieval Church, and make possible moral discussion across national and confessional boundaries.

A common theme in the natural law tradition is the unity of humanity, and consequently the existence of goods, virtues, and moral principles accessible to, and binding upon, men and women as such. Universal human rights also flow naturally from a natural law perspective, though not more easily than universal human goods and universal human virtues. Natural law theorists affirm, moreover, that questions of the good and right are matters of knowledge and truth in as good a sense as, or better than, that of natural science. Thus natural law rejects conventionalism and historicism, where these are understood as reaching all the way down, as versions of the ancient idea that might makes right. It also rejects those religious doctrines that affirm that human nature is so corrupt that we cannot attain moral knowledge by our unaided reason, whereas harmonizing with more moderate strands in the Christian tradition.

Philosophers have distinguished between morals and ethics. Morals concerns our day-to-day life, while ethics is a theoretical reflection on morals. Morals proceeds along its own paths, with only occasional interventions from ethics. Reasoning about ethical theory proceeds most easily among those who share a rich set of moral judgments—including a reasonably concrete conception of virtue. There are concrete moral positions characteristic of natural law ethicists, as of utilitarians and pagan Kantians. (I use this phrase to describe philosophers, such as John Rawls and even more so David Richards, who emphasize Kant's independence of moral and religious tradition, and in so doing depart from many of his concrete moral judgments.) Nor are theology and its analogues easily avoided: even among atheists, natural insight—the so-called "click of recognition"—is sometimes given a force comparable to that of divine revelation in Judaism, Christianity, and Islam—and there are secular counterparts to excommunication as well.

The most pervasive problem for philosophical ethics is the absence of consensus about moral issues, both among self identified philosophers and among the rest of the human population. Moral conflict presents a political as well as a philosophical problem. In the absence of shared premises, it is not possible to settle political disputes by rational argument. Hence mutual avoidance (including avoidance of "sensitive" topics), rhetorical intimidation, and coercion step into the gap. Moreover, people are entirely prepared to renounce shared premises when they have, or appear to have, unacceptable consequences in some sensitive area—often going beyond the requirements of logic when they do so. It is always possible to try to "bork" the most challenging of one's opponents, but positions consigned to the closet have a way of returning to haunt us. (To *bork* is to place outside the mainstream, after the would-be Supreme Court Justice against whom this tactic was used.) It is one aim of natural law ethics, as part of the broader enterprise of philosophy, to avoid such measures so far as possible.

The aim of this book is to continue the natural law tradition by providing a contemporary statement of the theory that assimilates some post-Kantian epistemological insights. In that way I hope to contribute to a reintegration of the Western ethical tradition, rather than producing an account of natural law ethics, that whatever its official claims to universality, abandons any attempt rationally to persuade the "gentiles."[2] I thus consider the anti-theoretical turn in ethics,[3] which challenges natural law as much as do Kantian and utilitarian ethics.[4] I also examine the critique of the ethics of rights and principles by some exponents of virtue ethics, the related appeal to the feminine as opposed to the masculine voice, the special appeal to narrative ethics; and the argument that we are dealing, not just with divergent moral views, but with at least partly incommensurable moral languages.

Even if there is a common human nature with normative implications, it is discovered in historical/social processes of human interaction, whose mark it always bears. The goods, obligations, rights, and virtues it implies come to us encased in the institutional and affective context in which we come to be as moral agents, and in which we receive our moral education. If we assert rights against society as a whole, we must appeal to shared moral and political beliefs, and not to our own private sense of entitlement. Burke, in his defense of private (and especially church) property rights, forgets Henry VIII's seizure of the monasteries.

Critics of appeals to tradition cite Franz Jäggerstäter who, despite the contrary judgment of the local religious authorities, refused service in Hitler's army and was hanged for it.[5] But, though Jäggerstäter opposed the dominant voices of both Church and State, he did so in the name of precepts that had long been given at least lip service within his community. He did not invent the just war tradition, nor was he in any other sense a moral radical. No moral theory can make decisions such as his easy.

I will formulate my response to moral historicism in terms of a weakened (though not utterly debilitated) sense of moral realism. Statements of principle and value, I shall argue, are true or false in as good a sense as those of science, but I will have little need or use for "moral facts" to which moral statements correspond or fail to correspond. The upshot will be natural law with a Kantian face, one that allows for postulates whose acceptance is a matter of rational faith and hope (emphasizing *rational* as much as *faith* and *hope*), rather than of knowledge in the strictest sense. Claims to moral truth and claims about human nature both are warranted by their internal coherence and their adequacy to prereflective moral experience rather than by self-evident insights into Being or supraempirical human nature.

Natural law ethics harmonizes with natural law jurisprudence. I take it to be central to natural law jurisprudence that moral argument is central to legal argument, though not necessarily that law is simply an arrangement for backing our moral judgments with collective force. Legislators, judges, and executives are people, too, and virtue and wickedness remains virtue and wickedness despite their offices. This consideration does not preclude taking into account the distinctive features of official role morality, only requiring us to insist that this morality cannot be isolated from the morality that applies to human beings as such. The importance of appeals to nature in unsettled times cannot be contradicted, but it is difficult to introduce natural law ideas into the day-to-day workings of a judicial system.[6] Moreover, as a school of jurisprudence asserting the existence of a higher law, natural law can use any brand of ethics.

There is no irreconcilable conflict between natural law legal theory and other schools of thought such as legal positivism[7] and moderate realism. All schools of jurisprudence acknowledge that our world is riven with deep conflicts, and that consequently a legal system requires more than the reasonableness of its rules to keep it going. A defender of natural law jurisprudence can concede that rules of law need to be promulgated by competent authority (and thus that a legal system requires "rules of recognition"); that moral considerations limit the use of the law to impose moral judgments, particularly on those who do not accept them; and that law, to be law, must be embodied in a set of working institutions.[8]

An inquiry such as this will inevitably be unfinished. I shall, for example, be able to consider non-Western conceptions of natural law only briefly, though the notions of *tao*[9] and *dharma*[10] are of relevance to the concerns of this book. Those who need more certainty than philosophy can provide to deal with the stresses of our public and private lives must seek it elsewhere.

Part I

Preliminaries

Chapter 1

What Can Philosophy Do?

Natural law ethics supposes that any person can reason with any other, regardless of either person's cultural formation, religious beliefs, or political allegiance. (Utilitarian and Kantian ethics are special cases of the natural law tradition in this broad sense, though both of them reflect a truncated view of human nature.) In this chapter, I first address the issues of whether clarity of language is enough, and whether philosophy can supply us with self-evident moral truth. I shall then defend the methodology of this book, which takes questions of moral epistemology as central.

IS CLARITY ENOUGH?

Heidegger held that the attempts, which go back to Socrates and Plato, to advance philosophical discussion by clarifying concepts, are examples of the cardinal "sin" of *Seinsvergessenheit.* He ended where the positivists thought he should have begun, in a silence reminiscent of the doctrine of the Nameless God (in this respect echoing the early Wittgenstein).[1] Yet an attempt at linguistic clarity is inherent in any drawing of the line between what is acceptable and what is not, and in any refutation of sophistical endeavors to erase the boundary, or move it for the sake of some interest or passion. To that end we have either to use existing language precisely, or to invent a new language to make the distinctions we are interested in making.

Nonetheless, the attempt to make philosophical problems go away by untying verbal knots has failed, and it is important to see why. There are concepts—call them *essentially contested*—whose sense, reference, and evaluative force is a matter not merely of philosophical but also of cultural and political debate. A title such as *The Real Meaning of Academic Freedom*[2] signals the presence of such a concept, since it expresses a need to combat false and distorted concepts that have gained currency among the users of the relevant language. Definitions of contested concepts are persuasive in intention, since, in regularizing usage, they extend good words to things we favor, and bad words to things we oppose. Hence analyses of contested concepts are normative descriptions.

It is not possible to resolve these issues by combining linguistic clarity with an emotivist theory of value. Rape, for example, cannot be defined as "intercourse without consent, boo!" since our disputes about its application concern the parameters of consent and the sorts of behavior that constitute intercourse. No doubt the desire to avoid or impose the *boo!* is an impulse shaping our analysis, but not just any *boo!* is at stake. For a man or woman may behave quite badly, even in a sexual context, without being guilty of rape.

THE QUESTION OF SELF-EVIDENCE

The association between the natural law tradition and claims to self-evidence has always been tight. Yet common sense in Lincoln, Nebraska, is not the same thing as common sense in Cambridge, Massachusetts; and common sense around Providence College is not the same as common sense around Brown University.[3] The issue here is whether there are self-evident moral truths, and if so, whether philosophy can discover them. We are here concerned, not with the right answers to disputed moral questions, but rather with which premises can be taken for granted in our attempts to resolve moral questions.

Most people's firmest moral convictions, to which they might easily attach the label "self-evident," are to be found at the concrete level. Even philosophers are often more concerned about defending their concrete moral judgments than with advancing their more rarefied investigations. (Unfortunately their judgments often differ, in much the same way as the judgments of nonphilosophers do.) Philosophers would do well to get their cultural anthropology right: despite a persistent legend among bioethicists, the Nuer did not justify infanticide by claiming that defective newborns were hippopotami.[4] Yet actions in breach of moral principles that intelligent people have regarded as self-evident have been entrenched in the practices of many societies, including our own. Thus "commonsense" approaches to morality end up as appeals to tribal sentiment, and invocations of self-evidence turn into demands for faith.

One can avoid these problems by appealing to principles at a sufficiently high level of abstraction. Defenders of bullfighting do not concede that the bull is tortured "just for fun": they adduce ill-defined cultural and aesthetic goods in defense of the sport. Nor did the Nazis concede that they were killing their victims for light reasons: they either denied that "subhumans" were people, or else provided a justification in terms either of protecting the Aryan race against pollution, or of putting an end to the misery of creatures whose lives were no longer worth living.

Although self-evident truths are hard to find, self-evident falsehoods are in abundant supply. John Finnis has persuasively argued that it is self-destructive to maintain that truth is not a good, since those who maintain this position hold that it is true, and call for our assent to it as such.[5]

Arguments from self-refutation, though very powerful, work only within a dialectical context. They depend, that is, on the assumptions I share with my opponents, many of which are tacit or embedded in a shared language. Hence their results can always be disrupted by the emergence of considerations or positions that no party to the original debate had imagined. To hold that truth is a good, however, is not yet to say how conflicts between truth and other goods such as peace of mind or social harmony are to be adjudicated. Nor is it to settle the question whether truth is to be understood as correspondence with extramental reality, as idealized warranted assertability, or in some other way.

However decisively we may think we have refuted our opponents, they may derive new versions of old positions by developing our language in a creative way, or even by inventing a new language. Descartes may have refuted the materialist position that he was nothing more than a body, but he did not refute the Hume-inspired view that he was entitled, not to *I think,* but only to *it thinks here.* Likewise, there is the constant possibility of new moral languages embodying moral attitudes whose expression we believe ourselves to have refuted; though nearly all of these will be foolish or evil, a few may make possible a better sort of life for human beings. Hence self-referential arguments do not establish a sufficient basis either for ethical theory or for moral reasoning.

That someone disagrees with me is no argument that I am wrong. It does tend to show, however, that my judgment is not self-evident, that is, that I am not entitled to assert it without argument (or at least defense).[6]

It is always easy to explain why someone does not find self-evident what I find so. Once a moral error becomes entrenched, some people will reject all the premises of any argument designed to displace it, even those I might find self-evident. A woman once suggested to me that the sexual judgments of males from puberty to middle age are distorted by testosterone poisoning. People raised in patriarchal or racist societies find it hard to believe that women or members of minority racial groups are, in the full sense, persons. It is hard for a job seeker facing a difficult market to evaluate calmly the arguments concerning the justice of preferential affirmative action. Those who habitually violate conventional norms of morality have an emotional investment in concluding that these norms are wrong and that those who enunciate them are fools or worse. Even the innocent beneficiaries of injustice acquire a vested interest in its continuance, which may make sound judgment difficult. As a last resort we can add the doctrine of original sin (the one Christian dogma for which there is powerful empirical evidence). These explanations of moral error are so powerful, however, as to engulf the practitioner of natural law himself. For we are not entitled to argue as if we, alone among our species, are without traits of character that distort our judgment.

The best procedure, in the light of these considerations, is to excise appeals to self-evidence from the corpus of natural law theory. For rational vindication is not the same thing as self-evidence.[7] It is sufficient that our conclusions be true, that we have good reasons for believing them, that we can refute all reasonable objections to them, and that we have reason to hope that our opponents will come to agree with us, if only they are prepared to listen to our arguments.

We begin with our practices as we find them, including the pervasive moral controversies that attend them, make the judgments they require, elicit and refine their governing principles, defend these principles against criticisms, and make such changes in them as critical thought may require. How far such reflection may take us from our starting point cannot be decided in advance. Our tradition—at least if "we" are either Christians or Americans—includes natural law elements. Critics of the resulting blend of natural law ethics and methodological conservatism maintain that it may counsel acquiescence in nefarious practices when they have become socially entrenched. But among the most important features of the natural law tradition is the insistence that the dissenter, even if opposed by the majority, the cultural elite, and those in power may nonetheless be right (Jeffrey Stout's "cautionary use of *true*").[8]

The abandonment of claims to self-evidence does not mean skepticism at the practical level. All versions of the *principle of preclusion,* which bars individual or collective action on a principle on the grounds that it is controversial, are to be rejected.[9] To abandon a principle of action because some people reject it with a show of reason is quickly to deprive oneself of any principles of action. (There is a show of reasons against liberalism, and for fascism.) Moreover, the principle of preclusion defeats itself, since many people reject it with considerable show of reason. For the same reasons, we ought to reject the suggestion that the fact that our having every reason to accept some practical principle implies that no one can reject it in good faith.

TRANSITION TO MORAL EPISTEMOLOGY

In a world in which divergent views about normative questions are advanced with vigor, the question, How do you know? cannot be long avoided. Some neo-

Thomists try to circumvent such issues by a direct appeal to "a metaphysical intuition of Being."[10] Not everyone claims to have such an intuition of Being, and people who do claim to have one draw very different implications from it. In any event, to begin with a developed metaphysics, and to generate one's ethics out of it, is to subordinate all other questions, however great their practical urgency, to that of persuading people to accept one's metaphysics.

The coherence theory of moral truth suggested by the argument so far leads to the worry that our thought might amount to "a frictionless spinning in a void," as John McDowell has put it.[11] If the only check on our reflections is coherence and agreement with our pre-reflective moral experience, what is preventing us from concluding that we may be deeply out of touch with moral or other reality? A fully adequate reply to this point must await a detailed working out of an alternative moral epistemology. For the moment it suffices to say that coherence is only one criterion of moral knowledge, and that spontaneous moral perceptions, though always contestable, nonetheless have some weight in moral judgment.

Chapter 2

The Epistemological Issues (1)

At the core of the natural law tradition are two propositions. (1) What makes for a good human being, and what is good for a human being, are functions of what a human being is. (2) It is possible for human beings to know what a human being is, and hence also to know what is good for a human being, as well as how human beings should live. The aim of this chapter is to articulate the state of the question in the theory of knowledge, in order to see what lessons can be drawn for the epistemology of morals.[1]

A NEW RESEARCH PROGRAM IN EPISTEMOLOGY

Many writers have maintained that epistemology is now undergoing a paradigm shift, away from that established by Descartes to one influenced by Wittgenstein and Heidegger. Charles Taylor goes so far as to reject epistemology as "the Hydra whose serpentine heads wreak havoc throughout the intellectual culture of modernity."[2] Alvin Plantinga, however, has persuasively responded that such claims confuse species with genus—in this case, foundationalist epistemology with epistemology generally.[3]

I here replace *paradigm* with Imre Lakatos's expression *research program*:[4] I understand a research program to be a set of working hypotheses and methods of investigation, whose validation rests in part on their success in practice. To propose a new research program is to issue a promissory note on the future of inquiry (as is also the case of those who resist such a research program in depth, rather than simply articulating obstacles to it). I thus invite my readers to accept provisionally the perception that the epistemological tradition that began with Descartes and reached its culmination in the logical positivists has exhausted its possibilities, and that a new research program is therefore required. The proof of this perception will be its fruits for our understanding of knowledge (in this book, knowledge of value and obligation).

The new research program rejects *foundationalism,* or the view that claims to know are warranted (note the legal metaphor) only if they are themselves self-evident first principles or are derived from such principles.[5] By *warrant* I mean whatever a belief must have, besides truth, to count as knowledge. My usage is thus neutral concerning the questions of *internalism*—whether warrants must always be accessible to the knowing subject himself—and *fallibilism*—whether there can be such a thing as a warranted false belief.[6] It also affirms that knowers do not passively receive, but rather actively construct, their pictures of the world. Finally, it affirms the social dimension of human knowing, as represented by scientific community. To the contrary, *classical realists* hold that we have direct knowledge of things as they are in themselves, whereas *classical foundationalists* hold that all our claims to know must either be self-evident themselves or derived from self-evident premises.[7]

There is no way to decisively settle the question of whether we have direct knowledge of things in themselves. Any attempt to prove such knowledge impossible must invoke premises concerning how things are apart from human knowing, and on their own principles, skeptics about knowledge of things in themselves cannot know that such premises are true.[8] Nonetheless, we have enough experience of the cultural conditioning of our claims to know, and of the distorting influence of culture on other people and our past selves, to place the burden of proof on those who would assert culture-independent knowing in any concrete case.

As for classical realism, so for foundationalism. To prove that self-evident foundations for knowledge are impossible would require the very sorts of premises antifoundationalists refuse to accept. We would have to deduce the nonexistence of indubitable first principles from indubitable first principles. Yet this sort of response fails to supply us with the foundations that, foundationalists hold, are required for knowledge.

SOME EPISTEMOLOGICAL PRINCIPLES

1. The Antifoundationalist Principle

Let us provisionally accept the *antifoundationalist principle:*

> Neither philosophers nor anyone else can refound knowledge *de novo* from self-evident principles.

This principle does not assert the nonexistence of such principles, only their inaccessibility to human knowers.

2. The Hermeneutical Principle

We can avoid skepticism by conjoining the antifoundationalist principle with the *hermeneutical principle:*

> All inquirers must proceed by interpreting and applying the standards of judgment supplied by their cultural heritage. As Otto Neurath observed, we are sailors required to repair our ship on the open sea, never able to put it into drydock.

Antifoundationalist principles are workable so long as we are engaged in an ongoing intellectual and cultural enterprise, whose rules are often enough observed in practice to make coherent discourse possible. In more extreme situations, when we are dealing with pervasive doubts about the seaworthiness of our epistemic vessel, as well as with persistent mutinies among the crew, antifoundationalism is of less use.

3. Methodological Conservatism

An immediate consequence of the hermeneutical principle is *methodological conservatism:*

> We are entitled to believe whatever we believe, for whatever reasons we believe it, until a persuasive argument for doing otherwise comes along. Doubt as much as belief requires a justification.[9]

One objection to methodological conservatism concerns beliefs whose grounds have been forgotten. Suppose someone keeps me supplied with scandal about my colleagues: I believe him at the time, but later come to realize that he is unreliable. Yet I continue to believe some of the stories he told me, at least insofar as they conform to my prejudices. It would not seem that I am warranted in so doing. Furthermore, my beliefs may be formed according to unconscious processes such that, if I knew of them, I would question their products.

My claims to know can be defeated, not only by direct refutation, but by discrediting the grounds on which I hold them.[10] I may have forgotten, or even never have been conscious of, the grounds of my judgments, but as soon as I realize that a belief rests entirely on an unreliable basis, I should abandon it. If I come to hold a philosophy that implies the unreliability of all my judgments (or all my judgments in a given area), I need not wait upon detailed refutation to abandon these judgments. But until a persuasive argument for such a philosophy is made out, I am entitled—as methodological conservatism implies—to believe whatever I believe.

Excursus: Coherence

1. To show that coherence is not sufficient for warrant, Plantinga[11] asks us to

> consider the case of the Epistemically Inflexible Climber. Ric is climbing Guide's Wall, on Storm Point in the Grand Tetons; having led the difficult next to last pitch, he is sitting on a comfortable ledge, bringing his partner up. He believes that Cascade Canyon is down to his left, that there is a hawk gliding in lazy circles 200 feet below him, that he is wearing his new *Fire* rock shoes, and so on. His beliefs, we may stipulate, are coherent. Now add that Ric is struck by a wayward burst of high energy radiation. This induces a cognitive malfunction; his beliefs become fixed, no longer responsive to changes in his experience. No matter what his experiences his beliefs remain the same. (p. 82)

2. To show that coherence is not necessary, he poses the following case:

> I am an arboreal expert giving a lecture on trees; among other things I claim that no oak trees grow in Washington State. Naturally I believe that I have never seen an oak tree in any part of that state. I suddenly notice you in the audience. Seeing you jogs my memory; I seem to remember a particularly luxuriant oak flourishing on the campus of Western Washington University in Bellingham. At the moment that it seems to me that I do so remember, the proposition that I have seen an oak tree in Washington has warrant for me, despite the fact that it does not cohere with my noetic structure. (p. 83)

In both of these cases, something has gone wrong in a person's cognitive apparatus. This is evident in Ric's case, but in the case of the arboreal expert, we must suppose that something has gone wrong as well. Otherwise, a conspicuous counterexample to the belief that no oak trees grow in Washington State could not have escaped his attention. We can thus understand coherence, not as a criterion of warrant, but as a standard that specifies what the believing subject can do of himself to achieve warrant (call it *justification*).

4. The Principle of Theory and Practice

One consequence of the hermeneutical principle is *the principle of theory and practice:*

> The way that some form of inquiry is carried on in fact is relevant to the normative methodological standards philosophers are entitled to assert. If theory conflicts with practice, there is no general rule which of them is to be preferred.

Our cultural heritage includes a variety of forms of inquiry, carried on in accordance with rough principles defining success and failure. Methodological conservatism and the principle of theory and practice do not exclude critique of these practices, but do prohibit proposals for change that would, if adopted, make any form of inquiry impossible.

5. The Principle of Context

The discussion so far implies the *principle of context:*

> The degree and sort of warrant required for our beliefs depends on the sorts of evidence available to us, and the moral and other issues at stake in the investigation.

Hence, for example, W.K. Clifford's critique of our right to hold religious beliefs on less-than-compelling reasons is unsound, since it treats as of universal validity principles drawn from cases where unwarranted belief endangers the lives and reputations of other people.

The principle of context coheres with a popular though controversial contemporary definition of *knowledge:*

> *S* knows that *p* if and only if
> (i) *p* is true;
> (ii) *S* believes that *p;*
> (iii) *S* has justifying evidence for believing that *p;*

(iv) There is no proposition *d* that factually defeats *S*'s evidence for believing that *p*.[12]

What counts as justifying evidence, and what counts as defeat, will be context-dependent.[13]

6. The Proactive Principle

Together with some elementary observations about the facts of inquiry, the principle of theory and practice implies the *proactive principle:*[14]

> We do not and should not passively receive data, but rather put questions to whatever sources of information we acknowledge.

It is the scientist's engagement with his subject matter, including the use of "theoretical" entities such as electrons to investigate other phenomena, that provides the most important source of support for a realist attitude toward microphysical entities.[15] Likewise, understanding what to do in complex and difficult situations begins by our doing the best we can in situations that are less complex.

7. The Social Principle

Even when we undertake inquiry alone, we use language and methods derived from the practice of others. Thus the principle of theory and practice also implies the *social principle:*

> Inquiry takes place within a context of shared belief (what "we believe" rather than what "I believe"). It is a collective activity, in which there is a place both for innovators and for conservers of tradition.

As C.A.J. Coady has observed,

> One needs intellectual autonomy to achieve a feasible degree of control over the beliefs one acquires and to ensure that one's thinking is appropriately responsive to one's actual cognitive history and present intellectual environment. None the less, the independent thinker is not someone who works out everything for herself, even in principle, but one who exercises a controlling intelligence over the input she receives

> from the normal sources of information whether their basis be individual or communal.[16]

Thus, for example, testimony as a source of knowledge cannot be reduced (to reasoning about the likely causal antecedents of other people's reports.[17] The evaluation of testimony is a complex practice in which historians, for example, blend considerations concerning the antecedent likelihood of the events reported with considerations concerning the trustworthiness and competence of the persons reporting them.

8. The Principle of the Inarticulate Background

The discussion so far implies the *principle of the inarticulate background:*

> The unstated assumptions within which we conduct inquiry can be articulated (and hence also evaluated) only in part. There always remains an inarticulate residue, which comes to consciousness only when it is challenged in some way.[18]

9. The Principle of Residual Pragmatism

Lastly, we may articulate the principle of *residual pragmatism:*

> When all other criteria of warranted belief have been exhausted, we are entitled to adopt those beliefs among the options remaining that enable us to pursue the good life as we understand it.

That pragmatism is for me a residual principle circumvents many of the standard objections to it (for example, that it presupposes standard conceptions of truth and knowledge).

10. Concluding Remarks

We may refer to the principles defended in this section collectively as "the antifoundationalist principle and its allies." The antifoundationalist principles and its allies also cohere with the "foundherentism" formulated by Susan Haack. In her words:

> (FH1) A subject's experience is relevant to the justification of his empirical beliefs, but there need be no privileged class of empirical

> beliefs justified exclusively by the support of experience, independently of the support of other beliefs; . . .
> (FH2) Justification is not exclusively one-directional, but involves pervasive relations of mutual support.[19]

Our claims to know are secure when there are pervasive relations of mutual support among inherited standards of judgment and the spontaneous beliefs generated by experience, and insecure when these beliefs come into pervasive conflict.

Our answer to the suggestion that our defeasible principles are all wrong must be the same as Haack's: that if we cannot trust our existing ways of knowledge, inquiry will be impossible.[20] The probability that our faculties are reliable is inscrutable, not in the sense that can be assimilated to 0.5, but rather in the sense that we do not even know what an inquiry into their reliability (or their reliability on evolutionary or theistic premises) would be like.[21] Views that imply that, under such circumstances, we should abandon our claims to know fail of warrant by their own criteria. An example is the reduction of our claims to know to our responses, as organisms, to our natural and social environment.

The antifoundationalist principle and its allies apply to all forms of human inquiry, ranging from scientific reasoning to the attempt of a group of believers to discern the will of God.[22] The argument for these principles rests, first, on their ability to explain the phenomena of human knowledge; and, second, on the failure of the foundationalist project (and in particular its failure to refute skepticism). We here observe a circularity built into the deep structure of epistemology itself: our evaluation of epistemological proposals must depend on our implicit theory of knowledge. Nonetheless, the antifoundationalist principle and its allies do well by hermeneutical principles, whereas, if we ask, Why accept foundationalism? no answer, on foundationalist premises, is forthcoming.

Chapter 3

The Epistemological Issues (2)

The argument so far supports a family of epistemological principles, whose gist is that inquiry never begins de novo, but always involves the application and interpretation of preexisting norms; otherwise, total skepticism would ensue. Such principles apply to moral as well as other forms of reasoning.

GADAMER AND HABERMAS

To invoke the antifoundationalist principle and its allies is to enter the debate between Hans-Georg Gadamer and Jürgen Habermas, on the relative roles of hermeneutics and critique in human understanding.[1] I shall be brief and dogmatic about what I take to be the outcome of this debate.

> 1. Gadamer persuasively defends a good sense for the word *prejudice*—namely, those implicit understandings from which inquiry begins. He himself, however, is engaged in a tradition-transcending inquiry into the possibility of interpretation as such. Hence he abstracts interpretation as an activity from the theological, literary, and legal contexts in which it arose and developed. The conclusions of this inquiry, however meager, are intended to apply to all forms of reasoning, including "the revolutionary consciousness which unhinges the tradition through emancipatory reflection."[2]
>
> 2. Habermas equally persuasively defends the necessity of critique. He himself, however, is not generating critique ex nihilo, but working within two complexly related traditions. The first of these is "a tradition of thought that unites Marx and Freud."[3] The second is the

Enlightenment war against "dogmatism," and its search for a form of "mature autonomy" *(Mündigkeit)* carefully distinguished from the nihilism associated with Michel Foucault.[4]

3. Habermas is vulnerable to the charge of uncritical reliance on the authority of the Enlightenment, and of limiting his critique of dogmatism to the dogmas of other traditions, whereas Gadamer can claim to be turning the weapons of the Enlightenment against itself. Nonetheless, logical tangles arise when one attempts to develop Gadamer's argument in a positive way.

4. All thinkers work within some tradition, and all traditions I know of contain resources for self-criticism (though these are sometimes stifled in practice). Both hypertraditional societies, in which reasoning is the mere application of inherited standards, and hypermodern societies, for which all reasoning is conducted without reference to past thought, are illusions. In all those traditions influential in the West, the resources of self-criticism are abundant.

5. Without tradition, critical thinkers could not distinguish ruptures prompted by serious conviction from those resulting from mere passion, or important from trivial issues. Nor could they propose and defend alternatives to existing ways.

6. All traditions suffer from internal conflicts and ambiguities, and all arise and develop in circumstances that by their own standards are oppressive or otherwise disordered. There is such a thing as prejudice in the bad sense, and disordered forms of social life produce what Habermas has called "pseudo-communication."

7. Nonetheless, as Alasdair MacIntyre has incisively put it, "Claims about hallucination, illusion, distortion of thought, and the like can be made only from the standpoint of claims that the contrast can be clearly drawn between the hallucinatory, illusory, or distorted mode of perception or thought, on the one hand, and genuine perceptions of reality or rigorous and undistorted reflection and deliberation on the other. Hence, to identify ideological distortion one must not be a victim of it oneself. The claim to a privileged exemption from such distortion seems to be presupposed when such distortion is identified in others."[5] Hence the generalized hermeneutics of suspicion brings discourse to an end.

8. Partisan versions of the hermeneutics of suspicion are equally available to radicals and to conservatives. Both versions of the hermeneutics of suspicion are destructive of dialogue.

9. What appears to some people as a breakthrough to undistorted communication may appear to others as a new and more dangerous form of mystification. For example, the therapeutic model to which Habermas has appealed neglects the reality of social conflict, as well as patronizing both allies and adversaries.

10. To uncover distortions in communication, we are required to use the existing critical apparatus, including inherited conceptions of the sorts of prejudice most likely to distort judgment. Evaluating utterances is an art rather than a science.

PRAGMATISM, RELATIVISM, MARXISM, THEOLOGY

The question of human nature is central, not only to ethics and politics, but to the theory of knowledge. Attempts such as suggested by Dieter Heinrich to ground epistemology in a metaphysics of the knowing subject need to confront the issue of what features of knowing subjects are pertinent to knowledge.[6] (Do such projects as feminist epistemology make sense, for example?)[7]

Human nature in the sense relevant to epistemology includes its social and historical aspect. Marxists link theory and practice in a way that offers some prospects for a synthesis of realism and pragmatism.[8] We understand the world by changing it, and the test of our understanding it is the success of our practical endeavors. If there were indeed laws of history that guaranteed that some forms of political practice would fail and others succeed "in the long run," this answer to our perplexities would be extremely powerful. As things are, history leaves standing a wide variety of practical-theoretical approaches. Hence the danger of relativism (and of cultural and intellectual tribalism) remains acute.

Since I have defended pragmatism as a residual principle, I need to answer the question of whether it may also be taken as the sole or sovereign principle of inquiry. Pragmatists, if they are wise, leave *true* undefined and defend their position as a theory of warrant. (They may go further and propose warranted assertability as a substitute for truth.) They hold that a belief is warranted just in case its adoption by an inquirer will serve his ends. (Recall that by *warrant* I mean whatever a belief must have, besides truth, to count as knowledge.) Likewise, for a pragmatist, defeat consists in events in the inquirer's environment that obstruct his attainment of the desired results—a felt obstacle to activity that leads the inquirer to ask what went wrong. Of the many objections to pragmatism, I here limit myself to those that arise when we attempt to apply it to contested cultural and political issues—a set of problems no honest pragmatist can ignore.[9]

Pragmatism appears to encourage arguments of a most troubling sort. Political allegiance is often more or less consciously allowed to settle even questions of fact. Moreover, even if we grant that pragmatism is appropriate, we are faced with the problem of supporting the necessary prudential judgments. Dewey had more political sense than some philosophers, but was hardly infallible: he supported American participation in the First World War, but strongly opposed our entry into the Second. Thus it seems to me that we have strong *pragmatic* reasons to reject pragmatism, even as an account of warrant—except as a residual principle, when the ordinary criteria of warrant have been exhausted.

But what "works" for us will depend in part on the tradition from which we approach the question. If tradition has a role even in philosophical reasoning, the question of the boundary between philosophy and theology takes on a new look. The cultural and intellectual tradition on which philosophers are dependent is an intricate mixture of truth and error, of which no element is privileged prior to inquiry, and it includes Christianity as one of its elements. Hence we can avoid Russell Hittinger's description of the epistemological condition of modern natural law doctrines:

> The subject of natural law was placed in the most unfortunate position of being organized under two extreme poles. On the one end, it represented the conclusions of church authority; on the other it represented what every agent is supposed to know according to what is first in cognition. We have Cartesian minds somehow under church discipline.[10]

Pope Leo XIII, commending Thomism to the Roman Catholic faithful, wrote,

> those . . . who to the study of philosophy unite obedience to the Christian faith are philosophers indeed; for the splendor of divine truths, received into the mind, helps the understanding, and not only detracts in nowise from its dignity, but adds greatly to its nobility, keenness, and stability.[11]

On a strong reading of this encyclical, Leo XIII is placing the methods, premises, and conclusions of philosophical investigation under theological scrutiny in such a way as to abolish philosophy (and hence also natural law). A weaker reading is that it is good for a philosopher, even as a philosopher, to be a practicing and believing Christian. The resulting ambiguity pervades the encyclical itself,[12] as well as the Thomist revival founded upon it.[13]

We need not, in any case, despair of reason. For truth can function as a regulative ideal even where not as a name for a secure achievement. Moreover, some human perspectives include belief in a transcendent Judge, Who stands above human knowing and defines which of our perspectives is true. There is no way a relativist can exclude such a belief as false. Nonetheless, the philosophical attempt to address the whole human race is an aspiration, which in practice must be furthered by addressing one's opponents one at a time (or at least group by group), on the basis of their particular positions and the arguments they give for them.[14]

IMPLICATIONS FOR ETHICS

In ordinary English, the word *fact* is used freely: we talk of facts as entering into causal relationships, and of negative and disjunctive facts. We also speak of moral facts, as in, for example, "The fact that many social reformers have behaved very badly in their private lives needs to be taken into account in any understanding of political history." (Virtually any sentence can be introduced with the words *in fact.*)[15]

There are circumstances in which talk of moral facts, and our experience of them through something like a moral sense, is natural. If, looking out of a window, I see children pouring gasoline on a cat and setting it on fire, I see cruelty in as legitimate a sense as that in which I see the color of the cat's fur.[16] (If I call the children's act cruel, I am describing and not just evaluating it.) In somewhat similar ways, I can see the beauty of a natural landscape, or the ugliness of an automobile graveyard. Likewise, I can see that a three-legged dog is defective as a dog, that some modes of life pursued by human beings are defectively human. Some of our evaluative beliefs are "cognitively spontaneous," and hence (unless we reject moral realism on other grounds) can be thought of as results of encounters with extramental moral reality. Most of the time, however, moral facts are best understood as shadows of moral truths.

Yet moral judgment is linked to the nature of things in another way. The most powerful objection one can bring against a writer in special ethics is that he does not understand the activity that he is trying to regulate. "Your rules," we can say, "might be just fine for some fictional activity, but they have nothing to do with what men and women do when they engage in business, sex, or adjudication." For example, as Camille Paglia has insisted, the "handshake model" of human sexuality is so removed from actual human experience that it is not so much wrong as irrelevant. More broadly, our ethics depends on a background picture, first of human nature, and then of the cosmos or chaos in which humanity must somehow find its place. (MacIntyre neglects the cosmos-or-chaos question.) Positivist-inspired objections to this sort of reasoning are fundamentally mistaken, since our worldview will incorporate, among other things, our answer to questions about the possibility of happiness and the nature of moral obligation.[17]

There is no way of getting outside the human world, to compare our moral judgments with moral facts. If I describe an act as one of adultery or theft, I am making implicit reference to institutions—of marriage and property—that contain moral standards as among their constituent elements, and to which I myself and the adulterer or thief stand in some sort of relationship. It is not as if there were some premoral act of sexual intercourse or appropriation on which I then put a derogatory label of adultery or theft. Murder may seem a different case, since it involves among other things the destruction of an organism, but for killing to be murder this organism must be linked to agent and evaluator by some sort of bond, if only as a member of the same species. Even if all human organisms are, morally speaking, persons, the two concepts are not the same.

Some differences between moral truths and facts and their nonmoral counterparts nonetheless remain. Suppose that I hallucinated the children igniting the cat: I would still be justified in saying that actions of that sort are cruel and, for that reason, wrong. This observation suggests an analogy between moral truths and the necessary truths of mathematics. We experience an intellectual compulsion when confronted with necessary truths, as well as an intellectual repulsion when confronted with necessary falsehoods. We can thus understand "cruelty is bad" as like "1+1=2" and "cruelty is good" as like "1+1=3." Moreover, claims to a priori knowledge founded on our intuitive grasp of the necessity of propositions are defeasible (and hence not in the strict sense self-evident) in the same way the principles of ethics are. For some supposed bits of a priori knowledge, in the theory of sets, for example, lead to paradox. Hence, that different people find incompatible moral propositions self-evident is not a reason for rejecting the idea of defeasible a priori knowledge in ethics: one or both of these "self-evident" intuitions may end up defeated.[18]

Moral perception is, I suggest, sui generis, containing within itself intellectual, perceptual, and emotional elements. It is not possible to improve on Bishop Butler's paradoxical formulation: conscience is both "a sentiment of the understanding" and a "perception of the heart." In the view of knowledge adopted here, which links knowledge of all sorts to the practice of societies and the endeavor to change one's world or at least to live well within it, the emotional dimension of moral judgment is no threat to our claims to moral knowledge.

We are already engaged, when we begin philosophy, in forms of life having a normative aspect. We live in a world in which certain forms of speech are taken as promises, and therefore are such in the absence of reasons to the contrary; and similar things are true of the principles of evaluation implicit in the fact that a person is a husband, a college teacher, and a friend. Our knowing is thus permeated by our desires, our purposes, and our felt obligations from the very outset: even the sorts of theories scientists find acceptable depend, in part, on their conception of the aims of science and the virtues of a good scientist. Hence there is no radical fact-value divide.

We can claim to know that an action is wrong without having a worked-out theory in which this and other conclusions are deduced from axioms (or even such a theory limited to bioethical questions, for example). Human beings exercise their moral capacities in actual (or plausible imagined) circumstances, far better than when confronted by abstract moral propositions or science-fiction examples. A concentration on real or at least possible cases is therefore in order. It is not necessary to formulate moral rules to cover naturally impossible situations, such as injecting kittens to produce supercats with human intelligence.[19] Nor do we need to make rules to cover situations presuming knowledge that human beings cannot have, such as if I have sexual intercourse now, my great-great-grandson will be a mass murderer (and I will not have a great-great-granddaughter whose good deeds outweigh his crimes).

To be sure, we do not always know what is naturally possible. It is, however, always in order to point out, when confronted with a weird case, that so much needs to be different for such a case to arise that we can neglect it in practical reasoning. In moral education, we should equip our children for the world they will have to live in, not for some philosopher's fantasy world.

CONCLUSION

Four implications of this part are the most important. First, arguments about "facts" and arguments about "values" are alike in fundamental respects; though they can be distinguished at the surface, at the deepest level they fuse. Our most important concepts are both normative and descriptive in their import. Gilbert Harman has observed of *reasoning:*

> Normative and descriptive theories of reasoning are intimately related. For one thing, . . . it is hard to come up with convincing normative principles except by considering how people actually do reason, which is the province of a descriptive theory. On the other hand, it seems that any descriptive theory must involve a certain amount of idealization, and idealization is always normative to some extent.[20]

And what is true of *reasoning* is also true of *knowledge,* of *human nature,* of *morals,* and even of *philosophy:* accounts of each must both touch base with, and be normative for, what people actually say and do.

Second, all sorts of reasoning—about facts as much as about values—proceed in broadly the same way. We work with a body of received materials, and modify and extend it as seems warranted in view of experience and the arguments presented.

Third, our principles of both knowledge and evaluation are embodied in a conception of human nature. That it makes knowledge impossible, either absolutely or for human beings, is an objection to a theory of knowledge. It is likewise an objection to an ethical theory that people not only do not, but could never come to, value the things the theory proposes as good, or recognize the moral requirements it asks us to observe.

Fourth, these results cohere with the natural law tradition, for which there is no radical break between fact and value, and for which the normative principles relevant to human life are based on what human beings are.

Some critics might wonder whether these conclusions ground a sufficiently strong sense of moral realism to make natural law ethics feasible. You are rendering beliefs about human nature subjective—such an opponent might say—rather than providing a ground for the objectivity of morals in human nature. If the objectivity asked for here involves knowing things in a way not conditioned by any of the characteristics of the knower, such knowledge is not available to human beings (even if it is available to God), and is therefore irrelevant to ethics. If, on the other hand, we admit a human dimension to our knowing, we can come to know that dimension more fully as we come to know its objects, and thus both theoretical and practical reasoning can proceed.

To foundationalists I therefore say: We have moral knowledge, and such knowledge is enough for our purposes without claiming that it is in some stronger sense self-evident. We can therefore admit the insights of the hermeneutical tradition without surrendering anything of importance for morals. To antifoundationalists I say: Granting everything (or everything defensible) that you maintain, moral reasoning is still possible. Both foundationalists and antifoundationalists, therefore, can join in examining our common humanity, in search of common ground (and we may hope, some common ethical results).

Part II

Human Nature

Chapter 4

The Quest for the Self (1)

From one point of view, the persistence of moral disagreement consists in other people's obduracy in error. Viewed from another perspective, however, it is our difficulty in reaching consensus about a large and important range of issues, and the resulting use of coercion and deceit as ways of getting people to coordinate their behavior. From yet another perspective, it is the quandary of the individual caught in more than one social environment, who must somehow mediate their conflicting demands. For we are dealing with multiple social worlds, and not just divergent moral codes. People who say that fornication is a mortal sin do not merely disagree with those who say that sexual variety is liberating; they understand sexuality, marriage, and human relationships in ways that deeply conflict with that of their opponents.

One of the aims of natural law ethics is to find a common humanity that will allow such differences to be bridged. The core axiom of natural law ethics is as follows: *What is good for a human being, and what makes for a good human being, are functions of what a human being is.* It is necessary, if we are to ground ethics in human nature in the way this axiom requires, to develop a conception of what a human being is. We are each of us entitled, moreover, to begin by examining that sample of human nature that is closest to each of us. This examination will not be value free, since no inquiry into human matters can be value free, but it should be at least some distance from the moral conclusions we are trying to reach.

THE SEARCH FOR THE SELF BEGUN

Hume held that there was no "self" underlying all the perceptions that are attributed to it; in his own words:

> The mind is a kind of theatre, where several perceptions successively make their appearance, pass, re-pass, glide away, and mingle in an infinite variety of situations. . . . Nor have we the most distant notion of the place where these scenes are represented, or of the materials, of which it is compos'd.[1]

He made no attempt to bring this conception into ethics (nor could he): his subsequent philosophy is dominated by the unexamined assumption that the Hume who flees metaphysical anxiety into backgammon is the same Hume who experienced this anxiety.

Sartre held that the self (what he calls the "for-itself") is Nothingness, that is, the perpetual denial of any attempt at definition. If I follow Sartre's counsel, I will define myself by progressively rejecting all efforts at definition—whether in biological, social, or theological terms. The removal of all limits can, perhaps, never be completed, but progress in this direction, if that is the word, can continue indefinitely—quickly overtaking whatever residues of ethics might remain in Sartre's philosophy. For any moral claim that Sartre might propose (for example, that it is wrong to deceive oneself about one's freedom) will be answered by the asserted right to redefine humanity so as to reject that claim.

Richard Rorty draws out the consequences of this way of thinking. When it comes to the choice between two ways of life such as liberalism and Nazism,

> I cannot appeal to such a "fact of the matter," any more than a species of animal that is in danger of losing its ecological niche to another species, and thus faces extinction, can find a "fact of the matter" to settle the question of which species has the right to the niche in question.[2]

At the level of moral decision making,

> We figure out what practices to adopt first, and then expect our philosophers to adjust the definition of "human" or "rational" to suit. For example, we know that we should not kill a fellow human being, except in our official capacity as soldier, hangman, abortionist, or the like. So are those whom we *do* kill in these capacities—the armies of the invading tyrant, the serial murderer, the fetus—not human? Well in

> a sense yes, and in a sense no—but defining the relevant senses is an after the fact, largely scholastic exercise. We deliberate about the justice of war, or the rightness of capital punishment or of abortion first, and worry later about the "status" of the invader or the murderer or the fetus.[3]

It is difficult to see what more is needed for a defense of ethnic cleansing.

There are objections to this sort of view independent of its morally and politically repulsive character. "We" do not treat either invading soldiers or serial killers as we do dangerous beasts. The first are entitled, if captured, to treatment as prisoners of war; the second to a trial before they are executed (assuming only for the sake of argument that we accept capital punishment). To say that we cannot be confined in any definition is to make a claim about human nature. To claim that the attempt to define human nature is oppressive is to treat human nature as carrying with it a normative claim. To the extent that people such as Sartre and Rorty attack the idea of a common human nature to overthrow traditional positions on moral issues, they also undermine the claim that it would be somehow a violation of our nature to sacrifice our autonomy by joining a cult whose leader had the power to dictate our every action. Finally, to deny that there is anything distinctive about human nature is to undercut the reflective inquiry in which existentialists on whom Rorty relies are engaged.

To the philosophical views considered so far there needs to be added the testimony of a mystic such as Thomas Merton:

> Every one of us is shadowed by an illusory person: a false self. This is the man I want to be but who cannot exist, because God does not know anything about him. . . . My false and private self is the one who wants to exist outside the reach of God's will and God's love. . . . A life devoted to the cult of this shadow self is what is called a life of sin.
>
> All sin starts from the assumption that my false self, the self that exists only in my own egocentric desires, is the fundamental reality to which everything else in the universe is ordered. . . . So long as there is an "I" that is the definite subject of a contemplative existence, an "I" that is aware of itself and its contemplation, an "I" that can possess a certain degree of spirituality, then we have not passed over the Red Sea, we have not "gone out of Egypt." . . . [Nonetheless,] this [external] self is not by nature evil, and the fact that it is unsubstantial is not to be imputed to it as a kind of crime. It is afflicted with metaphysical poverty: but all that is poor deserves mercy.[4]

At least the following propositions hold firm in the resulting confusion:

1. I am a physical being, having a certain mass, etc.

2. I am an organism of the human species—a species that reproduces by sexual union, and whose members constantly seek to keep themselves alive, but in the end always die. I am male rather than female, but a rough half of my species is female rather than male.

3. I am a conscious being capable of pleasure and pain among other states of consciousness.

4. I am a cultural being, who thinks and imagines in certain ways, initially at least because that is how I was taught to do so.

5. I am a social being who exists in a variety of roles, such as husband, brother, son, teacher, and friend; and in a variety of communities, political, religious, intellectual, and cultural.

6. I am a historical being, the result of a long history of biological and cultural transmission, and of the various crises, traumas, and ruptures that have taken place in the process of transmission. Some but not all of this history I accept as my heritage.

7. I am a critical being who can reject, reaffirm, or modify inherited standards of all sorts, and do so for reasons.

8. I am a moral being whose choices respond, or fail to respond, to standards of right and wrong, good and evil. Initially, at least, these standards are derived from my cultural heritage.

9. I also have a unique history and prehistory, a unique cultural and biological ancestry, and a unique story of actions and sufferings. It is not always easy to say how much of my life history was chosen, and how much happened against or without my will.

10. I at least like to think that the world in which I live has a meaning, and that my own existence contributes or can contribute to that meaning.

Such a collocation of different elements of the human person prompts a search for an organizing principle—what the Biblical writers call "the heart," and writers in the Aristotelian and the Christian traditions call "the soul." The resulting debates do not admit of an algorithmic solution. For all his flaws, Rorty is right in holding that the question of human nature "will be decided, if history allows us the leisure to decide such issues, only by a slow and painful choice between alternative self-images."[5] *Human nature* is in short a contested concept, and philosophers are only one group involved in the debate concerning its sense, reference, and evaluative force.

MIND AND BODY

We have the moral problems we have because we are embodied creatures—able to harm one another physically, and to conceal our thoughts from one another. More particularly, we are animals of a certain species, bisexual in structure, and reproducing by sexual union.

Naturalism in the broad sense treats our existence as animals as prior to, and explanatory of, those features of our lives which pertain to intellect and imagination—in other words, to culture. Three forms of naturalism can be distinguished: *eliminative materialism* holds that beliefs and sensations are illusions; *reductive materialism* holds that beliefs and sensations are physical events (usually brain states) under another name; and *emergentism* forswears both reduction and elimination and holds that mind arises out of bodily processes in some weaker sense.[6]

In dealing with materialist positions, there are two fallacies to watch out for. One is the promissory note on the future of science, which holds that if a position as now formulated is incoherent or otherwise deficient, these difficulties will be removed in finished science. No philosopher knows what scientists of the year 2998 will be maintaining, but it does not make sense to suppose that their theories will be both sufficiently like some currently unacceptable hypothesis to count as a vindication of it, and sufficiently different to remove our current objections to it. The other is equivocation among inconsistent versions of materialism. Reductive and eliminative materialism are not only different but mutually inconsistent philosophies: the first holds that there are mental events, that is, a subspecies of physical events; the second that there are none.

One persistent problem for physicalistic accounts of belief is that what a person believes is a function not only of the state of his brain, but also of the world in which he lives. (The technical name for this problem is wide versus narrow content.) A materialist might reply that it is not our particular beliefs, but a complete description the universe that includes them, that can be reduced to, or eliminated in favor of, a merely physicalistic version of the world. The prospects of doing anything like this in practice are negligible, however.

We can exclude eliminative materialism quickly, since it implies that no one believes—let alone knows—anything, including eliminative materialism itself. Hand waving in the direction of a cognitive science that will replace folk psychology with something better, but not include beliefs and other mental phenomena, is not sufficient. Likewise, the suggestion that belief is a product of the intentional stance rather than a feature of Things As They Are ignores the fact that intentions and stances are themselves mental phenomena (as Hilary Putnam has pointed out against Daniel Dennett).

Briefly, the argument against reductive materialism is that belief cannot be a brain state, for beliefs are true or false, and brain states are neither. (To deny that our beliefs are true or false is self-destructive, since it precludes asserting any theory whatever of mind-body relationships.) Moreover, from the standpoint of a thoroughly naturalized epistemology, all beliefs—warranted, unwarranted, or mad—are on a level, since they result from the interaction between the believing organism and its natural and social environment. Hence the sources of warrant cannot be reduced to physical causation, either. No doubt, in seeing, the physical world has causal effects on our eyes and brains, but seeing is of epistemological interest only insofar as it is a way of knowing. Even a bad reason for a belief is not merely an event that causes a person to hold it (as smoking marijuana sometimes induces paranoia).

A critic of this argument objects that it confuses two senses of *belief,* belief as a state of a person (hereafter, a *believing*), and belief as an object of believing (hereafter, a *proposition*).[7] Propositions are true or false: they either exist in Platonic heaven or can be reduced to some form of inscription. Believings are events in the self: they are either irreducibly mental events or can be reduced to brain states. Hence—it might seem—a reductive philosophy of mind can progress by distinguishing these two senses.

But belief is not merely a state of the self or a thing believed; it and the other propositional attitudes such as fear are relations between the self and a proposition. What distinguishes propositional attitudes from other states of the self is their relationship to a proposition; what distinguishes propositions from other abstract entities is their status as possible objects of propositional attitudes.

What needs to be understood is the believing-proposition complex: treating believings and propositions separately avoids rather than resolves the issue.

For the purposes of this discussion, the many different doctrines of emergence and supervenience[8] may be divided into two classes: those that imply or presuppose epiphenomenalism, that is, that physical events cause mental events (but not vice versa), and those that do not.[9] Epiphenomenalism is not acceptable, since it only halves the mystery of the mind-body nexus while entailing a significant sacrifice of common sense. Body-mind causation is as mysterious as mind-body causation, and among the data for our inquiry is the fact that we make a difference in the world outside ourselves through our actions.

Doctrines of emergence and supervenience that do not imply or presuppose epiphenomenalism either (a) restate reductive or eliminative materialism; (b) explain the obscure connection between mind and body by an even more obscure notion of emergence or supervenience; or (c) boil down to the uncontroversial point that body precedes mind both in the life of the human individual and in the development of the physical universe. This last interpretation of emergence is consistent with a belief that both mind and body depend for their existence on a supraphysical spiritual cause such as God.

Some metaphysical or methodological limitation on the scientifically acceptable is thus necessary to the definition of *naturalism.* If the limitation is metaphysical, it requires explication and defense.[10] If it is methodological only, it rests on broadly pragmatic considerations arising in part from the social role of the sciences in contemporary industrial societies. In the latter case, there is no reason to suppose that all possible truths are accessible through scientific methods. To distinguish scientific methods from other methods of inquiry, without giving reasons to believe that these other methods cannot attain truth, is to undermine the claim that science is the measure of all things.

John Searle contends that, whatever the intellectual deficiencies of philosophical materialism may be, we twentieth century people have no choice but to accept a materialistic world picture.[11] As a general statement about all twentieth century people, this proposition is surely false. As a statement about some communities of discourse devoted to the discussion of the philosophy of mind, this proposition is true. There are, however, also circles in which it is mandatory to accept the Bible as an infallible authority even about questions of historical fact.

DESCARTES

The persuasive power of materialism, despite the many objections to it, arises from the difficulty of understanding how the heterogeneous elements of mind and body can be connected on any other premises. Descartes' response is that God has created us as mind-body composites, and that we might as well accept this fact as given. God could have created us so that different motions in the body led to different mental events, but the conjunction He has chosen is for our good as mind-body composites, and evidences His power and wisdom.[12] Even if narrowly consistent sense can be made of what Descartes says about the mind-body connection, this connection is a dark spot in his philosophy. Other philosophers have not been able to avoid dark spots in their philosophies, either. St. Thomas, for example, holds that the soul is the form of the body, and yet transcends it (survives its destruction, for example). Moreover, he holds that the soul is not the self, but nonetheless enjoys the rewards of virtue and endures the punishments for vice. If, as seems to be the case, all pictures of human nature have their dark spots, we are entitled to bring our moral concerns to bear in understanding ourselves. For the purposes of this discussion, we are concerned with the issue of what picture of human nature makes best sense of ethics and morality.

In ethics we are primarily concerned with our ability to affect the world outside ourselves, including the minds and bodies of other persons. Even self-regarding acts affect our own bodies. Moreover, Descartes' own philosophy has minimal ethical implications, even on the most sympathetic reading.[13] Finally, if we extract from Descartes' philosophy a view of ourselves as "persons" to whom a human body is unessential, the consequences for ethics are devastating.[14] It becomes a serious question, why, for instance, it is wrong to kill a person in deep sleep or a reversible coma, or even a person so drunk that, if he survives, he will not remember the occasion. Hence we are entitled to prefer a broadly Aristotelian to a Cartesian philosophical anthropology for ethical purposes.

In any event, we are capable of knowing truth and pursuing what is good, rather than merely responding, as organisms, to our natural and social environment, and hence are more than merely bodily in our nature. It does not seem, however, that this argument supports *personal* immortality, since as knowers of propositions not containing indexicals, human beings are interchangeable. If you and I both know that 2+2=4, there is in this respect no difference between us. So far we have only the "divine spark" theory of Aristotle.[15]

Properly personal immortality cannot, so far as I can see, be established by philosophical argument alone. Even granted that we naturally desire immortality in this sense, I see no way of proving that the world will comply with our desires in this respect: the question would seem to be one of faith and hope, if anything is. On the other hand, once we envisage the resurrection of the body, the possibility of personal immortality is beyond question. The doctrine of the separated soul, which is sometimes used to bridge this gap, is mainly of religious rather than philosophical importance.[16]

Chapter 5

The Quest for the Self (2)

First to be considered in this chapter is the classical problem of free will, then the much disputed question of culture versus biology. I shall then return to the question of how the multifaceted human reality can attain some sort of unity (if indeed we want it to do so).

THE WILL AND FREEDOM

Our discussion of mind and body, and in particular the problem of mental causation, left open the question of how mental events such as beliefs and desires caused physical events. In one version, this problem is that of free will, or as I should prefer to say, freedom of agency or choice.

Aristotle neatly (and in my view correctly) blended intellect and will when he defined choice (or decision) as "either desiderative reason or ratiocinative desire."[1] The union of intellect and will throughout the process of decision making is also central to St. Thomas Aquinas's understanding of human action, on at least on one plausible reading of his doctrines.[2] This union also harmonizes with the epistemology adopted in this book, according to which our understanding is always already fraught with evaluations.

Sometimes St. Thomas writes in highly intellectualistic terms, however. He defined the will as a rational appetite, directed toward what appears to be good, though it need not be good in point of fact. This account works well for cases of honest error, where a person chooses what is bad for him in the belief that it is good. There are, however, a number of reasons why a less rationalistic account of the will seems plausible.

The impulse to distinguish intellect and will arises in large measure from reflection on the Socratic paradox that no one does wrong willingly. If we can know that *A* is the better course, and yet do *B,* it seems that there must be something independent of our understanding that determines our conduct. Desires and emotions are not enough to explain this phenomenon, since what is in question is why we act upon some desire when we know we ought not to do so. The "something" that shapes our conduct against our better judgment has been called "the will."

A second source of the distinction is medieval reflections on the power of God, questionably analogized to reflections on the power of human authorities.[3] The relevant distinction is that between what an agent can do, absolutely speaking; and that which he in fact does (and can be counted on to do).

A third source is encapsulated in Myles Brand's definition of volition as "a mental event involved with the initiation of action."[4] The focus of discussion here is Wittgenstein's question, What is the difference between my raising my arm and my arm's rising?

Fourth, we need to clarify the notion of will or choice to decide to what extent we are free and responsible for our actions, and in what circumstances some us are to be excused as not responsible. The insanity defense in the criminal law, and the legal doctrine of diminished capacity, pose some deep philosophical issues, issues that also arise in the day-to-day operation of our judicial system.

Fifth, some theories of ethics and politics take as foundational the concept of will or (as it is usually put) decision. In the face of a value-free universe, the individual or group must postulate certain norms or "values" in order to guide conduct. Since different individuals, and different groups, will postulate different "values," relativism is an inevitable consequence. Even if we lay down our postulates, in quasi-Kantian fashion, as universal laws, we have no reason to expect others to agree with us, except insofar as we are able to secure their consent by coercion or manipulation. Even uncoerced agreement, on these premises, would represent only the contingent convergence of fundamentally diverse sources of value.[5]

Gilbert Ryle begins his skeptical discussion of the concept of the will by arguing that *volition* is a technical concept: "We have to study certain specialist theories in order to find out how it is to be manipulated."[6] Although the line between specialist and ordinary concepts is by no means as bright as Ryle here supposes, it is sufficient to replace the Latinate *volition* with the Anglo-Saxon *will* to refute his argument. Concepts such as *strongwilled* and *weakwilled,*[7] and of doing things of one's *own free will,* join the commonsensical distinction between *will* and *whim* in testifying to the role of such concepts in ordinary speech. Likewise it appears to make perfect sense to ask at what age an immature human being acquires a will, or whether a nonhuman animal can ever have one. *Will,* in fact, belongs in the enormous family of contested concepts, whose meaning is a matter of debate both among philosophers and among ordinary folk.

Another source of skepticism about the will is the problem of infinite regress. If free acts are distinguished from mere motions of the body by being preceded by acts of the will, then either these acts are themselves not free, or they, too, must be preceded by acts of the will, and so on to infinity. We can stop this regress at the start: human acts are to be distinguished from what St. Thomas calls "acts of a human being," not by an antecedent act of the will, but by their having been done by the agent, as opposed to being mere occurrences in his body or mind. That certain events are our acts, that we are in some sense the masters of them, and that they (and we) are for that reason open to rational and moral evaluation, are central facts of our moral consciousness.[8] In appealing to these facts I may "have replaced a problem with a mystery," as a critic of an earlier draft has put it;[9] but, if so, this is a mystery we cannot get behind. The mystery is particularly acute when we choose to do evil: although we can understand the good for which we act, our reasons for consciously preferring the worse to the better remain opaque.[10]

Certain virtues—for example, courage, temperance, and patience—are usually said to involve willpower; they embody what Robert C. Roberts calls "the athletic side of virtue."[11] These virtues do not motivate action directly: courage, for example, is not a preference for risky situations. But they make it possible for the agent to resist impulses and emotions that might otherwise deflect him from the path of virtue. To see how such virtues involve the will, consider a virtue not considered by Roberts, that of decisiveness. Apart from the other possible sources of bad behavior in difficult situations, I may be tempted to dither endlessly, and as a result injure my own interests or leave important duties unperformed. Decisiveness is the virtue whereby I am able to set aside some considerations and embrace others in order to act effectively. It also provides an excellent counterexample to the alleged unity of the virtues: one might argue that courage in a bad cause is not true courage, but hardly that decisiveness with a bad result is not decisiveness.

Accordingly, we may define the *will* as the power of choice, and *willpower* as the power to make and carry out choices in the face of external and internal obstacles. The will is the point where our desires and our intellect meet, at which we decide to act for one set of goods (or apparent goods) and neglect others, and in that way define the sort of persons we are. A person is *willful* to the extent that he adheres to his resolutions even in the face of good reasons, moral or otherwise, to the contrary. *Weakness of will* is the lack of those virtues that enable me to make appropriate choices in difficult situations and stick to them in the face of obstacles. A person can be both weakwilled and willful, if he pursues transient resolutions in the face of reason, but abandons them for others that subsequently seem more appealing.

Acts of will are internal performances that the agent finds useful, or hopes to find useful, in exercising willpower and avoiding weakness of will. (I see no need to suppose unconscious acts of will.) Sometimes such performances are attempted to overcome limitations of bodily power rather than those of moral character. Belief, also, though not under the direct control of the will, can sometimes be brought about by deciding to attend to one set of considerations and neglect others. Some people are better at doing this than others.

Sometimes people act even against their clearest convictions, reached after taking into account the full complexity of human situations. Aristotle compares the avowal of good principles by the weakwilled person to the utterances of an actor speaking lines.[12] St. Thomas maintains that in such cases "passion fetters the reason" and thus prevents the agent from "assuming and concluding" under the correct principle (but rather under some other principle of less normative weight, such as the allure of pleasure).[13]

The two philosophers are describing different situations. In the one case, the weakwilled person discovers, in the presence of temptation, that the norm to which he gave lip service before he was tempted has failed to become authentically his; in the other case, an inconvenient moral principle is locked away, where it cannot interfere with the expression of a powerful desire. ("I can't think about that now," says the agent to himself.) In either case, the weakwilled person employs a line of reasoning that has as its premise the requirements of passion rather than those of moral obligation or self-interest.[14] This is how things happen in the standard cases, but the allure of pleasure and the heat of passion are not the only sources of weakness of will. People are often weakwilled out of deference to group custom or tribal loyalty, or in preferring obligations of lesser to those of greater weight.

In any event, St. Thomas's formulation conceals a paradox: how is passion able to act, so to speak independently of the person experiencing it, to remove from circulation the obstacles reason places in the way of its expression? If I know that an act is wrong or irrational, and my principles require me to rank morality or self-interest above pleasure, how can I consider the act under the description *pleasurable* instead of that of *wicked* or *foolish* when deciding what to do? If I simply decide to neglect my moral principles or what is good for me on the whole, the problem of weakness of will reappears in unchanged form. Nor does it help to speak of the conscience or will as an agent-surrogate, for, as Donald Davidson puts it, "how can the Will judge one course of action better and yet choose the other?"[15] At this point analytic philosophy and theological tradition converge: "What is special about incontinence is that the actor cannot understand himself: he recognizes, in his own intentional behaviour, something essentially surd."[16]

Our sense of agency is not all that is central to our consciousness. Also central is our sense of being acted on or constrained by alien forces. As St. Augustine noted,[17] our power over our minds and bodies is not perfect, and differs from individual to individual and in the same individual from occasion to occasion. A person in a doze who cannot get up however much he tries, a paralytic who attempts to move an afflicted limb, and the Augustinian poet who addressed his phallus with the words, "Down, wanton, down!"—all may be said to will (or intend) events in their bodies that do not take place. Likewise, if the present writer, who cannot wiggle his ears, nonetheless attempts to do so, he finds himself twitching his jaws, cheeks, and forehead in hope of moving his ears slightly (and then more than slightly).

Some of the forces that constrain us are straightforwardly physical, such as the force of gravity, the solidity of a wall, or a wind strong enough to blow us off our feet. There are, however, also powers that work within us and lead us to feel or behave in ways that we perceive as alien to ourselves. One might try, without success, to will away lustful, resentful, or anxious thoughts, or to summon up affection for a disagreeable family member. Sometimes powers acting within us, but experienced as external to us, so overwhelm us that we are bereft of agency as much as if we had been constrained by a physical force—or at least they threaten to do so.[18] Such powers work sometimes for good and sometimes for evil (and sometimes discernment is needed to discover which). In any case we lack adequate language to describe them: psychology either retreats into behaviorism or physiology, or else resorts to concealed mythology (as in the later Freud and in Jung), and there is no reason to expect this situation to change. We can therefore call good powers "angels" and bad powers "demons" without begging metaphysical or theological questions. Though we must avoid flirting with what has been called "the glamour of evil," the recognition of dark as well as light angels distinguishes Christianity from New Age doctrines (to the credit of Christianity).[19]

The problem of free choice is one aspect of the larger issue of whether our inherited conception of human action should be jettisoned as folk psychology.[20] It concerns the issue of whether choice is ever real, or whether the apparent exercise of choice is always a mask for the play of natural forces. (That choice is sometimes an illusion I take for granted.) We appear to have free choice, and we constantly speak, and conduct our individual and collective affairs, under that assumption. Hard core naturalists will maintain that this feature of our shared experience is a socially generated illusion, and that in reality nature is all there is.

In fact, however, the role of random mutation in evolutionary biology guarantees that there are many features of human reality that no scientist will ever understand. Yet it remains possible, on the argument so far, that agency is a mask for an irrational and unpredictable array of forces, even if naturalistic determinism cannot be established. Conversely, if the causal connection is understood weakly enough, as embodying mere regularities, it need not extinguish freedom of choice.

To deny the possibility of free choice is absurd, since it is to ask us to abandon settled habits of thought (which we by hypothesis have no power to do).[21] Yet this conclusion does not establish what features of our lives are within our power to change; for all we know, genuine choices are very rare. The law and other social institutions deal with such questions in a practical way, and history and literature portray the way they work themselves out in practice.

CULTURE AND BIOLOGY

Both our ability to know, and the constituent elements of our moral lives, arise in part from our biologically given nature, and in part from the society in which we were educated, and whose norms we spontaneously accept before we are able to reflect on them. Hence—setting aside the role of free choice—there is a dispute between those who take culture as the primary determinant of human behavior, and those who find the source of our behavior in our biology. This dispute is politically sensitive, not to say bitter, since many people assume that the cultural is modifiable by political and educational means and the biological not.

This supposition is, however, false. Increased longevity, reduced infant mortality, and improved techniques for controlling reproduction change our biology. On the other hand, that racism is a cultural trait, or even that (unlike xenophobia) it has a discoverable historical origin, does not mean that it can be willed away. Nor does the fact that a given phenomenon is a "social construction" entail that there is any alternative to it but chaos and dim night. For once we start deconstructing "socially constructed" notions, we cannot protect liberal individualist conceptions of personhood against dissolution, and our objections to even the most rigid caste systems would therefore vanish.[22] Michel Foucault puts the point dramatically:

> As the archaeology of our thought shows, man is an invention of recent date. And one perhaps nearing its end. . . . One can certainly wager that [if the structure of thought changed,] man would be erased, like a face drawn in sand at the edge of the sea.[23]

If, moreover, we ask, *who does the constructing?* and *with what materials do they work?,* no satisfactory resolution is available. Those who speak about social construction do not have in mind the idea that we are God's inventions (and perhaps even God's fictions). If we look for an uninterpreted stratum immune to the arguments of social constructionists, we are quickly led to some sort of Kantian noumenon, which can be invoked to disrupt any understanding of human life, but cannot itself sustain any position, radical or other. "Might makes right" is not a philosophy that will win much support among the clearheaded, since even secure members of the elite may find that, in some lonely place, power relations have been suddenly and radically revised.

One strand of feminism takes maleness or femaleness as external to the self, imposed upon us by some sort of conspiracy (or at least malign social construction).[24] This position is sometimes combined with a quasi-Marxist view, that men are (by nature?) the class enemy, in a way that makes for questionable coherence. In any event, "assimilationist" feminism embodies an untenable anthropology, deriving what credibility it has from a questionable analogy with race.[25] (Racialist theories assign crucial importance to physical differences that are not essentially connected to either sex or reproduction.) Homosexuals are as interested in the sexual characteristics of their partners as are heterosexuals. Even a bisexual, whether male or female, will sometimes prefer a man and sometimes a woman as a sexual partner, according to his or her frame of mind at the time.

In short, being male or female is an important element—though not the only element or the one most important in every circumstance—of what each of us is. The extent that "gender" is a social rather than a biological matter is largely unknown, and of limited practical importance. At the same time, the need of males and females to live together and cooperate in, among other things, the reproduction and the rearing of children, is a constant element in human society. How much we can distinguish the "masculine" from the "feminine" is a complex issue, to which I shall return.

THE PROTEAN SELF

It is self-destructive to maintain that it is our nature to have no nature. The doctrine is also absurd for independent reasons: we cannot decide to define ourselves as weightless and jump out of tall buildings with impunity. Nonetheless, any fair examination of the nature of human beings (or the particular human being that I am) will disclose our protean character.

There are many different ways of being human, and each one of us contains within himself tendencies toward at least a large number of them. And, to look ahead, data from anthropology, history, biology, and physics will only confirm our divided character. We are not only more complicated than, for example, horses; our nature partakes of a number of possibly incongruous elements in a way unknown among nonhumans. We are, for example, at the same time in the grip of our bodily impulses and uncomfortable with them, as such phenomena as prudery make clear.

We are both animals and rational, both part of the natural order and aspiring to transcend it. This fact about ourselves poses fundamental questions concerning the way in which we are to live—whether to seek to integrate the various aspects of our nature, or to allow one of them to rule us one-sidedly, or to compartmentalize our existence. It also means that the forces to which we are vulnerable, in that aspect of our existence in which our agency is limited or overridden, can be understood as working toward integration or disintegration.

Some features of our lives have an intermediate character: we share emotions such as fear and sexual desire with other animals, whereas nostalgia is peculiar to humanity. The history of ethical and social theory reveals a continuing tension between those such as Plato and Kant, for whom morality and rationality are convertible terms; and those such as Rousseau, who find emotion a surer guide than reason on moral issues; and Hume, for whom reason is impotent in the most important decisions about moral issues. Another stubborn issue concerns the capacity of human beings for fine-grained moral judgments: to what extent we can allow ambiguity in the standards governing moral choice, without licensing forms of arguments capable of justifying any action, however abhorrent.

The species as a whole is divided between male and female (with a few anomalies), but somehow both men and women need to accept themselves and one another as participating in a common humanity. There are three-way conflicts between the demands of humanity at large, the demands of particular communities, and the demands of the particular self. We are each of us idiosyncratic; so much so as to lead some people to regard talk of a common human nature, or even a common human situation, as oppressive. Yet we need other people, both for practical purposes and to realize what we take to be essential to our full humanity, and thus we require common standards (and more broadly a shared sense of humanity) to regulate our mutual relations or even to make communication possible. Our relations to others, and the norms we accept to regulate them, are marked both by a desire for union with at least some of them, and by a need to establish boundaries and limit the moral and material demands they make upon us.

One attempt to resolve the problem of the protean self identifies human nature with the deepest, or the most tightly held, conventions of some group; to be unnatural is on this view to be un-American. But all conventions defining group membership contain ambiguities and conflicts reflecting the tensions characteristic of human nature. Moreover, we belong to a number of groups ranging from friendships with one other person to the whole human species. There are persistent conflicts, say between the requirements of personal relationships and the demands of larger political communities.

Another view demands "liberation" from everything that ties me to a particular identity—especially the mores and habits of thought of particular groups. The Sartrean doctrine of the self as Nothing is, on this view, not a description of ourselves as we in fact are, but a program for what we should become. This position requires that each of us should have an individual nature, which social practices repress, but such individual natures are themselves quickly dissolved by programs of radical liberation. The one thing the liberated self is not permitted to do is to establish a fixed identity. But what moral authority could support a program so much out of keeping with what most men and women desire, escapes my understanding.[26]

We thus have arrived at the situation described by Michael Walzer:

> First, the self divides itself among its interests and its roles . . . in relation to the different social goods available to it and the performances required of it in different spheres of justice. . . . And, second, the self divides itself among its identities; it answers to many names, defining itself now in terms of its family, nation, religion, gender, political commitment, and so on. . . . Third, the self also divides itself among its ideals, principles, and values; it speaks with one moral voice—and that is why it is capable of self-criticism and prone to doubt, anguish, and uncertainty.[27]

The moral life on this account is a messy, and quite possibly chaotic, business. Each of us must attend to a heterogeneous array of moral critics, of whom Walzer writes,

> The critics that crowd around, speaking for different values, have not been chosen by me. *They are me,* but this "me" is socially as well as personally constructed; it is a complex, maximalist, whole.

In this context, we must somehow maintain a stable self, capable of forcible and spontaneous moral judgments expressive of its integrity. Walzer argues that "democracy of criticism saves [us] from the harshness and persistence of a single supercritic." But a democracy of internal critics can be quite as despotic, and quite as much given to putting us in double binds, as democracy (or capricious autocracy) in politics. We all sometimes experience an inner voice that finds emphasis on a plurality of consciences self-serving, and a society that accommodates it morally corrupting. Walzer gestures in the right direction when he writes of Randolph Bourne, "It is not his conscience that refuses [participation in World War I], but something deeper within, or more continuously active across, or more pervasive throughout, his inner life." The natural law tradition calls this "something deeper" conscience, and usually understands it as the voice of God in the soul (even in that of an atheist, since nothing requires God to speak only to those who believe in Him).

Chapter 6

The Testimony of History and Cultural Anthropology

Whatever else we are, we are social beings whose practices have arisen as the result of a long and complex historical process. Both our moral language and our moral codes testify to the complexity of our nature.

THE VARIETIES OF MORAL LANGUAGE

There is not one language of morals, but rather a multitude of competing moral languages.[1] If I talk about *honor* while you talk about *efficiency,* we do not merely disagree about our evaluation of some particular action or character. We are speaking from within different modes of life, which our differing languages and judgments reflect and in part define.

Some people insist that one way of understanding crucial moral words is right, and that those who defend other points of view are mere sophists. *Adultery* just means sex outside of marriage, and any further discussion of the matter is evidence of dishonest intentions. Likewise, words such as *truth* or *knowledge* have an antirelativist sense; other senses of the words are simply wrong.[2] This approach supposes that rational intuition or revelation (or both together) can supply us with a complete system of casuistry, making prudential judgment unnecessary.

On the other hand, there are devastating objections to the Rortyan[3] celebration of the human capacity to invent new languages, and redescribe ourselves, other people, our world, and our actions accordingly. First, some proposals for redescription, such as those that suppress the fact that we have bodies, are immediately refuted by experience. Second, some programs of redescription, and the languages they generate, are evil—for example, the redescription of persons as vermin or mere masses of tissue. Thirdly, some languages are designed specifically to restrain the human capacity to redescribe: the language relativist can neither honestly bar, nor consistently admit, those who speak the language of *orthodoxy.*

Finally, if moral languages are radically incommensurable, the only solution to the resulting social problems is the use of power—including a rhetoric that claims truth for one's proposals. It is hard to see how anyone would regard such a result as good: the more usual position, that "might makes right" represents the truth of things, supposes that at least this aspect of our situation is immune to redescription.

TABOO MORALITY

Human beings are not the rational contractors of individualistic fable; they are connected with one another, especially with members of their own families, in ways better understood by novelists and tragedians than by philosophers. Actions done and experiences suffered in earlier generations have important and often painful consequences for later generations. This interconnectedness affects our understanding of property: a family house or farm, less so a family business, and a family stock portfolio not at all, embody it—not always in happy ways.

Those aspects of life summed up in the expression "birth, copulation, and death" are in a special way productive of such consequences, for it is the departure of old members of a lineage, and the arrival of new ones, that defines the shape of a family history. (Hence, for example, Antigone's insistence on burying her dead brother was morally significant.) We are internally related to our family history, for it is to our ancestors, both literal and metaphorical, that we owe our being the sorts of people we are. We can understand why some people try to escape from the burden of the past or flee the emotional complexities of social life into the chilly rationalism of Benthamite calculation. But, even when connectedness is a source of pain, it still needs to be redeemed rather than denied.

Philosophers (here following their theological forebears) are much concerned with the maximum claims of morality: with impartial benevolence; or with treating all persons, oneself included, as ends in themselves and not as means merely. But of greater social importance are morality's minimum claims, prohibitions whose neglect marks a person, not as weak or selfish, but as warped. There is not only conventional morality but also conventional immorality, the latter conducted within limits that are, though hard to explain, nonetheless important. Acts such as cannibalism, suicide, and sex between adults and children sometimes elicit what Lord Devlin called "intolerance, indignation, and disgust."[4] The aversions at work here are not mere dislikes, but something deeper than ordinary morality, which may restrain a person even when moral constraints of the usual sort would fail.

Ordinary criteria of moral responsibility do not apply to taboos. Oedipus did not know that the man he was killing was his father, nor that the woman with whom he was copulating was his mother, but he tore his eyes out nonetheless. Where taboos are in question, a mere accusation is enough to stigmatize, and even the unwilling recipient of homosexual advances is likely to feel tainted thereby. Taboos can even taint persons who are in every sense innocent: the children of incest are tainted by the transgression of their parents, to which they were in no sense a party. The vexed question of "dirty hands" bears witness to the persistence of such notions. Many people believe that there are actions that contaminate, which an agent may nonetheless be sometimes obliged to perform as part of the responsibilities of public office.[5] An ancient pagan well understood what it was to be obliged by piety to incur pollution.

Sometimes we observe a dissociation of moral consciousness, in which the deep horror some actions occasion is hidden behind a sort of evaluation more acceptable in sophisticated circles. Not only sexual passions or other instinctive drives can get repressed: the same fate befalls the powerful emotions occasioned by transgression of the limits that define a way of life. We may half-believe that sex is a more intense version of a handshake—what an acquaintance of mine calls "an enjoyable and nice activity"—until something happens that rouses our latent feelings, or those of someone close to us, with powerfully disruptive effects. Hume's conclusion, that reason is and ought to be the slave of the passions, then exacts its price.

Roger Scruton defines *piety* as "the attitude that leads the present generation to defer to the last one and to assume responsibility for the next."[6] We need to preserve a sense of responsibility, not merely for the natural but also the social environment posterity will inherit, and a way of life cannot be created just because some philosopher thinks it desirable to do so. What is odd about Scruton's argument is his suggestion that we separate piety from the religion that, in every cultural tradition I know of, sustains it, and to which piety itself would lead us to defer. I am not sure whether he believes that God is dead, or is afraid that He might be alive.[7]

There are at least five reasons for not abandoning what is sometimes called "wagon train morality." First, the more primitive our moral consciousness, the surer is its hold on the human mind: the thought that some sort of act is "not done" has kept many people from actions any moralist would condemn—in the teeth of the fact that some people do such things and other people approve them. As Aeschylus showed in the *Oresteia,* "civilized" systems of ethics need to take primitive moral powers into account—not to give them unbridled rein, but to harness them to the task of establishing a good, or at least a tolerable, society. Some boats ought not to be rocked.

Second, the more precise a moral norm, the less scope there is for self-deception about whether one is, in fact, breaching it. Most people know when they are committing adultery, but whether their attitude toward their husband or wife is, in some deeper sense, morally good is much harder to discern. It is sometimes more important that a line be drawn than that we be able to justify the particular line we draw. Hence there can be good reasons for drawing a line whose precise definition is not amenable to rational scrutiny.

Third, it is one of the functions of taboos to protect the boundaries within our conceptual (and moral) scheme. Prohibitions on bestiality and cannibalism protect the boundary between human beings and brute animals.

Many social scientists believe that the social world is a construct without a natural basis (or whose natural basis determines little or nothing of its content).[8] In this view, what appears to be natural merely reflects the most tightly held of our conventions. This position, despite its initially radical appearance, provides a powerful reason for respecting cultural taboos. Cultural radicals find such conventionalist moves "antihuman," objecting that our social constructions violate the "disparity" or "accident and succession" that constitutes the truth of things.[9] Such radicalism is self-undermining, since despite itself it claims that accident and succession are natural, and that attempts to establish stability unnatural. Without some normative conception of human nature, it makes no sense to object to a practice or attitude as socially induced.

Fourth, one important feature of moral reasoning, even in philosophy, is its use of practical reductio ad absurdum. A moral philosophy that implies, for example, the legitimacy of adult-child sex can be rejected on that ground alone (though we will want a deeper understanding of what went wrong). In a world without taboos, it is always possible to "outsmart" such objections, and accept the conclusion of an opponent's reductio. Behavior which one had once thought was out of the question is constantly being defended in the contemporary world. Hence the possibility of many forms of moral reasoning is stymied at the outset.

Fifth, however sophisticated our understanding of moral issues, we need to retain our capacity to recognize evil, and not only in such trite cases as the Nazis. Especially where standards of public morality are in a downward spiral, there is a great need for points at which those attempting to maintain some sense of decency can rally. Any morality needs to distinguish minor offenses from grave faults, and grave faults from acts that are utterly horrible. But philosophy is of very little use in answering the question, when the time for discussion is over and we are required simply to say No. (Socrates relied upon a divine sign.)

Public assaults, both theoretical and practical, on the possibility of a coherent way of life are now too far advanced to make cautionary piety a sufficient response. A sense of moral limits cannot be sustained by a generalized conservatism: markets in infants, human genetic material, sexual services, body parts, and help in suicide are in the best entrepreneurial tradition. Our tradition of free speech likewise places limits on how much we can constrain the aggressive marketing of "alternative life styles," even through pornography.

We cannot endorse all our taboos just as they stand, since they vary from culture to culture (and from subculture to subculture). We cannot credibly prefer the taboos of our group on the sole ground that they are ours, whereas to accept our taboos as (nothing more than) legitimate conventions is already to weaken their force. Moreover, there are taboos—such as that on torture—that most of my readers want to promote, whereas there are others—such as that on interracial marriage or marriage across class boundaries—that most of us want to discourage. If morality were merely conventional, we would be left in our confusions.

THE PROBLEM OF HUMAN DIVERSITY

The appeal to diversity in contemporary political rhetoric is largely unserious.[10] Yet human beings are in fact highly diverse, and any attempt to place limits on the range of acceptable human behavior will face immediate challenge. "You neglect the fact," the critic will say, "that people are different, and their differences are given rather than chosen. For this reason, a morality that is healthful for some people may be deleterious to others."

Arguments that attempt to undermine the idea of common morality by stressing human diversity fail, however, to take our diversity seriously enough.[11] So long as we limit ourselves to a few formulaic forms of diversity—such race, sex, disability, and sexual orientation—it might seem that peace and justice among human beings could be attained by inculcating respect for difference alone. But in fact our differences are far deeper in than sheltered academics suppose. Our world includes Mormons, Jehovah's Witnesses, "rednecks," and tribal Masai, among others. And peace and cooperation among all these different sorts of purposes requires shared moral standards, or at least rough approximations to such standards. Hence insistence on human diversity, unless balanced by an equal insistence on a common human nature, is quietistic or fascistic rather than liberal in its implications.

We must begin with the postulate that what unites us is more important than what divides us. This postulate is frankly grounded in moral and political considerations, but that does not mean that the quest for a common human nature, once undertaken, is either hopeless or arbitrary. What we look for, we are likely to find.

If we accept this line of thought, some sorts of moral argument will be unpersuasive. Some people argue that conduct condemned by traditional morality would be wrong if ordinary people did it, but some people are different from the rest of us in ways that make it permissible (and perhaps sometimes even obligatory) for them.[12] This argument implies that any moral requirement whatever can be evaded by pleading individual difference. For instance, some people are temperamentally homosexual, others are temperamentally promiscuous, and still others are temperamentally violent or sadomasochistic (the classes overlap). In fact, human beings are infinitely various in their sexual persuasions and fantasies. Moreover, human beings do not group themselves into types in such a way that principles that apply to persons of one type cannot be applied to persons of another. An acceptable account of our shared humanity will have to respect the many sides exhibited even by a single human being.

What is true of sex is also true of other aspects of human nature. Yet an unusual propensity to road rage does not justify vehicular homicide or even reckless driving. The same sorts of considerations refute the claim that some men and women are *Übermenschen,* entitled to govern their lives by standards different from those of the common herd.

The role of choice, on the one hand, and of heredity and environment on the other, in making us the kind of people we are is something of a mystery. On the one side, it is dangerous to deny moral responsibility; on the other, we ought not to be quick to judge other people. But insofar as some deplorable feature of ourselves is given rather than chosen, this fact pertains to the excuse rather than that justification.

THE SEARCH FOR CULTURAL UNIVERSALS

Familiarity with the variety of human mores has been a fertile source of ethical perplexity since classical Greece. People reason: if members of other societies do things forbidden in our own, and with every appearance of good conscience and without immediate disastrous results, why should we not do so as well? One response to skepticism of this sort is to look for cultural universals, that is, goods, virtues, or moral rules recognized in every known human society. This project is made easier if we take moral requirements abstractly: for example, "dispose of the dead respectfully" rather than "do not burn (or eat) them."

Three different problems afflict this approach to ethical issues. First, the requirement of cultural universality is very strong: one maverick society is enough to defeat it. For example, manliness—defined in remarkably similar ways—is highly valued in very many societies, but there are a few societies which do not value it.[13] Probably, the best thing to say here is that certain *issues* require moral regulation: killing, communication, allocation of scarce resources, kinship relations, sex, reproduction, and possibly the disposal of the dead.

Second, it is a mistake to treat cultures as fixed entities, uniform in their attitudes and sealed against influence by one another.[14] If Margaret Mead and Derek Freeman found different attitudes and practices in Samoa, part of the reason is likely to be that they talked with different Samoans.[15] What constitutes a single society is itself a question: whether we can identify one that requires celibacy of all of its members depends on whether we take the Shakers as a society or a subgroup within a society.

Third, the fact that some set of beliefs and practices may be limited to a fringe group within contemporary Western societies proves very little. That group might constitute a society in its own right, which might moreover consider itself the advance guard of human progress.

Nonetheless, a wide range of cultural traditions grounds ethics in a cosmogony designating some aspects of experienced humanity as "higher" and others as "lower," and this tendency can be found even in "secular" thinkers such as Marx and Freud.[16] Even Kant's Categorical Imperative echoes the Word of God to Moses on Sinai, and those who reject the claims of the Is to determine the Ought work within a metanarrative in which humanity is seen as progressively freeing itself from the bonds of nature. "Autonomous" ethics arises when an old cosmogony loses its grip on a society, or when two rival cosmogonies struggle for ascendancy, even within a single mind.

THE QUESTION OF METANARRATIVE

One way in which men and women have attempted to resolve moral and political conflict is by designating one side (their own) as *progressive* and the other (that of their opponents) as *reactionary.* Sometimes this is just another way of saying *good* and *bad,* and sometimes it is mere rhetoric, used in an intellectual context in which it is impossible to take it seriously. Nonetheless, at least until 1914, many people took seriously the idea that history was inherently a movement for the better, and that certain groups—be they the working class or the builders of the British Empire—were doing God's (or History's) work in the world.

There is no metaphysical barrier between Is and Ought that Hegel, Marx, and Spengler somehow transgress. The difficulty lies with their factual premise—that there are laws of history that, by informing us of the wave of the future, can at least establish a presumption in favor of some moral and political principles. It is the complexity and unpredictability of human nature, not its irrelevance to normative questions, that is the most serious challenge to the project of natural law, including those versions that appeal to metanarratives. Neither technical skill nor scientific knowledge, of itself, makes us either better or happier: people can and do use them for evil purposes (or just plain stupidly). And the complaint that we are becoming slaves of our machines is too persistent to ignore. Nineteenth-century progressivism neglected what was valuable in colonized culture, and imposed merely local Western customs as if they were universally binding standards.

The "reactionary" (more politely, "restorationist") metanarrative holds that civilization took a wrong turning at some point in our past, and the more sophisticated its advocates are, the further back they locate this wrong turning. Some people think that everything went wrong in 1968; others think that everything went wrong in 1914 (when nineteenth century progressivism sustained a damaging blow); others blame the Enlightenment, Columbus, the Renaissance, the nominalist theologians of the fourteenth century, or the fall of the Church in the reign of Constantine. And so on back, to Socrates and Plato, the fall of the primeval matriarchy, and beginning of an epoch of decline that some Hindus see as having taken place in 3000 B.C.[17] Yet the past from which we have supposedly fallen always turns out to be idealized (when it is not fictional). Restorationists are in fact lamenting our expulsion from Eden, and between us and return to Eden stands an angel with a fiery sword.

Another variety of conservative regards existing forms of order, for all their flaws, as a precious and highly vulnerable achievement, which should not be cast away for the sake of abstract hopes of human betterment. In view of the outcome of many revolutions—even Gandhi's nonviolent revolution against the British raj led to bitter intercommunal violence—, we cannot dismiss this sort of conservatism as unreasonable. But nearly all forms of social protest find their root in revered sources, and the operation of existing institutions regularly produces dislocations that threaten our way of life. The doctrine of Original Sin has its limits as an apologetic strategy, and no society can be sustained by fear of the alternatives alone.

The rise and fall of social, political, and cultural orders exhibits something like a seasonal cycle. But, on any reasonable version of the cyclical metanarrative, there are a multitude of different cycles—cultural, economic, and political—and these interact complexly. Moreover, a dying movement can exhibit a terminal burst of vigor, and a vigorous movement might be reaching or passing its peak. In fact, the movements of history are like the movements of the ocean, viewed from a standpoint immersed in the water. Often the pursuit of ends good in themselves will have unexpected bad consequences, but sometimes disaster will have unexpected good consequences. Sometimes the forces of human betterment even win.

THE CORE TRADITION OF THE WEST

Nonetheless, core Western tradition provides a morally significant pattern in history. Invoking this core tradition means that there is no irreconcilable conflict between natural law theory and narrative or tradition-bound ethics, since the Western tradition can be understood as a carrier of the natural law.

I do not understand *Western* as a geographical expression: with the exception of the North and South Poles, every spot on the globe is both West and East of every other spot. Rather, I understand the West as that tradition that was forged around the Mediterranean between 500 B.C. (or B.C.E.) and 500 A.D. (or C.E.), and its cultural offspring all over the world. This tradition is a blend, and at least an attempted synthesis, of Greek and Hebraic elements. In both of its aspects the tradition is committed (though in different ways) to a conception of the unity of humanity and a transcendent ground for that unity. Another signal feature of the core Western tradition has been its selfcritical capacity: a few pioneering or prophetic individuals invoke its transcendent ground (in the Greek tradition, Reason; in the Hebraic tradition, YHWH) to evaluate existing practice and sometimes to condemn it.

In the course of the development of the Western tradition, universality has been understood in three different senses. First, the norms of Western ethics are understood as binding all rational creatures, at least if they have the opportunity to understand them. Second, all human beings are protected by these norms, having at least a right to live. And, third, human beings of every sort are in principle able to contribute to the tradition, so that works by Africans can end up in anthologies of classical writings of the Western tradition. It is possible for the centers of Western culture to come to include Argentina, Kenya, or the Philippines (this is not a prediction), quite as much as Germany, France, or America.

If Hindus invoke Western ideas against the West (as Gandhi did), their appeal will continue to be important beyond the political context in which they do so. Moreover, when Asians and Africans speak of "human rights imperialism," they are appealing to principles of communal self-determination having Western origins.[18] When they claim universal validity for non-Western values (and do not merely reiterate traditional forms of ethnocentrism), they mimic Western missionary claims.

All relativistic positions involve a paradox closely related to Nietzsche's truth that there is no truth. If we reject the universal claims of our tradition, but nonetheless affirm it as *our* tradition, we quickly find that our tradition in all its modes affirms the existence of universally binding truth. The manifold hesitations of post-Heideggerian skepticism, which puts into question principles it cannot firmly reject, are the inevitable consequence of this paradox.

Nonetheless, tribalism has often been the prevailing pattern even in the West, and rejection of critics as smartalecks or worse has been as least as common as the willingness to give them a hearing. Moreover, self-criticism sometimes threatens to destroy the cultural tradition that sustains it. The television playwright Dennis Potter, for example, observed, "Perhaps the noblest task of the popular historian should be to make us ashamed our forefathers."[19] Yet it is these forefathers who articulated the moral standards by which we condemn Western injustice, and to discredit our ancestors is to discredit these standards as well.

Chapter 7

The Testimony of Biology and Physics

For the sake of goodness and love, man shall let death have no sovereignty over his thoughts.

—Thomas Mann[1]

Donald ("Dax") Cowart is a survivor of a propane gas explosion in the summer of 1973 that left him totally blind, permanently disfigured and severely maimed. Despite his massive handicaps, he now leads a reasonably secure and productive life. He is financially secure by virtue of an out of court settlement with the energy company whose leaking pipeline caused the accident. He recently graduated from law school and has set up a small legal practice in his hometown of Henderson, Texas. But, had Dax Cowart been given his way, he would never have survived his horrifying ordeal. Through fourteen long months, he repeatedly demanded that he be allowed to die. He pled with his mother and lawyer to be discharged from the hospital. He raged against the treatment his doctors and therapists provided. But neither his family nor his physicians would consent to his demands. He remained in the hospital and received treatment until he was well enough to be released to his mother's care. Thereafter, he languished through years of virtual helplessness until he finally began to build a new personal identity and public life for himself. Though his efforts have been successful beyond anyone's expectations, he remains convinced to this day that he should have been allowed to die.

—Lonnie D. Kliever[2]

PROGRAM FOR THE CHAPTER

Professional bioethicists tend to maintain that Dax ought to have been allowed to die as he requested.[3] James Childress and Courtney Campbell make relatively traditional arguments, reasoning that the principle of respect for persons in this case outweighs the principle of beneficence.[4] William F. May, in contrast, starts from an acknowledgment of his own aversion to burn victims and poses the ethical question in apocalyptic terms: "How does one respond to one's death, to a total, comprehensive, all-penetrating, sun-blackening, oxygen removing, flesh-charring, chilling, stilling, numbing, and isolating death?"[5]

Although favoring May's experiential approach, Paul Lauritzen points out that May leaves out the experience of Dax's mother Ada, who saw to it that her son survived contrary to the advice of learned bioethicists. Nonetheless Lauritzen sides with Childress and Campbell and May in rejecting the arguments of Dax's mother. Her position, he writes,

> would simply not cohere well with the best philosophical account we have of how to deal with conflict between respect for persons and beneficence, nor with our understanding what continued existence must have meant for Dax, given the deep aversion others would have for him and he would have for himself.[6]

I do not attempt here to "solve" Dax's case, but to use it to draw some lessons for ethical theory. On no account are we obliged to preserve a human being in every possible way and at whatever cost. But it is disturbing when ethicists find a justification for letting a person die (and by plausible implication for his killing himself), not in the pain he is suffering, the supposed impossibility of his return to relatively normal functioning, or even in his desire to die—but in our instinctive inability to acknowledge the full humanity of the disfigured, an inability into which a disfigured person himself has somehow been conscripted. The impulse to turn away from those who are somehow marked or scarred is not one a sound ethics should encourage.

THE CONTRIBUTION OF NARRATIVE ETHICS

Narrative ethics cannot do what many bioethicists want it to do and provide a basis for consensus about health care issues in a culturally divided society. For there are too many stories to tell, and too many different ways of establishing relationships among them.

There are stories of heroic struggle against the odds, and of miraculous rescue from the brink of doom, as well as stories of courageous acceptance of inevitable fate. Beethoven has often been used as an exemplary case against abortion on "sociomedical" indications, but he also provides a case against physician-assisted suicide. If anyone is a plausible candidate for the ministrations of Dr. Kevorkian, it is a man whose whole life has been dedicated to the composition of music, who finds himself profoundly deaf. Whether Beethoven is a paradigm of how human beings can triumph over adverse circumstances, or an unusual case that can be neglected in day-to-day bioethical reasoning, depends on what set of stories we take as central.

All of our stories represent important aspects of human experience, and it is impossible to establish a hierarchy among them by anything approaching algorithmic reason. We will be inclined to give a relative privilege to those stories that harmonize with the Big Story as we understand it, and people in the contemporary world do not share a common Big Story. Even attitudes toward dead bodies have controversial metaphysical ramifications. Hence *narrative* has come to be, in many academic circles, a euphemism for propaganda.

But casuistical approaches to bioethics fare only slightly better than do the narrative variety. Even if we assume that suicide is wrong, we still have to ask whether Dax's intentions were suicidal. If they were, then we have to draw the line between wrongful cooperation with wrongdoing and mere failure to interfere, that is open to prudential considerations. And, if his intentions were limited to refusing treatment which he found, in the circumstances, unduly intrusive, still other prudential considerations arise. For intervention did save Dax's life. Still, we must avoid the fallacy of retrospective judgment, that is, of arguing that since Dax is now happy to be alive, his wishes ought to have been overridden and treatment imposed on him. No one knew at the time what the results of imposing treatment were going to be.

Any system of casuistry, however detailed, will include judgment calls, and such judgment calls engage a person's entire sensibility, as shaped both by his own experience and the Big Stories that have played a role in his education. My own bioethical outlook, for example, was influenced by a brief period of employment in an animal shelter—which prompted the thought, how easy it would be to dispose of unwanted human beings as we dispose of unwanted kittens. It was shaped as well by the Biblical story of the massacre of the innocents.

Likewise, our Big Stories affect our understanding of the principles applied in bioethical casuistry. Consider the principle of respect for persons, in contexts where it is thought to count against the preservation of the very person demanding respect. Even where killing in the core sense is not at issue, some people will find it harder than others to sever respect for a person from a felt obligation to preserve and protect the human organism that person in some sense also is.

POSITIVISM AND SCIENTIFIC NATURALISM

The phrase "the place of value in a world of facts" suggests a residual positivistic picture that continues to be influential. On the one hand, there are those who believe that facts about human nature are morally irrelevant; on the other hand, there are those who use words such as *real* to suggest that normatively infused convictions are for that reason somehow second-rate.

No one denies that facts about human beings are relevant to moral judgment. Even Bentham turns to account the fact that we ordinarily and for the most part prefer pleasure to pain, and other sorts of utilitarians use the fact that we are ordinarily and for the most part happier when we get what we want. All concede in practice that data about human nature provide one element necessary to sound moral judgment. Moreover, all cognition is value laden. Scientific investigation reflects a desire to control nature not universally shared, or given the same weight among human ends by those who share it. Judgments of simplicity, coherence, and the like also reflect the value-commitments both of the individual scientist and of the scientific community. The way we interpret ambiguous data reflects our vision of the world.

Human beings give every appearance of having been designed, mind and body, to survive and continue their kind (and to protect their offspring once born). The requirements of human survival encourage the motives that moved Dax's mother to insist on his being treated despite his objections. (The *Pietà,* representing a mother mourning her only son, is not merely a Christian icon.) For Dax represented to Ada Cowart the possibility of the future, indeed a certain simulacrum of eternity. Each one of us is the descendant of numerous human and animal ancestors who managed to survive long enough to reproduce, often against staggering odds. Natural selection favors the disposition to attempt to survive, even when the objective probabilities suggest that it is hardly worth the effort. Inference from single, vivid examples, when these involve triumph against the odds, makes evolutionary though not logical sense.[7]

Yet the orientation of human beings toward survival and reproduction plays itself out in a universe in which—if we are to believe the dominant scientific story—all forms of energy are transforming themselves into heat. The forms of order exhibited by human and other organisms, and even more so the motivational structures favored by natural selection, work contrary to the dominant tendency of the physical universe. Hence children, and children's children, can only represent a simulacrum of eternity. The conventional scientific wisdom is not necessarily the last word, even scientifically, but we have no right to presume that the future of science will in some fundamental way alter our intellectual situation. Yet we need not assume, either, that the regnant scientific picture of the human situation is complete.

Biological nature also teaches less benign lessons. The ordinary forms of predation are easier to accept than the perversity of the parasite: moreover, some species kill their young, and some insects eat their mates after or even during intercourse. We can recognize a diseased organism as diseased, and see something contrary to nature in the lovelife of the praying mantis, but how this is so is something of puzzle. In view of the incongruity between nature and our moral sense, Annie Dillard is led to observe that "either this world, my mother, is a monster, or I myself am a freak."[8] "When nature . . . owns her sovereign Death," as the Sacred Harp hymn puts it,[9] naturalistic vitalism ceases to be an option.

There is a conflict between Eros and Thanatos, developed in quasi-mythological form by Freud in *Civilization and its Discontents,* and given powerful literary expression in the novels of Thomas Mann.[10] There is a conflict between the attitudes that tend to sustain life and the requirements of consequentialist ethics. Even limited forms of consequentialism require that possible outcomes be so far as possible appraised according to their objective probabilities, whereas human beings notoriously commit systematic fallacies concerning probability.[11] A person struggling to survive against the odds is more likely to survive if he overestimates his chances of survival; at times and places where many women die in childbirth, the reproduction of the species requires that they underestimate both pain and risk. Hope is the most precious of commodities, for which men and women have been known to sacrifice even their own lives and the lives of their children.

Some might attempt to solve the resulting dilemma by saying that physics gives us truth, whereas morality or even biology is only a human projection. (This is the "God's-eye" or "no-eye" point of view of contemporary materialism.) But physical theories are as much and as little social constructions as are moral codes and biological observations. To find the physical universe harsh and unfeeling—to be terrified, as Pascal was, by the silence of those infinite spaces—is to place physics within the human world. Considered merely as a physical reality, the space between the galaxies is neither hostile nor friendly nor indifferent; the question about its attitude toward us is a category mistake.

Other people attribute primacy to the vision embodied in physics, on the grounds that physics concerns the whole universe and biology only a tiny part of it. Whether biology can be reduced to physics is an open question, but no one has responsibly proposed to reduce physics to biology. From the standpoint of the moral life, however, it is biology that matters: moral issues have to do with what we do with our own and other people's bodies, but not with the microparticles that compose them. Even such notions as purity of heart would make no sense if we did not have a notion of bodily cleanliness. In moral contexts, extension in space and time are not the most important issues.

RESOLVING THE CONFLICT?

Sometimes the existence and pervasiveness of both moral and physical evil is taken to establish that the power or powers that rule our universe, if indeed any powers do so, are hostile or indifferent to humanity (and in particular to the claims of morality). To argue this point successfully we would have to show that there is no possible good to which the evils we experience are a necessary condition, and this cannot be done. Contemporary atheism is usually content to announce itself as a self-evident insight, which cannot be rejected by those who have confronted it clearly.

Another way of dealing with these problems is to provide a decisive argument for the conclusion that the regnant scientific image, though true so far as it goes, is not complete. The argument here is strongest for consciousness, since both reductive and eliminative materialism faces severe difficulties. This argument leaves open the possibility that materialism, though strictly false, might as well be true for all practical purposes—a result that reproduces, in another form, the dualism between the biological and physical visions set out above.

Let us, finally, consider the possibility that we are the creation of a wise and beneficent God, Who among other things endows us with the capacity to know moral truth (and, in some versions, gives us further assistance toward its discovery). There may be good arguments for at least part of this picture, though much of it is on any account a matter of (possibly reasonable) faith and hope. But none of these arguments will satisfy the sort of skepticism that the defeatist vision is likely to generate. For, on any account, God, as an infinite (or perhaps better, inexhaustible) Being, is radically different from His creation. Hence there will be a conceptual gap between any concept applied to Him—for example that of Creator or Designer—and the same concept as instantiated among created things. The perplexities of analogy defeat any attempt to establish a contentful theism by watertight argument.

A PRAGMATIC RESOLUTION

Naturalistic defeatism and Jewish or Christian theism do not exhaust the field of possible outlooks. Merely to simplify discussion, I shall address the issue in terms of only two rival visions, and leave to others the task of putting Hinduism and Marxism into the picture. The methods of argument appropriate to a limited choice will also prove useful when the choice widens.

When the resources of ordinary argument have been exhausted, pragmatic considerations step into the breach. To put it precisely, *when all other criteria of appropriate belief have been exhausted, we are entitled to adopt those beliefs among the remaining options that enable us to live (and live well).* "Living well" here has a moral component: belief systems that authorize massive injustice are not acceptable.

Even in this-worldly terms, there is a strong pragmatic case for some form of theism, at least when compared with the most important contemporary versions of atheism. There are powerful reasons for promoting a sense of the solidarity of the human species, and the most persuasive ground for this solidarity is our common condition as having been created in the image of a Creator God. One popular alternative—solidarity based on rebellion against the Cosmic Tyrant (in one version, Thanatos)—is self-destructive: once its adherents convince themselves that God is really dead, they have no reason not to turn their fury on one another, whether as individuals or (more likely) as tribes.

The force of pragmatic arguments depends on the desires of the people to whom they are addressed. Those whose deepest disposition is to pursue liberty or death (or both) will not be impressed by any argument that requires them to accept any avoidable suffering or renounce any possible pleasure. Perhaps a version of Pascal's Wager will impress such people.[12]

Theists believe in truth in a stronger sense than do atheistic humanists of any description; hence, although such humanists can ignore or persecute theists, there is a sense in which they cannot prove them wrong. If the vindication of theism must take place outside the confines of space and time, well then so be it.

References to eternity raise, however, some questions that threaten to undermine morality. Why should we not rely on God's Providence to make up for the evil that we do? Why, for example, should we not kill a freshly baptized infant, confident of his salvation and trusting in God's mercy for our own? But few if any people these days believe (and perhaps ever believed) in a future life with enough confidence to act coherently in such a fashion, and those who do so will not mix secular and religious systems of ethics in a way that reduces religious morality to incoherence. If indeed there is a God who secures our moral code, He will not so arrange matters that moral decisions are inconsequential both in this world and in the next.

Part III

From Goods to Rights

Chapter 8

Goods

This part takes as its concern four crucial moral concepts—*goods, virtues, obligations,* and *rights*—and the theoretical and practical implications of understanding them appropriately.

HEDONISM

The simplest understanding of the good—*hedonism*—holds that all and only pleasure is good, and all and only pain is bad. We need to avoid confusing *pleasure* as used by philosophical hedonists with the popular sense centered on the so-called physical pleasures of eating, intoxication, sexual activity, and scratching itches. (It is not clear to me why the pleasures of bicycling, swimming, and petting cats should not be accounted physical pleasures as well.) Even these are not phenomenologically homogeneous: most strikingly, sexual pleasure—even apart from the emotional and symbolic elements characteristically embodied with it—involves a transformation of the self, a concentration of consciousness in one part of the body, and the taking of another person, real or imagined, as an object of appetite—aspects that do not have any analogue the other sorts of physical pleasure.[1]

No one believes that only physical pleasure is valuable, but Bentham is, I think, guilty of treating all pleasures as if they were physical pleasures. Thus we can define hedonism as the doctrine that

> A state of affairs is good to the extent some conscious subject likes or enjoys it, and bad to the extent some conscious subject dislikes it or finds it a source of suffering.

If we were differently constructed, hedonism would be true. Creatures who always knew what they wanted, were always pleased when they got it, and never looked back on their past choices with disgust or regret, could still have moral problems arising from their relationships to one another, but the only issue in the conduct of one's own life, so far as it affected oneself alone, would be to get as much of what one wants as possible. To describe such creatures is to describe what human beings are not, and the same considerations tell against accepting desire, choice, and retrospective sentiment as final criteria of value.

People frequently desire what they, upon getting it, find worthless or bad. Anyone, however content with his previous satisfactions, can face Ivan Ilych's question, What if my whole life has been wrong? Likewise, I have read of a man who discovered that what he was looking for through pickups in bars could be attained only in the selfless devotion of a dog. And people sometimes look back on experiences (in the army, or at school) that they found painful at the time, and conclude that they were in fact good for them in ill-defined ways. Revisions of our evaluation go on so long as we live, and even what we most value now we may come to consider bad or worthless later. Hence St. Augustine's saying: Our hearts are restless until they rest in Thee. Hence also there are bad pleasures, such as those of cruelty, which (or at least we so hope) those who enjoy them will come to reject. There are also false pleasures, such as those of being subjected to lying flattery, which turn to ashes upon knowledge of the facts.

Hedonism falsely supposes that one can evaluate pleasures independently of the sort of person one is. The following grant proposal would then make sense: I will spend a year in (say) San Francisco, enjoying both those pleasures commonly deemed high and those commonly deemed low. At the end of the year, I will be able to speak with authority about the relative merits of the views of pleasure defended by Aristotle, Bentham, and Mill. But I have already decided—in deciding which pleasures to pursue and which to shun—what sort of person I am and therefore how I shall rank my pleasures.

THE GOOD AS THE OBJECT OF STABLE DESIRE

We may provisionally define the good as the object of stable desire, and the bad as the object of stable aversion. But what stabilizes desire is, in part at least, a conviction that there is something about the object that makes it good, even apart from my desires. Hence our concept of the good will have an intellectual as well as an emotional dimension. We can regard knowledge, friendship, and the like as good in themselves, and not merely because they satisfy our desires (though, if no one ever desired them, we could never recognize them as good).

R.B. Brandt defines the good as the object of those desires that survive maximal cognitive therapy.[2] On this premise, an inextinguishable desire to eliminate some form of behavior from one's social environment is rational, and its satisfaction therefore good—and for no other reason than that some people have that desire, and cannot get rid of it however they try. Brandt is mistaken at a more fundamental point, however: what makes for a rational desire is not drenching oneself with information, as too much knowledge of the details of digestion might ruin one's appetite. Rather, desire needs to be schooled according to a conception of virtue, and hence also according to a conception of the right. Virtuous people do not desire sadistic pleasure, and hence it is not good.

In any event, we desire not just episodes of want-satisfaction, but also complex goods such as friendship. Such complex goods not only stabilize our desires: they also provide a framework in which we can pursue other goods in cooperation with others. Happiness or flourishing in the Aristotelian sense means a life structured around such complex goods.

WHAT IS GOOD?

There is less dispute about fundamental goods than about what to do when their requirements conflict. I here list some things that are objectively valuable. We like them because they are good; they are not good because we like them, and hence their acknowledgment helps stabilize our desires. I do not attempt to avoid overlap, nor do I claim completeness or originality.[3]

1. Life and health, both in themselves and as preconditions of other goods.
2. The continuation of life beyond one's own span, though literal and metaphorical procreation.
3. Friendship of all sorts, from intimate personal relationships to membership in transgenerational communities.
4. Participation in the imaginative life of culture.
5. Aesthetic experience, including the enjoyment of natural beauty.
6. Knowledge.
7. Play, or the exercise of one's powers for their own sake.
8. Being the part author of one's own life, in accordance with a conception of the good arrived at after due reflection *(autonomy)*.[4]
9. Making a difference in one's world.
10. Harmony with whatever Power or powers are in control of oneself and one's world, and the integration that comes thereby.

All the goods listed except the first pertain to how we constitute ourselves as persons. We have the life we have, and our physical, emotional, and mental constitution is largely beyond our control. But for the rest what we choose, and what we enjoy, both reflect and define the kinds of people we are. Hence a judgment of what sort of person we should become essentially enters into the sorts of friendship or play that we value.

Friendship (good 3) includes, in a special way, sexual relations insofar as they fulfill what is traditionally called "the unitive good." Heterosexual union, even apart from its reproductive potency, brings together the two halves of the human species, in a way that has a social importance larger than the satisfaction obtained by the parties. (Observe a traditional wedding, without being oneself one of the spouses or closely connected to one of them.) The distinction between the sexes is more central to the natural history of human beings than that between races, for example. (This is no objection to interracial intercourse, but it is not humanly central, either.) That the differences between men and women often make their relations difficult is one more reason why union between them is of special value.[5]

This traditional judgment receives confirmation from unexpected quarters. The word *queer,* which some homosexual activists have revived even in public contexts, testifies to a sense that homosexual desires are somehow off target (although homosexual advocates, being hostile to natural law ideas, are prepared not only to defend but even to celebrate that fact). Again, a novelist describes the discovery, in medias res, that his partner was a man rather than a woman in the following way:

> I felt the longing for pleasure and abandonment inside me, but I also sensed that I had been accepted too readily, that everything had suddenly become very predictable. All that we could do was to exist for each another solely as a reminder of the self.[6]

The context of this observation is tales of sexual degradation and violence, in which moral issues in the usual sense are far from the author's mind.

The existence of persons constitutionally unable to achieve heterosexual union does not give us any reason to question the heterosexual ideal, since we are dealing here with what is good rather than what is obligatory. These results would not apply to homosexuals if they were a third sex in the science-fiction sense, but the existence of bisexuality makes it clear that they are not.

One rival to the heterosexual ideal is an androgynous approach to sexuality, in which the physical structure of the person desired is irrelevant—as if one could ever experience sexuality that way.[7] A more serious challenge to the heterosexual ideal defends bisexuality, and emphasizes the range of sexual fulfillment available through contact with bodies of both sexes. Polymorphous sexuality—including such things as bestiality, the use of sexual toys, telephone (or Internet) sex, and sexual fixation on an automobile—carries the search for variety in sexual stimulation to its logical extreme. Pornography, especially in its most exotic forms, celebrates the infinite malleability of human sexuality (and implicitly that of human nature). There are also people who find heterosexuality not merely unattainable or insufficient, but repulsive. A determined advocate of ecological ethics might argue that if transcending the gender barrier through heterosexual intercourse is of special value, transcending the species barrier through intercourse with beasts is even more so.

The highest court of appeal here is educated intuition: we perceive heterosexuality as natural and normal, independently of moral strictures on other sexual possibilities, or of moral issues concerning the sort of heterosexual relationship that is morally appropriate. It is the views most distant from what most people spontaneously regard as natural that are the hardest to refute.

The good of friendship is of special theoretical importance, since it grounds moral demands in the interests of the agent. If I sacrifice something for my friend, I am serving both my interest in friendship and whatever interest of his the sacrifice may serve. Yet the inclusion of friendship among goods does not dissolve the problem of egoism. To be sure, my good includes the good of my friend, but it will not include only that good (even if, as is unlikely, I have only one friend, or the interests of my friends never conflict). Conflict is possible even between the most affectionate spouses, and a man may be pulled between the conflicting demands of his wife and his mother. Moreover, when egoism is magnified by group membership, it becomes even more virulent.

Robert George maintains that autonomy (good 8) cannot be a fundamental good, since it cannot be an ultimate reason for action, insisting instead on John Finnis's "practical reasonableness."[8] He argues:

> One may choose a certain possibility over its competitor(s) because that possibility is the practically reasonable one. One cannot, however, choose a certain possibility over its competitors because that possibility is the autonomous one.

One can, however, decide to protect one's autonomy, say by refusing to join a religious or political group that attempts to extinguish its adherents' capacity for choice. The deep issue is whether autonomy, even in the upright version affirmed by Kant, is just the sin of pride by another name (as Calvinists hold).[9]

Claims to autonomy imply a sphere of discretion in pursuit of a genuine good (say knowledge). A scientist who performs morally objectionable experiments may, if in good faith, exercise a valuable sort of autonomy, though he may have to be punished nonetheless. Freedom to do as one pleases, where one's choices have no special importance, may be a matter of providing oneself with the space necessary for morally valuable endeavor, but it may also make for an aimless rather than a properly autonomous life. Arranged marriages under favorable circumstances (including the child's right to veto a proposed spouse) may be morally acceptable, but resistance to them is not merely a matter of a perverse will.

In light of these considerations, I agree with John H. Garvey that politically recognized freedoms exist in order to make it possible for us to pursue important goods such as love, the practice of religion, or the pursuit of knowledge.[10] Freedom of religion, where it does not rest on individualistic or subjectivistic premises, depends on a judgment (which requires both philosophical and theological defense) that "imperfect participation in the good of religion" nonetheless has value.[11]

The implications of these considerations, especially for "morals" legislation, are complicated by the difficulty of discerning when people have honestly concluded that their way of life is a good one, at least for them. My entirely fallible impression is that a considerable number of homosexuals and people who commit suicide, but a negligible number of heroin users and readers of pornography, have done so. In any event, life in society always requires some restriction even on desirable forms of autonomy, and no society, however repressive, has ever succeeded in extinguishing the human capacity for choice or prevented its members from using it in destructive fashion.

Evils are distortions or deficiencies in the goods listed. Thus death and disease are evils, as is the dying out of cultural and biological lineages, hatred and indifference, doltishness, ugliness, error and ignorance, lack of control over one's own life, inability to act (or act meaningfully), and being out of harmony with the world. Such evils are attended by pain and suffering, but do not cease to be bad when the person suffering them has become so numbed as not to feel them any longer.

Among the goods listed here, knowledge (good 6) has a special position, insofar as the whole inquiry presumes that I regard it as good. The same is true also of autonomy, since if I were not in the business of making my own judgments I would not be writing a philosophical work (and the same is true of George, who is entirely ready to criticize Aristotle and St. Thomas Aquinas—who for him form the "central tradition"—on various grounds.)[12]

The question finally arises of whether we should include pleasure as a good in its own right, and pain as an evil, apart from the objective goods enjoyed and the objective evils suffered. Play is one of the basic goods listed here, and one can enjoy one's organic life as a manifestation of health. The question, whether sexuality can legitimately be used for mere recreation, cannot be decided by listing goods. Pleasure is notorious for its instability, and the goods listed provide sufficient sources of happiness to make appeal to pleasure outside them unappealing.

LIMITS OF THE STABILITY CRITERION

The understanding of the good as the object of stable desire is subject to some important limitations. First, the more complex the good, the more vulnerable it is to fortune. If those to whom I am bound by merely economic ties despise me, or attack some of my most cherished convictions, that misfortune is relatively easy to bear. But if my wife or close friend turns against me, or I find a chasm opening between me and a larger community through which I have defined myself, the result is tragedy. The vagaries of social and economic life can also have a severe impact on friendship: one of the saddest contemporary experiences is to call a friend long distance, and discover that one is relieved to get no answer. Even if all goes well in a friendship, one of the parties is likely to die first and leave the other alone.

Second, death is a prime exception to the continual revision of evaluation that forms a part of our moral and evaluative life. It is possible to feel a desire for death, whether or not one acts on it, but if one puts to oneself the question, Is death really good for me now? no answer is forthcoming. For one cannot ask whether, after death, one will come to regret one's choice. When we attempt to envisage death, in order to decide whether to choose it, we encounter a blank traditionally filled in with myths (including those that portray death as sleep).[13] Even if we desire, not death, but escape from pain or disgrace, there is no answer to the question, how great an evil death is, and thus how much suffering should be accepted to escape it. Since we are among other things animals, our desire for life requires no justification, but if it did require one, we could not provide it by comparing our prospects—in old age, for example—with the alternative. Hence death implies an important limitation on the good of autonomy.

Third, our ability to revise our conception of the good is never extinguished, however much satisfaction we may attain. Sometimes the question of the worthwhileness of our way of life is prompted by acute suffering, but we must not forget the experience of disappointment upon getting what one wants. Even the notorious experience machine has its appeal under some circumstances. On the other hand, the inadequacies of earthly happiness prompt some people to press beyond happiness and seek, in traditional language, for beatitude.

Finally, we cannot separate questions of the goodness and badness of states of affairs from the acts that in some way produce them, for we evaluate not merely the outcome of our acts, but our acts in themselves. Acts of friendship are part of the complex good of friendship; acts of betrayal undermine that good, even if one can conceal them from one's friend. Garvey astutely compares our situation to that of mountain climbers.

> Their objective is to climb one of the Rocky Mountains (say Grand Teton). They want, of course, to reach the top. . . . But the climb is important in itself. It wouldn't do to take a helicopter.[14]

Chapter 9

Virtues

THE RECOVERY OF VIRTUE

There has been recently a revolution (or counterrevolution) in ethical theory, resulting in the recovery of the ancient idea that virtue rather than obligation or rights is central to morals.[1] Virtue ethics links moral questions in the narrow sense to the question of what sort of person one is (or wants to be). Thus a moral standard is not just a proposition one accepts; it is embodied in a way of life to which one is committed and that contains other elements linked to it in various (and not always well understood) ways.

A virtue is a trait of character that involves renouncing or postponing some pleasure, or accepting some pain or other harm, for the sake of a good that is non-hedonistically conceived (the most accurate expression in English is *flourishing*). Once we fully acquire virtue, we do not miss the pleasures we renounce for its sake: temperate people do not mind doing without orgies. We may even find the pains required by virtue less burdensome, though this is more difficult to achieve. Despite the frequent use of the English word *habit* to describe virtue, becoming virtuous is not a matter of mere repetition but of learning the art or skill of living well.

Virtue provides the motivation for adherence to a moral code, and protects it against wholesale abandonment, against casuistical whittling, and against legalistic rigidity in which the point of the code is lost. In all moral discussions, we must presuppose a certain modicum of virtue: there is no point in discussing biomedical ethics with someone who sees nothing wrong with raping a patient under anesthesia, or sexual morals with someone who sees nothing wrong with sex with young children. Hence also, change in our moral beliefs is both more difficult and more risky than is sometimes supposed. There are many more ways of further corrupting an admittedly inadequate social morality than of improving it.

Virtue theorists protest the exclusion of "self-regarding" questions, such as How would a good philosopher handle this opponent? from the central concerns of moral thought. In any view, some virtues are primarily self-regarding, such as careful stewardship of one's resources, whereas others, such as generosity, seek primarily the good of others.

If we are consequentialists, we make moral decisions one at a time, given our understanding and evaluation of the alternatives available. Hence the master consequentialist argument:

> Anyone who resists consequentialism seems committed to the claim that morality tells us to do less good than we are in a position to do, and to prevent less evil than we are in a position to prevent.[2]

The virtue ethicist responds: What alternatives we consider, and how we evaluate their consequences, depend on previous moral choices. There is no morally neutral list of alternatives and evaluation of possible consequences to which to apply our moral theories.

This result makes possible some progress on a core question in the philosophy of punishment: whether the suffering and death of those who blow up public buildings with child care-centers attached is a good in itself, or valuable only as a means to some other good such as the prevention of crime. Many people persistently and intensely desire retribution, and leaving vengeance to the Lord depends on theological assumptions not open to the philosopher. The philosophical issue is whether a virtuous person, aware as virtuous people are of his own moral and other limitations, would desire an evil person's suffering or death as such. J.R.R. Tolkien phrases the issue:

> Many that live deserve death. And some die that deserve life. Can you give it to them? Then do not be too eager to deal out death in judgement. For even the very wise cannot see all ends.[3]

Virtue ethics also at least partly bridges the gap between *ought* and *can.* If I find myself recognizing some moral requirement that I do not have the inner strength to put into practice, I need not despair of my ability to live a morally good life, nor need I cut down the requirements of morality to fit my capacities. I can strive to try to become the kind of person who can do what I ought to do, perhaps even gladly. Moreover, our moral journey is not a lonely one, but consists in being introduced to practices linked to our shared past by a common tradition.[4]

But the concepts of *tradition* and *practice* are no guarantee of anything. Torture can be considered a practice, that is, an activity containing within itself its own standard of excellence. (A good torturer knows how to keep his victim alive and conscious in order to inflict maximum pain and degradation.) This and other morally repellent practices can be carried on with increasing skill from generation to generation.

Machiavelli spoke frequently of virtue (or at least of *virtù*),[5] and some people admire shamelessness, that is, the willingness to accept or even provoke other people's disapproval for the sake of some supposed good. Among more moderate people, there are disputes over whether patriotism or tolerance is a virtue, and if so to what extent. Even among those who accept the same table of virtues, there are important disagreements: for some people suicide is the coward's way out, whereas for others suicide missions on the Kamikaze model are paradigms of courage. Finally, the requirements of the virtues, even if we agree what they are, sometimes conflict, as do honesty and kindness, and generosity and thrift.

VIRTUE AND TRADITION

Because virtue has to do with traits of character acquired before we are capable of moral reflection, the connection between virtue and moral tradition is tight. There is no way of entirely transcending our moral reflexes, and these are inevitably affected by our shared cultural past. Moreover, virtue ethics raises doubts about the project of making our morality entirely transparent to our understanding. For to understand our morality fully we would have to understand ourselves fully, including the history that has gone into making us the people we are. Many unbelievers acknowledge that their moral consciousness has been to some degree formed by Christian (or Jewish) tradition, and admit some need for distinctively Christian virtues such as hope and patience. Even the most zealous Christian will have to have acquired some degree of the pagan virtues, such as moderation, courage, justice, and prudence, if he is able to live in society at all.[6]

Nearly all of us have been also influenced by the Romantic movement and the Enlightenment; we thus admire, even if within limits, both sincerity (even a in bad cause), and a critical spirit. The discovery of a new virtue (or the invention of a spurious one) does not merely change our principles of evaluation: it opens up new possibilities of acting, and even of being. It was not always possible to try to be sophisticated (or to repudiate sophistication as a false ideal), or to find a way of life romantic.

Though blind adherence to inherited moral ideas is not an option in contemporary society, reflectiveness poses dangers to which an ethics of virtue is sensitive. The first is that the reflective person will conclude that everything is permitted, and then go on to do horrible deeds. The second is a form of opportunism, in which we tailor our morality to our current needs or even our current mood. Third, reflectiveness may undermine morality in a broader way, turning the moral life into a search for the morally correct positions to the neglect of morally uncontroversial requirements. Finally, the abstractness of philosophical discussions of ethics favors the moral habits of the judge or bureaucrat over those of the moral amateur.[7]

MORAL EDUCATION

All education, including moral education, requires the concept of virtue and a supporting concept of human nature. Unless we have a conception of what the human material is, what we want to make of it, and what elements in the material offer resistance or support to our endeavors, what we say about education will make no sense. We need, moreover, a sense of the stages of our lives—of what is appropriate to childhood, what to adolescence, and what to maturity. One important dimension of education is instilling in children an appreciation of the complex goods that are central to the flourishing of adults.

Issues in moral education center about the competing claims of autonomy and directiveness.[8] Though any society requires citizens who are spontaneously disposed to accept and obey its rules, many people have opposed directive education as violative of the autonomy of the child or of the subsequent adult. Yet very young children cannot be autonomous; if they are not controlled by their parents and teachers, peer pressure and their own spontaneous desires will dictate their behavior. And adults will always be affected by their childhood memories when they make moral choices.

Children, however, start asking philosophical questions—such as why it is all right to kill animals but not people for food—at a very young age.[9] (In addition, we do not have any right to assume that children are without independent spiritual life, so that religiously based moral education will always be an imposition from without.) The solution is to use both directive and argumentative methods of moral education, reducing the former and increasing the latter as the child matures. Raising children to avoid moral opportunism, on the one hand, and fanatical zeal on the other, raises issues that cannot be resolved by any formula.

As Marx observed, the educator himself must be educated. If the educator himself has received a morally defective education, or has fallen short of the sound aspects of his education, he will transmit his deficiencies to his pupils. Moral progress presupposes something sound in existing moral understandings. It was because American society before the Civil War had a generally sound public morality that it was possible to argue that slavery was unjust (and convince at least some people). Only external intervention can serve as a remedy when a bad pattern has been entrenched.

MASCULINE VERSUS FEMININE VOICE

Contemporary attempts to define a feminine voice in ethics are in part a protest against Lawrence Kohlberg's claim to have discovered the "universal invariant sequence of moral development."[10] An ethics of principles, of well-defined, usually hierarchical social relations, and of a sharp distinction between person and body, they argue, fails to capture the moral experience of women.[11] The same argument could be made, though not in exactly the same terms, about the moral experience of strongly religious groups and of non-Western peoples (and of other groups that differ from standard Cambridge liberals).

George Sher has questioned whether the feminine voice adds anything to the traditional disputes in moral theory concerning the roles of abstract principle and the particular features of situations.

> Even the most unbending absolutist, who believes (say) that no promises should ever be broken, must allow moral agents to pay enough attention to context to ascertain whether a particular act *would* break a promise; and additional attention to context is required by the notorious problem of conflict of duty. Yet, on the other hand, even the most ardent proponent of "situation ethics" must acknowledge that moral decision-making requires some abstraction from total context. . . . Thus the proper question is not so much *whether* context is relevant, but rather how many, and what aspects of it are pertinent to our moral decisions, and how these interact to generate moral duties.[12]

But the "feminine voice" thesis can be understood as pointing to two different sets of virtues rather than two different sets of principles of action. Both masculine and feminine virtues include dispositions not only to act in certain ways rather than others, but to regard certain aspects of a situation as salient and others as less so.

Masculine virtues include adherence to principle and courage to act in accordance with one's principles in the face of danger and temptation—or even to act on them ruthlessly at serious cost to self or others. They include a disposition to stand up for one's rights and respect those of others—rights here being defined by either a scheme of hierarchy and subordination or a strict juridical equality. They include an ability to distance oneself from one's emotions and bodily urges in order better to control them—perhaps in response to the way sexuality invades the consciousness of males from about age fifteen to about age thirty-five. Lastly, they include the ability to grit one's teeth and do a morally questionable deed when circumstances require it. ("A man's gotta do what a man's gotta do.")

Feminine virtues include the ability and willingness to make compromises, and to avoid moral conflicts through forethought. They include attention to the needs of the particular other, and the ability to tolerate relationships (such as contemporary marriage) in which the authority structure is ill-defined. Feminine virtue accepts the legitimacy of emotion and is not afraid of the body. A determination to preserve relationships and adjust competing claims precludes, so far as possible, situations in which any person or interest is sacrificed. There is also a feminine form of situationism, more willing than the masculine version to depart from received moral rules, but less given to overt acts of violence. One wing of contemporary feminism argues that feminine virtues are equal or superior in importance to masculine virtues (if indeed masculine virtues are virtues at all).

A tension between the *feminine* and the *feminist* thus arises.[13] To the extent that we value the qualities needed to care for young children, we will be out of sympathy with political and social movements whose point is to liberate women from the care of small children, and in that way among others make them more like men. To the extent that we believe that traditional female roles are oppressive, and are prepared to neglect the question of who (illegal aliens, perhaps?) will care for small children, we will have little use for the feminine virtues—even when exhibited by men.

There is a dark side to both the masculine and the feminine approach to ethics—a ruthless rigidity prepared to shed large amounts of blood over relatively trivial issues, on the one side, and a penchant for deceit and manipulation, on the other. (This development of the feminine voice has been called amoral familism.)[14] All people need both masculine and feminine virtues, and a man or woman who completely lacked either of them would be some sort of monster.

PRUDENCE

We all make prudential judgments in our personal, professional, and civic lives.[15] (Consider for example the question, to what extent problems within a group should be shared with the press.) Though judgment calls may be difficult to make and evaluate, it is easy to discern want of judgment, at least in others. Though it may be hard to discover the Aristotelian mean, it is easy to identify people who habitually run to extremes. Prudence is more than risk avoidance[16] or worldly wisdom[17] or moderation:[18] it links good character with the intellectual capacities required for virtuous action in complex circumstances. It sometimes requires boldness—on what occasions is itself a matter for prudential judgment. It does not concern means-end reasoning alone, but allows for critical reflection upon our goals.

Prudential judgment responds to the question, What is to be done? as well as to the question, How shall I respond to what Jones has done (or is doing)? rather than to the question, Is act *A* morally permissible? The attempt to give an account of prudence does not encourage theoretical optimism. We should avoid both the quantitative language that bedevils prudential reasoning, and a cynical elitism, which holds that "we" are entitled to bend the rules for our purposes, whereas "the people" are to be held to the letter of the law.

Prudence is directed to a comprehensive good, that is, the flourishing of human beings in society, rather than to winning a particular political battle. This comprehensive good permeates the means a prudent person chooses to attain it. It is for example incoherent to suppose that one can build a just society by massively unjust means. Hence, prudence compares and mixes goods in a way that respects their diverse and partly incommensurable character, without freezing us into an impracticable rigorism. Even if there are absolute moral rules, the moral life cannot be reduced to their observance, and the strongest advocates of exceptionless rules are often lacking in prudence when their moral code proves inadequate to a particular situation.

Abstract reasoning will never grasp the complexity of lived experience, but immersion in the present moment in all its concreteness fails to guide action; somehow these heterogeneous sorts of reasoning need to be combined. The messiness of human life, and the difficulty of knowing the right thing to do in complex circumstances, should make us understand why political leadership is often thought of as a special gift of God, and why it makes sense to precede a difficult moral or political decision with prayer.

Prudence involves trained attentiveness, of the sort needed by an artist or writer who needs to know when his work is finished. It constructs an imaginative representation of the situation, or of the act requiring a response, which so arranges its features that the proper course to follow (or the proper judgment) becomes apparent—or so one hopes. Intuition, conceived of as "gut" feeling reflecting the agent's cultural background, has a place in prudential reasoning, but it is not the same thing as an in-the-last-analysis prudential judgment.

A certain effort at detachment from the pressures of the moment is involved in prudential judgments. They nonetheless engage one's whole personality, and hence also one's cultural background (which is one reason among others why philosophy cannot make our prudential judgments for us). One of the most difficult problems for prudential judgment is balancing the detachment characteristic of moral judgment with the identification with a given community our dependence on a moral tradition implies.[19] Hence also, it is difficult or impossible to advise those whose outlook is importantly different from one's own.

The virtues most necessary to the cultivation of prudence are those, such as patience and self-control, necessary to the maintenance of long-term commitments. For such commitments require one to attend to the less obvious consequences (and more broadly, the less obvious aspects) of one's actions, and this sort of awareness is an important element of prudence. They also lead us to picture ourselves as connected to other persons, rather than as isolated selves entitled to pursue our own goals without regard to their interests.

Martha Craven Nussbaum (drawing upon her reading of Henry James) tries to correct what she regards as the excessive intellectualism of the Aristotelian tradition.

> Moral knowledge is not simply an intellectual grasp of propositions; it is not even intellectual grasp of particular facts; it is a perception [here she cites Aristotle]. It is seeing complete, complex reality in a highly lucid and richly responsive way; it is taking in what is there, with imagination and feeling.[20]

Such knowledge includes awareness of the character and motives of all the people concerned, including those of the agent himself (who needs to know what sources of distorted judgment he needs to fear).

Yet Nussbaum's account neglects the role moral rules play in the judgments of even the most sensitive agents. She describes a difficult situation in the relationship between a woman and her father, but the resolution they adopted would not have been possible if incest were an acceptable option for them. Concentration on the complex ways in which the various sides of human life interact in real situations is a valuable exercise, but carried beyond a certain point it paralyzes judgment, and may even prove morally corrupting. Our description of a situation will contain many morally laden words. And our equipment for picturing situations includes not only the subtler considerations she favors, but also a moral language that includes words like *murder* and *adultery,* as well as rules of prudence, such as *Do not go to the limits of the permissible except for compelling reasons.* Prudent moral agents are well aware of their need for rules and principles, lest their actions be altogether chaotic or opportunistic. Nonetheless, rules, principles, and maxims are not substitutes for prudence, but guides to it.

We need to be able to recognize prudence in others, to get help in resolving questions that exceed our own capacity. Yet disagreement about who is prudent is as possible as disagreement of any other sort: Plato and Aristotle disagreed about Pericles.[21] We are therefore forced to evaluate persons and not just positions, though even a vile person may be right about some things. The argument here is from authority, and only virtuous people are authorities in matters of morals.

Prudence is not middlingness, but it often supports it. The defense of a middle-of-the-road position must begin by rejecting both extremes on more substantive grounds than they are extremes. The adherents of extreme positions use the rhetoric of final struggle: the moment of truth has arrived, and either we or they must triumph. Some historical struggles do take this form, but often the rival parties fight one another to mutual exhaustion. In such a case moderate positions—for example, a liberal regime of religious toleration—begin to make sense.

CONCLUSION

Morality is concerned not merely with the harm we do one another, but also with the sorts of people we are. Other-regarding and self-regarding morality differ in their structure and texture—one might say that they represent analogous rather than strictly equivalent senses of *moral.* Yet even Mill prefers a reflectively chosen way of life to one dictated by appetite, habit, or custom, on something like moral grounds. Moreover, he writes,

> Though doing no wrong to anyone, a person may so act as to compel us to judge him, and to feel toward him, as a fool, or a being of an inferior order. . . . We have a right, also, in various ways to act upon our unfavorable opinion of any one, not to the oppression of his individuality, but in the expression of ours.[22]

Self-regarding acts also affect what has been called the "moral ecology" of our society, and thus affect other people as well.[23]

Virtue is a necessary condition of sound moral and evaluative judgment. Even at the level of moral theory, a morally bad person may accept repellent conclusions rather than abandon doctrines that enable him to justify his bad behavior to himself. Likewise, naivete may lead a person to adopt moral positions of whose real world consequences he is unaware. Virtues such as humility and charity are required to prevent the degeneration of moral discussion into character assassination.

In order to practice virtue, we need to know what is good and right, at least in those instances where we are required to make decisions. A partial solution to moral perplexity moves from the better to the less well known. In any society, some genuine goods will be pursued, some rudiments of morality will be observed, and some of the traits people admire will be genuine virtues. Though it is possible to give reasons for our moral judgments, they remain to a significant degree a reflection of the sorts of people we are. The answer of virtue ethics to moral perplexity—"become a virtuous person and then you will know"—does not require perfection, only improvement. Nor are all virtues equally necessary for all kinds of decisions.[24]

Chapter 10

Duties

Virtue ethics does not excuse us from the question of what we are to do in difficult cases. I here defend a natural law reading of Kant (or a Kantian reading of the natural law), and apply it to some moral issues.

CONSEQUENTIALISM, PROPORTIONALISM, AND ANTIPROPORTIONALISM

Utilitarianism means consequentialism plus hedonism. But there are morally relevant considerations that are not strictly consequences, such as that a proposed act breaches or strains a relationship, or shapes the agent's character in an undesirable direction. Such considerations shade off into what may be called *moral consequences,* such as the creation or reinforcement of bad habits, or bad patterns of interpersonal relationships, beyond what is intrinsic to the choice itself. The sort of moral thought that results from modifying utilitarianism in this way is called *proportionalism,* and, in its pure form, is open to much the same objections as is pure consequentialism.[1]

Objections to consequentialism and proportionalism point in two different directions. First, the consequences of adopting a consequentialist ethics are bad (and likewise it seems on the whole best not to adopt a purely proportionalist approach to moral questions).[2] This objection supposes that consequentialist reasoning is possible, even though difficult and dangerous—especially in a world where passions are strong, time and information limited, and deliberation itself has significant costs.

To reject consequentialism on consequentialist grounds is to raise the issue of rule-consequentialism (or rule-utilitarianism as it is usually called). Without some sort of nonconsequentialist backing for its norms, however, rule-consequentialism leads to unacceptable indeterminacy. The range of possible rules is indefinitely large, and much of the utility of rules consists in their being shared. Moreover, no human being could apply rule-consequentialism as a general moral system. If we think in terms of an ideal moral code, rule-consequentialism approaches act-consequentialism, since difficult cases can be resolved by a rule fashioned "for this day and this train only." If, on the other hand, our criterion is the consequences of the adoption of some rules by actual human beings, we end up evaluating an entire way of life. The consequences of accepting a rule depend on the other rules in the system. They also depend on the moral and semi-moral attitudes that surround the code aspect of one's morality. Likewise, the consequences of one person's moral rules depend on those adopted by others. In a novel by Susan Howatch, two brothers—one liberated in his views, the other traditionally religious—combine to destroy a vulnerable young woman.[3]

In practice, rule-consequentialist arguments have to do with modifying an existing morality, not with creating a morality ex nihilo. Even so, there are moral changes which it is desirable to exclude ab initio, such as proposals to sanction the killing of people by reason of their ancestry.

Rule-utilitarianism also poses special motivational problems. Act-utilitarians ask us to weigh the interests of persons distant from us, and even of brute animals, equally with our own and those of our friends and family. It is difficult to see, on the view of human nature implicit in utilitarianism, how this feat is to be accomplished. But rule-utilitarianism asks even more: it asks us to value the observance of a useful rule even under circumstances where its violation will do great good and little or no harm.

The New Natural Law Theory

The second argument against consequentialism maintains that such reasoning is not difficult and dangerous, but impossible. Thus John Finnis and Germain Grisez[4] have founded what has been called "the new natural law" school[5] on the rejection of proportionalism, even as one method of prudential judgment among others. (Merely technical [means-end] commensuration, however, they admit as legitimate [e.g., FE IV.3].)

As Finnis puts the two authors' master argument,

> once a moralist accepts a proportionalist method, even as one methodological principle amongst others, he can produce arguments in favour of any solution which he already favours. All such arguments will be illegitimate, i.e., mere rationalizations. Moreover, to the extent that he

> seeks to deny his proportionalist method the exclusive status which it has in the classic utilitarian and other consequentialist systems, he can find no grounds for so restricting it which are not either (a) rationalizations or (b) grounds for excluding the proportionalist method altogether. (FE p. 95)

Grisez argues that a proportionalist cannot satisfy two requirements that any moral method must meet: giving results, and making moral error possible. In Grisez's own words:

> If the first condition is met and the morally wrong action could be chosen, then its morally acceptable alternative must be known. Otherwise one could not choose wrongly, for one chooses wrongly only when one knows which option one ought to choose and chooses a different option. But when the first condition is met, the second cannot be. The option which promises the definitely superior proportion of good to bad cannot be known by a person who chooses an alternative which promises less. If the superior option were known as superior, its inferior alternative simply could not be chosen. (WLJ 1:132)

Finnis and Grisez reason further that, since every argument for rejecting stringent moral norms can be rejected as proportionalist, a morality that commands unconditional respect, in each and every act, for each and every basic human good, is the only rationally available option. Hence Grisez formulates the core antiproportionalist moral principle as follows: "One should not be moved by a stronger desire for some instance of an intelligible good to act by choosing to destroy, damage, or impede some other instance of an intelligible good" (WLJ 1:216).

Finnis and Grisez conclude from these arguments that artificial contraception is always wrong, on the ground that it involves a direct attack on the basic good of reproduction (or on the good of life in its procreative aspect). At one point they join Joseph Boyle and William May in arguing that "contraception should be regarded as homicide is regarded" (THV p. 37), thereby rejecting the guidance other sorts of natural lawyers (and the new natural lawyers in other contexts) find in patent differences of biological fact.

Yet natural family planning, quite as much as the use of a condom or diaphragm, involves an intention to enjoy sexual intercourse while avoiding offspring, and thus would seem to be not only wrong but even homicidal on this argument. Finnis responds that

> the system of identifying fertile times and avoiding intercourse at those times can . . . be followed by couples who form no intention to impede the coming-to-be of a new child, and who in following that system of avoiding intercourse intend only to avoid the bad side effects which having a baby may bring about. (MA p. 86)

But such a couple takes active measures (discovering the woman's fertile period, for example) to achieve their goal, that is, to enjoy the other goods involved in sexual intercourse without producing offspring. One can, moreover, manifest an impermissible intention by inaction, such as by failing to provide a patient or prisoner with food.

The theoretical question here is to what extent differences of intention can be cashed in terms of overt action, and to what extent very different intentions can be expressed in what to all appearances is the same act. Finnis both displays and conceals the central difficulty when he writes:

> Aquinas puts the point starkly when he says that a conjugal act of intercourse and an act of adultery are *acts* of different types even though the behavior, the physical and psychosomatic activity, may be identical. And he does not mean to make the logical, empty point that the two types of act are morally right and morally wrong. Rather, he is saying that the reason that there can be this profound moral difference is precisely that, despite their physical identity, they are different types of human act: the wills of the parties relate to the human goods at stake in intercourse quite differently. (MA p. 38)[6]

There is, however, no reason to suppose that all married, all unmarried, or all adulterous, lovers relate their wills to the goods involved in sexual intercourse in the same way.

The closest thing to an answer to this difficulty is to be found in the following passage:

> To judge one's option right, one must consider all morally relevant circumstances—*bonum ex integra causa.* But one can judge an agent's action wrong as soon as one identifies a morally significant defect in one's motivation, or an inappropriateness in relation either to the circumstances or the means involved in that option—*malum ex quocumque defectu.* (MA pp. 16–17)

We cannot assume, however, that, in every problem situation, a solution free from every "defect" is possible.

Capital punishment takes the death of an individual as an end in a way self-defense and possibly even abortion do not: even on the wildest science-fiction hypotheticals, if the convicted criminal survives, the execution has failed. Nonetheless, Finnis defends the death penalty on the grounds that "the defining and essential . . . point of punishing is to restore an order of fairness which was disrupted by the criminal's criminal act" (FE p. 118).[7] The missing premise here is that the "order of fairness" outweighs this criminal's life in the scales of moral reasoning—a contention which looks proportionalist to me. Grisez has the better of the argument when he rejects Finnis's argument, and expresses the hope that Christian doctrine will develop in such a way as to exclude the death penalty except in rare and extreme cases (WLJ, vol. 1 chap. 8, sec. H, para. 10).

In any event, applying the doctrine of respect for human goods requires proportionalist judgments. Reproduction is a basic good. Suppose that a fertile man with a barren wife finds himself attracted to a fertile woman. If he reins in his sexual desires because he wants to remain faithful to his wife, it would seem that he is at least "impeding," if not exactly "damaging" or "destroying," the basic good of reproduction (a choice that, let us recall, is not merely wrong but homicidal for Finnis and Grisez). If he does so because he does not want to beget a child out of wedlock, he is rejecting reproduction even more clearly. Only a sense of the overriding value of marital fidelity or the proper upbringing of children could lead us to say that one is not exactly choosing, in such a case, to impede that good.

Moreover, all moralities distinguish between more and less serious offenses. In moral theology, this distinction takes the form of a distinction between mortal and venial sin, or more exactly the distinction between light and grave matter: the "subjective" requirements of mortal sin—sufficient reflection and full consent—are not currently at issue. Grisez would make life easier for himself if he adopted the view that he attributes to the theorists of fundamental option, that "grave matter is the sort of thing which is likely to be an occasion for making or reversing one's fundamental option" (WLJ 1:385)[8]. Such a view would reduce his need to distinguish between graver and lighter offenses in terms of the nonspiritual damage they do. In fact, however, he asserts that the distinction between grave and light matter must be maintained "rigidly," rather than adapted to the vagaries of individual psychology and cultural formation. He appeals here to the judgment of the Church, "which perhaps defies easy articulation" (WLJ 1:396), but cannot on his premises be proportionalist.

Politics makes proportionalist judgment indispensable, even for those with strong deontological convictions in morals. The resulting problems of judgment could perhaps be mitigated by adopting a steeply Augustinian distinction between the city of man and the kingdom of God. But there are questions of church as well as secular politics. Both Finnis[9] and Grisez (THV pp. 7–32) are on record as calling for solemn ecclesiastical condemnation of moral views advocated on proportionalist grounds. In fact, a need for excommunication is built into the new natural lawyers' arguments. For root and branch rejection of proportionalism requires walling out much human experience—of believers quite as much as of unbelievers—a fact that perhaps accounts for some of Grisez's more annoying intellectual habits.[10] In any case, popes and bishops, before taking Finnis and Grisez's advice, are required to weigh, not only the truth of the matter, but the effect of their actions on the well-being of the Church.

Although Finnis and Grisez hold that proportionalism is meaningless, they still have a clear idea of the atrocious sorts of behavior it will bring about, or be used to justify—including the nuclear holocaust that has not, yet at least, taken place.[11] Even if we grant that proportionalism is the culprit in such cases, this argument is self-destructive, for on Finnis and Grisez's showing, proportionalism cannot logically imply approval of such behavior. If causal relationships are the issue, then the evil done on proportionalist grounds needs to be balanced against the good so done.

Robert P. George faces a similar difficulty when he observes that "perhaps every generation must learn for itself that 'private immoralities' have public consequences," and that

> to say whether a certain form of what one reasonably judges to be immoral ought to be prohibited or tolerated by law . . . requires an understanding of the complex circumstances of particular political communities at particular times.[12]

For his arguments call for an examination of the consequences of competing policies, and where these consequences are mixed, a weighing of their good consequences against their bad ones.

Whether proportionalist reasoning is impossible, or only difficult and dangerous, cannot be resolved by inspection. But no moralist I know of has ever refused an appeal to consequences when it suited his argument. Considerations such as the bad effects of divorce on children, the value of religious belief and ritual in maintaining group identity, and the likely decline of insufficiently assertive religious bodies are now the stock in trade of conservative religious argumentation. Once a moralist has made such an argument, he cannot honestly refuse to attend to his opponents' consequentialist arguments. For if the good consequences of a rule or institution support the claim that it was ordained by God, then its bad consequences support the claim that it is of merely human origin.[13]

Goods impose a vague and unspecified hierarchy of claims on us before choice, and by our choices we give this hierarchy a clearer structure. Defects in temperament or moral education for which the agent is not to blame may lead to good faith moral error, which we can understand as a failure of perception. On the other hand, habitual wrongdoing, understood at least initially by the agent as such, can also warp his moral capacities; this is traditionally called the darkening of conscience. It is also possible to reason wrongly, either because past decisions of the agent or others, or conditions of human life for which the individual agent is not to blame, have muddled our understanding of the order of goods. Reasoned decision is also possible, however, because reflection, given a virtuous disposition, illuminates the situation and enables us to appreciate the proper hierarchy of goods. The messiness of the resulting picture of morals is no greater than that inherent in human life.

KANTIAN PRINCIPLES

Kant's second (and in my view, most central) major principle—*treat humanity as an end in itself, and never as a mere means*—implies that we should respect other people as rational decision makers, and hence that there are (unclear) limits on the extent that we are entitled to endeavor to prevent their acting in accordance with their best judgment. But we are not mere rational decision makers; we are also animals who eat, mate, and die in ways not that different from dogs and horses. It is not "humanity," but flesh and blood men and women, who have moral problems, and it is the effect of actions on men, women, and children that must centrally concern us in ethical reflection. Murder is possible only because abstract humanity is presented to us in a fleshy form. Thus the following revision of Kant's principle is the closest thing to an ethical axiom possible. *Always respect human beings, in the full complexity of their nature, as beings at once rational, social, historical, and embodied.*

The modified Kantian principle (hereafter "the Kantian principle") is preferable to a "Thomist" principle that focuses on human goods.[14] It provides us with a reason for valuing those goods—that is, respect for the person who embodies or enjoys them—and makes possible a rich array of forms of moral reasoning, connecting abstract principle to the moral problems experienced by human beings. Moreover, it makes it possible to ground ethics in our solidarity with creatures like ourselves, in this case human beings (or rational creatures generally).

The morality defended by Kant also includes duties to self that require us to set aside even powerful desires for the sake of a higher good. There should be no difficulty about such duties, so long as we do not think of morality as solely a matter of maintaining social peace rather than also the attainment of individual perfection. Both self and others are human beings, and as such are entitled to be treated as ends in themselves rather than means merely.

MORAL ISSUES

In discussing applications of the Kantian principle, I follow the traditional distinction between duties to self and duties to others. I also follow Kant in concentrating on violations rather than affirmative requirements.

1. Duties to Others: Lying

One implication of respect for persons is refusal to admit maxims that make an exception for oneself, since such maxims treat other persons as mere means. Thus, though there is no clear way of distinguishing acceptable maxims from those cooked up to serve the needs of a sophistic casuistry, Kant's argument against lying is persuasive unless the defender of lying is prepared to make some very extreme arguments. A liar depends on his statement being taken as a serious expression of belief. "Dear" at the beginning of a letter, and "sincerely yours" at its end, are never lies, however much malice and insincerity may be found between them. If lying were the accepted rule, even the most solemn statements would be regarded as mere courtesies. Hence, unless the liar isolates himself from common humanity by claiming a special privilege, or is prepared to destroy all forms of social life by abolishing all our reliance on one another's word, Kant's argument for honesty is compelling.

A falsehood is not a lie, however, when no reasonable audience would take it as a serious expression of belief. Jokes and speeches in a play are easy examples. Statements exacted under duress cannot be reasonably trusted either. Jews entering an extermination camp cannot be reasonably expected to inform their captors of their correct ages, when both the very young and the very old are destined for immediate death.[15] In all such cases we should speak of deception rather than of lies, since the trust between human beings that is breached by lying does not exist. The difficulty here is determining how far we can exempt the oppressed from the duty of honesty to their oppressors without undermining the possibility of human society (imperfectly just as human society always is).[16]

2. Duties to Self: Suicide[17]

The first step in a philosophical discussion of suicide is to face a powerful, even though by no means universally shared, intuition that suicide is horrible in a way the murder of another, at least as such, is not.[18] The more we have struggled against difficulties, and the more we value the sort of courage that embodies the will to live, the more we are likely to think of a suicide as a traitor, who has broken the solidarity against Death that defines the human community. In lenient moods, we suppose more and more obscure sources of temptation, to alleviate the horror this sort of breaking of ranks engenders.

Suicide of all human acts most engages our metaphysics of the self. Sometimes it reflects a perverse metaphysical motive—a desire to destroy a world (including a human world) that has thwarted one's desires. Thus A.E. Housman writes:

> Here is a knife like other knives,
> That cost me eighteen pence.
> I need but stick it in my heart
> And down will come the sky,
> And earth's foundations will depart
> And all you folk will die.[19]

Some suicides, to be sure, want to go to sleep and escape pain and suffering. Yet even they attempt to escape the burdens of humanity and become a mere part of nature. Nature for Kant involves a moral order, so that a suicide's refusal to consent to it can be unfavorably evaluated from the moral point of view.[20]

Suicide engages the metaphysics of the self because agent and patient are the same. Moreover, it has to do, not with some aspect of our existence, but with our existence as such. Under bizarre circumstances, there can be self-homicide without suicide: as Oedipus cursed himself without knowing whom he cursed, so someone might kill himself without knowing whom he killed. But suicide kills oneself precisely as such. As Michael Wreen well puts it,

> Our being in and of the world, and our not being in and of the world; our total freedom to act and the most basic constraint upon our freedom—life itself; our agency and patiency; our dual, seemingly irreconcilable nature, subjective and objective—all are viewed, from both the subjective and objective perspective, in suicide. . . . And yet it is also the repudiation, the ontological repudiation, of our very humanity, but a repudiation which is metaphysically possible only for humanity.[21]

The possibility of metaphysically perverse motivation makes the principle of double effect of special importance when dealing with suicide. Socrates, who intends to do what the law of Athens requires of him, the soldier who throws himself on a grenade to save his comrades, and the patient who accepts morphine to ease his pain even though it may also hasten his death do not commit suicide in the relevant sense. The argument so far, however, does not help us in the more notorious casuistical cruxes, such as that of the spy who kills himself to avoid telling secrets under torture, or of self-starvation as a means of spiritual cleansing as recommended by Schopenhauer.

The resulting issues cannot be considered in exclusively self-regarding terms. The suicide of the parent of the same sex can have especially debilitating effects upon a child, since it conveys the message that the outcome of life's struggles is despair. To legitimate suicide is to put those who are chronically ill, disabled, or in disgrace under pressure to make things easier for the rest of us by removing themselves from our environment. Just about the most pernicious message we can send to young people struggling with life's difficulties is the attempt to legitimate suicide as a "lifestyle option": the anger toward self such arguments counsel can easily be turned outward.

Yet if effects on others were the only consideration, then there would be many circumstances in which suicide might seem to be mandated (for example, to reduce the welfare rolls or even overpopulation). A more adequate understanding of the common good includes not just an individual's role as economic producer, but the value we place on one another as persons (and hence also on the virtues of compassion or generosity). For society is not something other than its members, and the well-being of society consists in the well-being of its members.[22] Hence we return to the question of whether suicide can be warranted as beneficial to the suicide himself.

Suicide is a breach of one's duty to oneself. To kill oneself because one's life lacks the appropriate "quality" is to treat one's existence as having, not a dignity, but a price. A code of duties to oneself that allowed suicide without restriction would be like a moral code that limitlessly tolerated killing of others. It is a breach of one's duty to oneself deliberately to extinguish one's capacity for moral choice—say by joining a cult where one's every decision is made by a religious authority (whether this ever happens I do not know).[23] If moral suicide is wrong because it violates the autonomy of the agent, then physical suicide is wrong because it violates the agent in every aspect. We cannot set against the case against suicide a balance sheet of goods and evils, whereby a person might conclude that he is better off dead than alive. For death is opaque and for that reason incommensurable with whatever prospect life may extend to us.

Alan Donagan permits suicide in overloaded-boat cases, to avert a threat to others (or spare them excessive burdens as caregivers), or "to obtain release from a life that has become not merely hard to bear, but utterly dehumanized."[24] Yet to jump out of an overloaded boat is not to purpose one's own death, but only to accept it as a foreseen result of one's withdrawal from a situation. In cases of threat to others, suicide is legitimate only if those benefited by it would have at least a good case for killing the prospective suicide on their own. If capital punishment is ever legitimate, it seems that the condemned may be appointed his own executioner. If someone considers killing himself to prevent disclosing a vital secret under torture—or if a dangerous maniac, who cannot be kept from killing in any other way, considers killing himself in a lucid interval—there may no leisure "to commit [oneself] to the judgment of others," as St. Thomas Aquinas puts it.[25]

The most plausible other exceptions involve suicide to escape, not pain or disability, but situations in which one's human dignity is systematically denied. No pain need be involved in such situations: imagine killing oneself to avoid the use of one's comatose body as an organ farm or for purposes of nontherapeutic experimentation. So long as I am alive, however, I retain, if not the limitless freedom supposed by Sartre, but a freedom to redefine my situation and alter my course of action accordingly. Suicide may "misfire," and if so I may subsequently judge my decision to have been one of cowardice. Therefore, it is possible to say of a successful suicide, that had he survived the attempt, he would have regretted it, and preferred to have redefined his situation in ways that affirmed his own dignity. Nor is it a point in favor of an action, that the agent has, in a way irrelevant to its merits, cut off the possibility of regret. We admire those slaves who did not kill themselves, or even bring about their own deaths by hopeless rebellion, but managed either to escape or to live with some dignity as slaves.[26]

Hence, a strict moralist can respond that, even in cases such as the use of a person's body as an organ farm, there is no degradation of the victim, as long as he does not consent to his being abused in this way.[27] In Kantian terms, the issue involves the complex question of the relationship between the noumenal and the empirical selves, and in particular whether the noumenal self is entitled to discard the empirical self when it no longer manifests its dignity. The relationship between these two selves or aspects of the self is one of the darkest spots in Kant's philosophy; in any event, we are required to accord some respect to the empirical self if we are to avoid the notorious argument of the *Gita,* that since the Soul is immortal it does not matter whom we kill.[28]

A further issue is whether we ought to revive the older language of self-murder.[29] In most cases, suicide will involve temptations of a sort that make the language of murder inappropriate. But suicide as the last resort of the bored aesthete, or suicide motivated by an unjust desire to hurt other people, requires the strongest language of moral condemnation, of the act, even if not of the agent. (Another case in which severe judgment is appropriate is when one person undertakes to encourage and assist the suicide of another.)

From the *Phaedo* on, the question of suicide has been discussed, not only in terms of duties to oneself and to other people, but also in terms of one's duties to the gods (or God). It is not possible for human beings to benefit or injure God, and Locke's appeal to God's property rights as a ground for human dignity is highly questionable. Nonetheless, the demands of society on me, and my understanding of my own good, need not harmonize even on the highest level, and an appeal to divinity as transcending them both is therefore in order. David Novak treats God in philosophical contexts as a reminder of human finitude. In Novak's own words,

> The suicidal person must be patiently taught to see and accept his own limitations so that he can affirm a world outside himself; only thus can he be helped to draw vitality once again from natural inclination, to converse with other persons, and to be silent in the face of what he cannot know, which for some is to wait for God.[30]

If we cannot make the awesome judgments necessary to justify suicide, the normal claims of human life can be brought to prevail.

3. Sex

The central moral principle advocated here is a form of modified Kantianism: *Always respect human beings, in the full complexity of their nature, as beings at once rational, social, historical, and embodied.* I now propose, as an auxiliary to this principle, the *overflow principle: Act toward that which, though not a person, is closely associated with persons, in a manner coherent with respect for persons.*[31] The moral status we accord to persons overflows to those entities and processes closely associated with persons. This principle will enable us to deal with those issues that arise from our embeddedness in biological lineages—with the domain of "birth, copulation, and death."

Because animals share with us such things as a capacity for pleasure and pain, they ought not to be injured without good reason; because corpses issue from people and resemble them, they ought to be respectfully disposed of. Since the existence and character of future generations depend on reproductive and other choices made now, future generations cannot be treated as persons like ourselves, only "downstream" in time. Nonetheless there ought to be future generations,[32] and we ought to be concerned about the quality of their natural and social environment. Likewise, because human reproduction involves the coming-to-be of a person, it is important that it be carefully distinguished from manufacture.[33]

Sexual passion easily escapes from moral and rational restraint, and can be separated from the rest of a person's moral and emotional life. The connection between sex and procreation also implies that sexual issues are not merely questions about the good, but moral issues as well. Because sexuality is the way new persons are brought into the world, it should not be treated merely as a source of entertainment or emotional release.

As Karol Wojtyla put it before becoming John Paul II, "The problem for ethics is how to use sex without treating the person as the means to that end, and so as an object of use."[34] Some moralists might even argue that sexual activity is always immoral, since it involves treating a person, oneself or a real or imagined other, as an object of appetite. Nor does it help to defend sex as necessary to reproduction, since for a man to use a woman as a means for the production of an heir is no better than his using her as a means to his pleasure. It is chiefly Kant's common sense that keeps him from condemning all forms of sex, even in marriage for purposes of procreation. Nor is it sufficient to appeal to love to resolve the difficulty, since cooperation may involve exploitation, which feelings of affection may mask.[35]

Donagan proposes the following principle of sexual morality: *"Sexual acts that are life-denying in their imaginative significance, or exploitative, are impermissible."*[36] Exploitation, we may agree, is wrong in sexual contexts as well as outside them. What some people most value in sexual experience—the release of psychological forces normally kept under wraps by the requirements of civilization—also makes sex dangerous both to the person and to those others toward whom his sexual impulses are directed. Nonetheless, the concept of "life-denying imaginative significance" is very hard to apply; I here limit myself to one timely and sensitive example.

An unfavorable judgment on homosexual practices is deeply rooted in our philosophical and religious traditions, and is not necessarily dispelled by familiarity with homosexuality as a way of life. Plato, who of all philosophers of the first rank had perhaps the best opportunity to examine what the homosexual life meant in practice,[37] wrote that "the crime of male with male, or female with female, is an outrage on nature and a capital surrender to lust of pleasure."[38] The question at hand is whether this judgment can receive rational support in a contemporary context.

The "new natural law" theory has difficulty supporting a prohibition on homosexual practices since, unlike the use of contraceptives, these need not involve a decision not to reproduce (and heterosexuality is sometimes sterile).

Finnis gives the gist of the new natural lawyers' answer to this objection in the following passage:[39]

> Sexual acts cannot *in reality* be self-giving unless they are acts by which a man and a woman actualize and experience sexually the real giving of themselves to one another—in biological, affective, and volitional union in mutual commitment, both open-ended and exclusive. . . . A husband and wife who unite their reproductive organs in an act of sexual intercourse which, so far as they then can make it, is of a kind suitable for generation, do function as a biological (and thus personal) unit and thus can be actualizing and experiencing the two-in-one flesh common good and reality of marriage, even when some biological condition happens to prevent that unity resulting in generation of a child (LAS, pp. 30–31).

Judged by this normative understanding of marriage, homosexual acts are "radically and peculiarly non-marital, and for that reason intrinsically unreasonable and unnatural" (LAS p. 25).

If sex is legitimate only in marriage, and if marriage is by definition heterosexual (or procreative at least in intention), then homosexual acts are illegitimate (and homosexual relationships especially bad because they cannot ever become marriages). This argument is valid, and its premises are believed by otherwise reasonable people without direct appeal to revelation. There is nonetheless something unsatisfying about this argument.

The claim that homosexual acts are inherently nonmarital requires more defense, in view of the marital quality of some sterile heterosexual acts. One source of difficulty lies in the concept of a "reproductive-type act." (In the view of the new natural lawyers, all marital acts are reproductive in type, though not all acts reproductive in type are marital.) As Robert P. George and Gerard V. Bradley explain the concept,

> The concept of a reproductive-type act is biological-functional. It refers to a species-specific pattern of behavior suited to the reproductive function. Although that function is completed only if certain nonbehavioral conditions also obtain, the pattern of behavior remains the same even if these conditions do not obtain. . . . The marital quality of spousal intercourse is not vitiated . . . by the fact that reproduction is impossible for all married couples most of the time . . . and for some married couples all of the time.[40]

Homosexual acts cannot be "open to new life," in the sense that the parties can seriously envisage possible reproduction, any more than can a shepherd who has intercourse with a goat while fantasizing about breeding a faun (LMS, pp. 28–29 n.46). But the same is true of some heterosexual acts that most people regard as normal (and the new natural lawyers as properly marital)—such as vaginal intercourse with a woman who has undergone a hysterectomy. Not every objection along these lines turns on the premise that our sexual organs are "equipment," whereby men and women achieve ends ranging from reproduction to pleasure.[41] The question is whether the anatomical and physiological differences between a wombless woman and one with a womb render the former sort incapable of "reproductive-type acts."

In relying on the surface features of action to determine their moral quality, the new natural lawyers depart from the insight that governs their arguments elsewhere—namely, that it is not what an act looks like that determines its moral quality, but the way the agent orients himself to human goods.[42] In the light of this consideration, Grisez moves too fast when he asserts that

> the experience of intimacy of the partners in sodomy [homosexual lovers] cannot be the experience of any real unity between them. Rather, each one's experience of intimacy is private and incommunicable, and is no more an experience of the common good than is the mere experience of sexual intimacy and orgasm (WLJ 2:653).

Though the question remains, why homosexual lovers choose sex rather than conversation to express their friendship (WLJ 2:653–64).

The new natural lawyers rightly insist that "marriage, as a one-flesh communion of persons, is intrinsically, and not merely instrumentally, good" and that the acts that consummate and sustain it are consequently good as well (and not merely means to the production of offspring or other extrinsic ends). They further maintain that sexual acts that are *merely* reproductive—in which an heir is sought without regard to affection or the other goods of marriage—fail to achieve the goods characteristic of marriage.[43] Nonetheless, their claim that the moral acceptability of homosexual acts turns on their marital quality is highly implausible.

It is coherent to accept some forms of nonmarital sexual behavior while rejecting homosexual practices, as do the customary moralities of many groups. The traditional conception of marriage is a very demanding one, from which many married couples, or persons customarily regarded as such, fall short in various ways. Somehow we must draw the line between acceptable and unacceptable forms of imperfection, and, at least ordinarily and for the most part, nonmarital forms of heterosexuality approach the ideal more closely than do homosexual acts. It remains to be shown, however, that all instances of homosexual practice fall below the admissible threshold, and that some nonmarital heterosexual acts rise above it.

Second, marriage is more than the union of the spouses: it is also a social institution, one of whose purposes is the regular procreation and upbringing of children. Homosexuals can have children, but such children are not products of their union. As for adoption, if we are prepared to place children under the care of avowed, practicing homosexuals, it seems absurd to worry about their marital status (though some assurance of stability might be required).

Despite these difficulties, we have reasons to believe that homosexual practices are at least ordinarily and for the most part vices, though in the case of persons incapable of realizing the heterosexual norm, excusable vices. Sex is a morally significant matter, and morality is not merely a matter of what we owe each other, but of our own perfection. And heterosexuality is normative, both by reason of its reproductive potency and because it represents the union of the two halves of the human species.

In fact, the human race is not divided into "homosexuals" and "heterosexuals" with a chasm between the two groups. Nonetheless, the hard core homosexual who manages to find stability in a relationship with a member of his own sex must excite our sympathy and respect, for his way of life is at least an improvement on the promiscuity now common among heterosexuals and homosexuals alike. Nonetheless, an unusual psychological disposition, although it may excuse, cannot justify deviations from the norm. If homosexual practices were legitimate, they would be legitimate for everyone—for example, natively heterosexual men and women whose experiences have soured them on the opposite sex. Detailed sexual casuistry must be left to the moral theologian, the expounder of the customary morality of some group, or the deliverances of the conscience of a virtuous agent. The moral theologian will remind us that we all fall short of what we ought to be, sexually as in all other ways.

4. Nonhuman Nature

It is relatively easy to argue for a duty to preserve nature as an object of the aesthetic enjoyment and practical interest of human beings, including those of future generations. The more difficult question is whether morality requires respect for nature for its own sake. Reverence for the natural order is a likely implication of one way of understanding a natural law approach to ethics. For we did not create the universe, and not everything in it serves our purposes. This line of thought proceeds most smoothly in theological terms: we were created, not to destroy our world, or limitlessly to exploit it, but "to till it and keep it" (Genesis

2:15 RSV). Thus ecologists rightly protest the species self-worship that results from decapitating the Christian worldview and leaving humanity the sole reason for the existence of nature.[44]

If it would be wrong to put an end to the human species by refusing to reproduce, the community (or the species) has some claim upon us apart from that made by individual people, and this way of thinking can then be extended to the biotic community as well. What we lack is a solid intuitive morality against which to check our theories. Ethical theory is dependent upon an agreed-upon, working morality, and in the absence of such a morality, beats its wings in thin air.

The extremes to which ecological ethics can go are illustrated by some remarks of John Aspinall:

> I would be very happy to see 3½ billion humans wiped off the face of the earth within the next 150 or 200 years and am quite prepared to go myself with the majority. Most of you sitting here are redundant in every possible sense of the word.[45]

In a more moderate vein, many ecologists value the "integrity, stability, and beauty of the biotic community" in a way that requires overriding the interests of individual animals (including human animals): some ecologists defend hunting, at least of species whose excessive numbers threaten the balance of nature (and some of their rhetoric suggests that they would defend the hunting of human beings, too). In such a philosophy, the interests of domesticated animals will count for very little.[46]

To deny any singular status to human beings is to undercut the entire ecological project, for it is not tigers or snail darters, but men and women, who are asked to restrain their appetites (including their appetite for domination) for the sake of the natural order. Hence, those who prefer sagebrush to people are something of a menace, for the outcome of their philosophies is more likely to be moral nihilism, and a reactive return to extreme anthropocentrism, than a stable concern for the environment.[47]

Chapter 11

Rights

Central to our political rhetoric is the invocation of natural or human rights, which override the laws and customary morality of any society.[1] For example, it is one of our firmest convictions that police who torture suspects violate their rights, even apart from some law forbidding them to do so.

ANCIENTS AND MODERNS

Nonetheless, a group of writers inspired by Leo Strauss find the concept of natural or human rights tainted in its origins and questionable in its application.[2] They argue that everything that we can say using this concept can be said more clearly, and with fewer subjectivistic overtones, without it.

Ernest L. Fortin treats the issue as a conflict between the ancients and the moderns (at some risk of homogenizing both groups of thinkers).

> According to the original natural law theory, human beings are social and political by nature. . . .They do not have from the start all that they require for their well-being and attain their full development only by engaging in activities that involve them in a web of reciprocal relationships typically structured within the context of civil society—ideally the *polis*—the comprehensive and truly self-sufficient human association and hence the only one capable of satisfying their longing for completion or wholeness. . . . In contrast to the natural law theory, the natural rights theory proceeds on the assumption that these same human beings exist first of all as complete and independent wholes,

> endowed with prepolitical rights for the protection of which they "enter" into a society that is entirely of their own making.

He illustrates his argument by contrasting two ways of opposing abortion:

> The old argument was mainly concerned with what abortion does to the person who performs it or allows it to be performed; the new one, with what it does to the aborted fetus. . . . The question, bluntly stated, is whether the two approaches are fully compatible with each other.[3]

St. Thomas Aquinas makes life difficult for his commentators by placing himself on both sides of the underlying question: sometimes he insists that the claims of human society are qualified by the superior claims of God; elsewhere he compares a criminal to a diseased body part that may be amputated for the good of the whole.[4]

The argument from tainted origins, to be sound, would have to meet two conditions. First, the principles which undergirded early modern natural rights theory would have to be, not just incomplete, but perverse—examples of what is sometimes called "the epistemology of sin."[5] Second, there would have to be so close a connection between these principles and any doctrine of natural rights that it would be impossible for someone who rejects the principles to coherently advance a natural rights doctrine. In our world, there are hardly any deists but abundant rights-talk, nor is everyone who talks about rights a disciple of Hobbes or Locke. Pope John Paul II, for example, uses rights-talk frequently.[6]

Those who deny the reality (or at least the accessibility) of the morally well-ordered world both natural law and natural rights thinkers have supposed pose the deepest questions about rights.[7] Traditionally, God was understood to have created us in such a way as to endow us with rights against one another (though not against Himself), and hence the problems of radical moral incoherence did not arise. This was the position of eighteenth-century deism, which could be followed without inconsistency by Christians and Jews. Invoking a theological background does not, however, excuse us from grappling with disturbing theoretical and practical issues.[8]

On a mundane level, critics of rights-talk point out that our conception of rights is closely connected with a liberal regime; and that theoretical developments within the liberal tradition reflect and legitimize changes in that system—from its origins in the downfall of feudalism to its present "postmodern" condition.[9] The issue here is what impact this observation has on the use of rights-talk by those who are critical of regnant liberal institutions. The reasons why Catholic spokesmen have adopted the language of natural or human rights, after having for a long time resisted it, are not hard to find.[10] They have wanted to say things that easily lend themselves to the language of human rights: not only about abortion, but also about religious freedom and social issues. Since such language has had wide currency in our world, it provides a context in which their teachings, even if they do not win agreement, are relatively unlikely to be ignored.[11]

As Robert P. George observes, "some, but not all, claims about justice can be conveniently translated into the language of rights."[12] Justice is an exceedingly complex concept.[13] In its broadest, Platonic sense, justice is equivalent to the whole of virtue, and includes self-regarding as well as other-regarding qualities. In a somewhat weaker sense, it includes what we owe God as well as what we owe our neighbor, even though our neglect of our religious duties does not injure Him. In a weaker sense still, justice includes whatever we owe our neighbor, even if our duties do not ground correlative rights. A still weaker sense excludes such claims, but includes our duties to those in authority, though the primary point of such duties is the welfare of the community for the sake of which such people exercise authority. Only in the minimum sense of *justice*—that which correlates with specific interests of other individuals—does justice directly ground claims of right.

As Thomas Nagel puts it, "Rights cannot be discovered by pure intuition: They must be justified by their role in making it unreasonable for anyone to reject a system that protects them, and reasonable for some to reject a system that does not."[14] In order to have natural rights, we need not be asocial creatures who enter into social relations for limited purposes. In defining a scheme of rights, and hence also such an understanding of justice, the needs of social life can have a large place.

THE RIGHTS WE HAVE

Rights-based theories are appealing because they attempt to give us moral and political guidance without opening up the endless controversies about the good life that other approaches to ethics invite. But it turns out that such theories are undermined by the vices latent in their virtues. It is not sufficient to appeal to a right to life, whose contours are discovered in intuition, to settle moral issues about killing.[15]

Nonetheless, one ought not to express this conclusion as a denial of the right to live. Nor are our rights wholly at the mercy of our societies, which might be tempted to redefine us as subpersonal to advance some collective goal.

We may distinguish a wider and a narrower sense of *rights.* A right in the wider sense is the blend of a value and an obligation—in other words, an obligation viewed from the standpoint of the beneficiary. Thus if being tortured is bad for dogs, and it is wrong for me to inflict this evil upon them, then they have a right against me, and all people with similar obligations, not to be tortured. The question of justification is simply the relatively easy one of justifying the relevant evaluations and moral principles.

Discrepancies between the rights we ascribe to people and their desires cannot be resolved on analytical grounds alone. A person's real interests may be closer to his rights than are his apparent desires. We may hope that a servile person will come to value self-respect and autonomous choice once opportunities to experience them are made available. Likewise, we may hope that a disabled, ugly, or dying person may cease to regard himself as a burden, and come to value his right to live, when chances to contribute to family or other community life are presented to him.

Rights claims may be also supported by considerations other than the interests of the apparent beneficiaries. Slippery slope considerations can enter into our ascriptions of individual rights (assuming, as I believe is the case, that slippery slope arguments are not fallacious as such). It would be very dangerous to create an institution of voluntary slavery for the benefit of those Dostoevskian folk who might prefer it to freedom. On the other hand, it is not clear to me that the sole or even the most important criterion of a good society is the range of choices available to its members, especially if many of the alternatives are bad or trivial, or if the celebration of individual choice leads to social disintegration.[16]

There is also a narrower sense of rights, in which human beings (in this capacity, "persons") are the primary rights-bearers.[17] However difficult it may be to specify exactly how, human beings differ from the rest of life by virtue of their capacity for choice. (Animals are wild, but not free.) Human beings who lack this capacity may be considered persons by virtue of their potentiality of acquiring it, or their solidarity with other beings of the same species, but normal, awake, adults remain our paradigm of personhood. Their distinctively human capacities can be destroyed, damaged, or impeded by the action of others, in a way that at least requires powerful justification if it is not to be wrong.

The fundamental principle of rights in the narrower sense is derived from the fundamental principle of duty. *Each of us has a right to be treated with respect, as a being at once rational, social, historical, and embodied.* This principle and the rights it grounds easily extend to those human beings whose lack of human abilities is only temporary, but auxiliary principles are required to derive rights in the broader sense, such as, those of nonhuman animals.

Our argument warrants a number of supraconventional claims of right, which correspond, though only in part, to stock American notions. First, the right to life remains fundamental, since we cannot make choices if we are dead. Second is the right to freedom, and in particular to pursue happiness in our own way. This means primarily the right to live as we think right and good. Third is a right to those goods that are necessary to make it possible for the ordinary person to make significant decisions, or at least to the opportunity to obtain them. In cases of conflict life comes first, then the degree of freedom necessary to act as a human being, as well as welfare rights beginning with goods necessary to life such as food and minimum health care. Least important is the right to do as one pleases just because one so pleases, though even this should not be interfered with without reason.

All of us lose our capacity to act as persons for longer or shorter periods. Those temporarily unable to act as persons, such as children and the curably insane, retain the right to life—that is, to a future in which (or so we hope) they will be able to make choices. This argument applies to the fetus also.[18] The most challenging alternative to potentiality is the *conventionalist principle,* that is, that persons (other than awake adults) are those whom society, or those powerful and articulate enough to make their voices heard, designate as such. But no consensus about abortion exists in any but the most homogeneous societies,[19] and a plain implication of the conventionalist principle, that might makes right at the deepest ethical level, is offensive to conventional opinion (for excellent reasons).[20]

Even in the narrower sense, someone who is bewildered by choice, or otherwise unable to handle liberty, may nonetheless have a right to freedom. For it is, by and large, in the interest of human beings that their freedom should be respected, even if in some particular case a person would be better off, even in his own eyes, if his freedom were restricted. Yet paternalistic arguments might still lead us to qualify or override the right to freedom in special cases.

Likewise, a presocial being has only a right to become social, including the right to life (and the right to be free of gross damage), and the right to access to, and education in, a set of social practices (always some concrete tradition). The right of adults to transmit their cultural and religious traditions, and the right of children to be educated into some tradition or other, frequently comes into conflict with the right of individuals to pursue untraditional ways of life.[21]

The rights of those members of the human species permanently incapable of human choice are, logically speaking, of the wide sort we attribute to nonhuman animals, and the same is true for future generations, who do not exist to have rights (and whose very existence depends upon decisions made now). But such rights need not be for that reason less important than the rights of persons in the full sense. In some cases, they may be reflections of the rights the person had when capable, which may extend even to the disposal of his dead body. In other cases, they represent a concern for the maintenance of human community, which is threatened by attacks on its most vulnerable members as much as by neglect of the human future. The Nazi genocide campaign began, not with Jews, Slavs,

Gypsies, or homosexuals, but with Aryan life deemed unworthy of continuation. Thus a fetus is not merely a person by virtue of its potentiality; it is also morally relevant that it is a human being by virtue of its species membership.

Another important set of rights upheld in our political and legal tradition concern process.[22] The most elementary of these rights is a person's right not to have collective sanctions imposed on him without notice of the charges against him, and an opportunity to defend himself against them (and appropriate advice in so doing). It is a precept of the natural law (*audi alteram partem,* as the Latin jurists put it) that no one ought to be condemned unheard—and this precept is largely independent of the other characteristics of the legal system of which it is a part.[23] Rights-talk, as opposed to talk about goods, duties, and virtues, receives its clearest warrant in a procedural context. The virtue of justice, in the sense proper to a judge, consists in respect for the rights of the parties before one.

The principles that apply to the state do not apply without more ado to communal institutions, but a communal context does not make questions of justice irrelevant. The right to a hearing binds private associations, including churches—at least if we regard excommunication as a serious deprivation.[24] The maxims *An unjust law is no law at all* and *Take away justice, and what are kingdoms but great robber bands?* apply in church contexts as well as in any other. No theologian I know of holds that ecclesiastical authorities are infallible in matters of discipline.[25]

A RIGHT TO DO WRONG?

John Courtney Murray describes the proposition "that a man has a right to believe what is false or to do what is wrong" as "moral nonsense."[26] A critic representing the error-has-no-rights tradition responds: "It is just such nonsense that is established by the First Amendment."[27] Many liberals would conclude from this exchange: so much the worse for the concept of moral and religious truth. Independently of the question of religious truth, many people are prepared to assert that we have a right to do certain actions (e.g., to spend a windfall on racehorses and champagne, or to vote for a racist party), and at the same time to hold that such an action would be wrong.[28] An adequate understanding of rights will, however, both vindicate the First Amendment against the charge of moral nonsense and at the same time uphold the notion of religious and moral truth. There is, I shall conclude, a (limited) right to do wrong, but this right does not preclude moral judgments about the actions I have a right to perform.

We human beings have rights against one another, not against God, against nature, or against truth. Likewise, human beings have rights, not propositions, even true ones. Whether God has rights is a complex question, but, since we can neither injure nor benefit Him, rights-talk is not the best way of presenting His claims.

A bare liberty to do *p* consists in the fact that one is not under a duty to abstain from *p,* but implies nothing about the obligations of others. A *liberty right* is the right to be left alone in the enjoyment of some good, or the doing of some action. It need not imply a *claim right,* or a right against some person, that he or should assist one in its exercise; or a *welfare right,* or a right to the help of some group, including society as a whole—through tax dollars or otherwise. *Manifesto rights* involve some group of persons getting together to demand their rights, often ill-defined with respect to the distinctions just made.[29] The right to life does not by itself imply the right to be rescued, though its existence may be part of an argument for recognizing such a right. All that it means is that other people are under a duty not to kill me. I can have a right to believe something without anyone having a duty to approve my beliefs, or fund their dissemination; or a right to do something wrong without anyone having the duty to cooperate with or fund my wrongdoing. The line between criticism of a person's behavior, or refusal to cooperate with it, and coercion is not always clear, but the difficulty of drawing a line does not imply that there is no line to be drawn.

Interference with other people's conduct has moral implications larger than merely stopping that behavior; it may, for example, curtail a sphere of liberty that we believe is important for men and women to enjoy. Any system of property—and not just a capitalist one—requires that there be forms of behavior that, although those who control some resource ought not to engage in them, are none-theless "within their rights." Though feeding children is of greater value than col-lecting Elvis memorabilia, we cannot just seize the property of Elvis fans to support a welfare program.

George maintains that rights to do wrong "exist only as 'shadows' of govern-mental duties not to intervene, which duties are not themselves grounded in the rights of individuals to perform immoral actions."[30] In the case of the right to hold and advocate false ideas, however, the government's duty not to interfere rests on respect for honest error and the value of the public dialogue to which such errors contribute—even supposing that, in extreme cases such as that of Nazi advocacy, this duty no longer applies.

Error is bad, and ideally everyone would believe the same (true) things. The right to free speech arises in important part from our need to consider false hypotheses in order to discover truth, and to understand its presuppositions and implications. The risks of pluralism, let us suppose, are not so grave as to cancel this argument, at least in view of the risks of governmental interference with truth seeking, for governmentally imposed consensus is very likely to be consensus in error. Hence it is necessary to have the liberty to put forth dissident views, even if these views themselves should turn out to be false. In religious matters, governmental support for true belief may bring with it the danger that religious teachings will be bent to the convenience of politicians, and that religion will wither when the state loses interest in it.

There are, in any case, wrongs so grave that we may breach any conventional or moral boundary in order to prevent them—in shorter form, wrongs so grave that no one has a right to commit them. The self-determination of nations, for example, does not include the right to exterminate minorities, and international law sanctions humanitarian intervention in extreme cases. Likewise, individuals have no right to hold slaves[31] or commit murder.[32] I want to say that the soldiers on both sides of a war are within their rights when they kill each other though not when they kill civilians—and hence that their acts, though wrong, are not murder—but extending this approach to domestic killings has disturbing implications.

THE CENTRALITY OF HUMAN RIGHTS

Both contemporary public morality and the theory advocated here take human rights as central—not surprisingly, since the parties to the conversation are all human beings. Yet a critic of my work on the ethics of homicide observes:

> Imagine that *we* (members of a dominant race) were to offer an analogous justification for counting lives of subject races as of less importance than our own: "Of course, one might say that whites are unable adequately to judge the richness of the lives of blacks, and thus to determine whether their lives are or are not as valuable as ours. But one is forced in any case to judge matters from one's own point of view, and there is nothing inappropriate in the actions of whites being guided by the perceptions of whites." . . . If we base ethics on self-assertion, as . . . Devine do[es], we can morally exclude oysters and pigs, but we pay a price: those who are asserting themselves can, with equal justification, exclude Jews or Blacks, the retarded, me, or, even, you.[33]

If it is self-assertion to live according to one's own tradition, as purified by scrupulous conscientious reflection, then even the most ascetic morality rests on self-assertion. For our reflections must employ shared criteria of good argument, without which there is nothing to say against the claim that what appears to me an unreasoned screed in fact reflects a sort of logic I am incapable of understanding. Nonetheless, the possibility that the best understanding we have is nonetheless corrupt, as judged by some superior standpoint, represents the deepest challenge to the natural law tradition in ethics.

Chapter 12

The Question of Absolutes

Goods, virtues, and obligations are equally central moral categories. Rights are a bit less central: they attempt to bridge the gap between ethics and politics, but even they are more central to our moral scheme than the concept of *vulgarity*. For all four central concepts the same question arises: Are there acts so bad that no possible good result can justify them? Are there acts no virtuous person will ever commit? Are there obligations that hold whatever the circumstances or consequences? Are there absolute rights?

A FALLACIOUS ARGUMENT

Moral disputes, especially those with wide cultural ramifications,[1] take place on at least two different levels. One concerns particular normative issues; the other concerns the nature and sources of moral authority. Although there is no one-to-one correspondence between views on the first and views on the second level, a person or group's position at one level has a significant impact on his or its position on the other. The sorts of arguments, and consequently the sorts of fallacies, that arise at different levels vary significantly. I now consider a moral dispute conducted, and a fallacy committed, at the second level.

Joseph Margolis defines (and defends) relativism as a "philosophy of the free spirit, of all those unwilling to let *any* premise count as privileged or fixed." Acceptance of this doctrine is for him a brute historical fact: "'Man is the measure' is now entrenched in a remarkably powerful way in all of our thinking."[2] Margolis's dogma has many applications, including the denial of infallible moral and spiritual authorities, and of necessary propositions with interesting content, and belief in the possibility of a completely open mind. Here I shall consider one version of this dogma, the belief that there are no moral absolutes—that is to say, no moral principles of a substantive and even moderately concrete sort that hold regardless of the circumstances or consequences.

Some defenders of absolutes weaken their case by beginning with controversial sexual examples: John Finnis starts with remarriage after divorce, and thereafter heavily emphasizes contraception.[3] But it is much easier to defend the belief that rape and torture are always wrong. Even here, counterexamples are legion, but eventually a plausible counterexample to a plausible moral absolute will be a hard case, no resolution of which will entirely satisfy the conscience. Appeal to the Common Moral Consciousness alone cannot support (or refute) the dogma. Hard cases will have to be resolved on broader theoretical, possibly even theological, grounds.[4]

The denial of moral absolutes sometimes rests on a consequentialist moral theory, so that any moral judgment can be reversed by adducing new unintended consequences. But the deepest source of the denial of moral absolutes is the seductive but fallacious argument that I shall expound and refute here. John McDowell rightly observes that

> if one attempted to reduce one's conception of what virtue requires to a set of rules, then, however subtle and thoughtful one was in drawing up the code, cases would turn up in which the *mechanical* application of the rules would strike one as wrong—and not necessarily because one had changed one's mind; rather, one's mind on the matter was not susceptible of capture in any universal formula.

But it does not follow, as McDowell thinks, that "the best generalizations about how one should behave hold only for the most part."[5]

A fuller statement of the fallacious argument is as follows. Human beings are highly complex creatures living in a highly complex world. Every human being is different from every other, and every interaction or relationship among human beings is unique. Hence every occasion for moral choice is also unique, and all those action kinds (homicide, for example) on which moralists are accustomed to pass judgment include an enormous variety of differing transactions, which ideally ought to be evaluated one by one. Moreover, each proposed action has a variety of different aspects—intention, foreseen consequence, conventional meaning, and symbolic significance, for example—that bear on moral choice in a variety of ways. Moral rules are therefore open to exceptions whenever persuasive arguments for making them are provided.

Our moral capacities are bound to the natural order in which they are exercised. Hence it is not necessary to formulate moral rules to cover naturally impossible situations. There can be no practical need for rules covering such cases, and any result one reaches for them will sound odd, if only because of the oddness of the situation envisaged. Miracles pose a special problem here, but we have no right to count on their occurrence. And a God Who gives us supernatural knowledge of the future will presumably instruct us how to act on it.

Human situations are complex and ambiguous enough without invoking science-fiction/fantasy examples, and this ambiguity and complexity might seem sufficient to support a categorical bar on moral absolutes. Yet an argument that can equally well be used to support both sides of a given controversy does not support either, and the argument against moral absolutes can be inverted. Given the complexity of human situations, a morality that allows practical reasoning an unlimited range quickly becomes unmanageable. If every nuance can make a moral difference, we can never have good reason to suppose that we have specified a situation in sufficient detail to make sound moral judgment possible.[6] Married life, in particular, is complicated enough as it is, without taking on the added sources of difficulty that arise if the spouses are open to other relationships. Thus Aristotle, despite the centrality of practical wisdom to his account of ethics, nonetheless upheld an absolute prohibition on adultery.[7]

Casuistry endeavors to combine the stability of moral absolutes with the flexibility necessary for life. For let us suppose that we acknowledge a moral rule to which we do not—at least as yet—recognize any exceptions. When someone presents a hard case, there are three responses possible: (1) strong-mindedly uphold the moral rule against "sentimental" pleas for an exception, (2) allow an exception in this hard case (and in a potentially unlimited number of hard cases of other sorts), and (3) argue that the sort of conduct in question is not, upon careful consideration, really a violation of the rule. It is not possible, at this level of abstraction, to decide which strategy is appropriate to what cases. But strategy (3) extends the hope of fine-tuning moral judgment to the complexities of moral decision making without opening it up to limitless ad hoc judgments about what seems best at the time.

Faith in the possibility of doing this is not shared by all religious moralists; Lutheran moral theologians have been the most serious questioners here. A fortiori many secular moralists have found it unpersuasive.[8] But the faith of the casuist cannot be overthrown merely by adducing the complexity of moral situations—a complexity of which adherents are well aware.

We are faced with an argumentative situation akin to Kant's antinomies, in which contradictory conclusions follow with equal persuasiveness from the same set of considerations. On the one hand, a skeptic can punch plausible holes in any supposed moral absolute; on the other hand the nonexistence of moral absolutes leads to an endless casuistry, in which more and more horrific possibilities get placed on the table. Even if these possibilities are not accepted in practice, a society in which proposals for genocide are openly debated is a worse society than one in which they are not.

My critique of the most common argument against moral absolutes does not, however, show that there are such absolutes; nor does it provide any way of discovering what they are, should they exist, or even give any grounds for hope about our ability to discover them. The complexity of human situations suggests our need for absolutes, but it also stands in the way of attempts to discover what they are.

DOING EVIL TO ACHIEVE GOOD

St. Paul's maxim *Never do evil that good may come* (see Rom. 3:8) suffers from many ambiguities. The first of these is whether the phrase "that good may come" is redundant: in some views, there is no other way of doing evil. The youthful St. Augustine, when he stole inedible pears, was moved by a desire for excitement and adventure, and the bond his escapade would create with his fellow adventurers.

It is absurd to refuse ever to do evil to achieve good, if doing evil means doing an act with some bad aspect or consequence. For there are many circumstances in which whatever we do is bad in some respect. Nor is it always wrong to intend a bad result, such as the amputation of a limb. The most plausible interpretation of the Pauline maxim is that one ought never to do *moral* evil, to achieve any end whatever. Since from the agent's perspective there is no difference between moral appearance and moral reality, we can also say that one ought never to do what one believes to be wrong. In short

(W) In no circumstances must one do wrong.[9]

W is not to be confused with two related nontautological principles also asserted by Socrates in the *Crito:* (1) One ought not return injury for injury; that is, the fact that someone has injured you does not make an otherwise wrongful action right. And (2) it is never in a person's interest to do wrong.

The denial of *W* is incoherent; as Thomas Nagel has put it,

> The notion that one might sacrifice one's moral integrity justifiably, in the service of a sufficiently worthy end, is an incoherent notion. For if one were justified in making such a sacrifice (or even morally required to make it), then one would not be sacrificing one's moral integrity by adopting that course; one would be preserving it.[10]

W does nothing, however, to tell us what acts are right and what wrong.

When dealing with other people's moral integrity, some distinctions have to be drawn. If it is wrong to do an act, it is wrong to intend that another do that act on one's behalf. If it is wrong for me to kill a colleague, it is also wrong for me to put out a contract on him. If my agent and I differ in moral judgments, two cases need to be distinguished. I may believe the act in question is wrong, whereas my agent has no scruples about doing it. (I employ a hired killer for whom *business is business* trumps even the rule against murder.) In that case I remain guilty of murder, but at least I have not corrupted anyone.

In the other case, I believe the act in question innocent or obligatory, but my agent regards it as wrong. A doctor, let us say, strongly urges a Jehovah's Witness to have a blood transfusion to save his life, or invokes coercive means to get him to do so, although the Jehovah's Witness believes that receiving such a transfusion is a major sin. The doctor may believe that the strength and sincerity of the patient's opposition to blood transfusions may legitimately be tested, so that if it turns out to be merely conventional he will be able to save the patient's life, whereas if it is sincerely held he will admire him for his integrity while watching him die. Or he might hope to persuade his patient that his religion is, at least in this respect, unreasonable, and so to consent in good faith to the transfusion. Or he might be indifferent to the effect of his behavior on the patient's soul, as long as he manages to do the transfusion. Or he may hope that, by being pressured into violating his convictions—and perhaps by being convinced that, if his religion were true, there would be no hope for his salvation—the patient would be led to renounce the Jehovah's Witness faith in favor of, say, liberal Protestantism.

The testing of the patient's conviction is easiest to defend: there need be, on the doctor's part, no intention that the patient act against his own convictions. It is harder to defend efforts at religious persuasion. Since persuasion in religious matters is notoriously difficult, it merges into the other and more difficult cases. Indifference to religious questions is harder still to defend. Ignoring the patient as a moral being, and showing concern for him only as a diseased body, is one of the banes of contemporary medicine. Hardest of all to defend is pressuring a patient to act against his convictions. Playing with another soul in this fashion shows the marks of satanic evil.

In any event, we have a principle that can demand acceptance as absolute if such things are possible:

> (S) It is always wrong to intend that a person do what he himself regards as wrong.

The violation of this principle is called *scandal;* it reflects the fact that a person's moral integrity is a good of a different order than the other goods he may also pursue.

But if we hold a view of morality according to which exceptionless first-order principles are impossible in principle, then we will be reluctant to attribute such principles to others. If we regard an alleged moral conviction as unreasonable beyond a certain point, we may regard it, instead, as an emotional aversion or social prejudice. To be sure, in order to gain the respect of others, a scruple of conscience need not be exceptionless, at least not in the simplest way.[11] Still, if a person's judgment of conscience is responsive to any changes in circumstance however small, those who have the power to change the circumstances of his choice cannot be expected to have much respect for scruples that stand in the way of what they regard as imperative projects.

Now consider the following sentence from Pope Paul VI's controversial encyclical on contraception.

> (V) It is never lawful, even for the gravest reasons, to do evil that good may come of it—in other words, to intend directly something which by its very nature contradicts the moral order.[12]

If by "something which by its very nature contradicts the moral order" is meant moral evil, we have here *W* or *S*—principles that yield no specific results about contraception or any other first-order moral issue. If it means something nonmorally bad—such as a disease—two difficulties arise. First, it is sometimes right to infect a person with a mild case of a disease in order to prevent a severer one later on (the process is called inoculation). Second, it is not a bad thing that a couple should have intercourse without procreating, that a woman should be temporarily sterile, or that a spermatozoon should be ejaculated without fertilizing an ovum. This last event takes place massively in fertile intercourse.

Nor is it clear what it is to "directly intend something" in this context. Do homosexuals directly intend the sterility of their relations? Do those who practice artificial insemination by husband, or versions of in vitro fertilization employing the husband's semen, take as the object of their intentions something different from what married people intend, when they try to have intercourse at the best time for conceiving a child? What do those who practice natural family planning intend, if not to enjoy the other goods of sexual intercourse but not offspring? If we cannot answer the questions of intention, and of the moral acceptability of what is intended, except by way of a moral judgment on the form of activity in question, *V* does not function as an independent moral criterion, but only as a way of expressing a conclusory moral judgment.

THE SEARCH FOR ABSOLUTES

To say that a norm is a moral absolute is to say, in part, that it is never permissible to breach it, no matter what the circumstances or consequences. But not every norm that meets this requirement counts as a moral absolute in the relevant sense.

1. Preliminaries

First consider the following principles:

> (D) One ought always to do one's duty.
> (F) One ought never to engage in sexual immorality (in one sense of that word, fornication).
> (L) One ought never to engage in wrongful deceit (in one sense of that word, lying).
> (M) One ought never to engage in wrongful killing (in one sense of that word, murder).

Duty in *D* can be read in the sense of "my station and its duties," and *immorality* in *F* in the sense of breach of conventional (or traditional) moral standards. But, taken in their most straightforward sense, these standards at most point out zones in which transgression is likely and dangerous.

Consider, second, moral axioms such as

> (A) One ought always to do good and avoid evil.

If *A* is true, one ought never to break it. Moreover, it directs our attention toward nonmoral goods to be promoted, preserved, or respected in our actions, and away from an ethics of duty for duty's sake. But the sorts of absolutes with which moralists are concerned give far more guidance in decision making than, on the most optimistic assumptions, *A* can do.

A more difficult case is

> (P) It is wrong to inflict serious pain just for one's own or another's pleasure.

P seems to be both true and exceptionless, but does not satisfy the demand for moral absolutes. For there may be no such thing as doing something merely for pleasure: there may always be something about the action or its results that pleases one, such as emotional release or the exercise of power. And the desire to please another involves either the expression of some sort of friendship, or else some ulterior end, such as placating someone in power.

Also tricky is the following:

> (H) One ought never to act out of (mere) hatred for a person.[13]

H implies that one has no sufficient reason, other than hatred, for injuring (or attempting to injure) a person. It is thus only apparently a moral absolute.

Another tricky case is

> (X) It is wrong to kill your boss because he has refused you a promotion, where you have been working at your job with reasonable but not extraordinary diligence for less than three years and need the money to buy a second yacht, where neither you nor your boss are members of a caste in which killings of honor are an accepted custom . . . (and so on for a complete description of the action in question).

Such statements, if true, have no exceptions. Nor do the descriptions they include contain an adverse moral judgment by way of logical implication. Nor do they restate moral axioms. Yet they do not count as moral absolutes in the needed sense, since they do not enable one to conclude that an act is wrong independently of a complete evaluation of the situation.

2. Murder

Murder is often defined as the intentional killing of the innocent, but the term *innocent* is ambiguous: it ranges in meaning from "not at fault morally" to "not harming," with all the ambiguities of the word *harm.* Consider the following cases:

> (M1) the execution of a killer for a legacy, who is now rendered harmless;
> (M2) the killing in war of an enemy soldier, who may or may not believe in the justice of his own cause;
> (M3) the killing of a prisoner, in a war in which we regard our enemies not just as wrong but as criminal (as traitors, for example);
> (M4) the abortion of an unborn child whose growth threatens his mother's life, or whose existence threatens a country with overpopulation or a family with destitution.

(M5) the shooting of an insane person who is on the verge of shooting someone else;
(M6) the killing of an infant rival to the throne.

Spelling out one's reasoning about *M1-M6* will reveal how much moral judgment goes into designating a person as innocent, and therefore into designating killing him as murder.

The views of St. Thomas Aquinas on the (almost) sacrifice of Isaac make a similar point.[14] Aquinas does not argue that Abraham does not intend Isaac's death but only accepts it as a side effect of his religious obedience. Rather he argues, in Patrick Lee's words:

> The direct object of Abraham's act here is the justice God intends in the act, even if Abraham does not understand *how* it is just. That is, Abraham does not do anything, or intend anything, other than to execute God's intention. . . . The executor of a superior's project (intention) has no project of his own distinct from that of the superior.

Thus, when God commanded Abraham to slay Isaac, He changed the species of the act from murder to sacrifice. This change of species was possible because, as a result of original sin, Isaac deserved to die "the death of nature." Murder and sacrifice are in this view physically similar, but morally different, sorts of acts.

There are circumstances under which such an analysis is plausible. Socrates, who condemns suicide before drinking the hemlock, intends only to obey the decree of the Athenian court. But this analysis will not work for Abraham: he must form plans and intentions of his own to carry out what he believes to be God's will—such as securing Isaac's compliance or at least acquiescence. The claim that Abraham did not intend to kill Isaac, even as a means (and, had he killed Isaac, would not have done so intentionally), is not tenable.

The supposed moral absolute at stake in Abraham's case would seem to be

(K) One ought never to kill a person unjustly.

This principle might have some content, insofar as it excludes killing someone on grounds of public or private benefit alone. But Aquinas's argument requires him to understand *K* as permitting the killing of anyone except Adam, Eve, Jesus Christ, and the Virgin Mary, so long as it is carried out at the behest of God. The question then arises, who is authorized to interpret God's behests, and by what criteria.

One understanding of *K* is

> (K*) It is wrong to kill a person, except by public authority for the common good.

*K** might support the killing of the tsar and his family by the victorious Bolsheviks, to prevent civil war, or the view that many people take about abortion, which accords sovereign authority to the pregnant woman's conscience.[15]

Finnis objects that the ordinary language/phenomenological approach to moral issues, adopted here, is fundamentally flawed.

> Common speech, which is not systematically oriented toward precise moral understanding and is impressed by behavioral and consequential similarities and by legal categories, is not a safe guide. It uses the action-related terms, including even *act* and *intention,* with an ambiguity which can be overcome only by careful attention to the importance of the end and means united in a proposal shaped by intelligent deliberation (however rapid), and adopted by choice.

What behavior looks like has little or nothing to do with its moral acceptability.

> The physical behavior and causality and outcome can be exactly the same, when completely different acts are done. . . . Equally, acts can be identical in every way relevant to a moral absolute's nonevaluative act-description, even though the physical behavior differs very noticeably.[16]

Yet we need public criteria of intentionality that include, among other things, the look of an action and its expected consequences. If we efface the common-sense distinction as between acts that shed blood and acts that do not, we lose all claim to represent the morality of the ordinary person, even in a purified form. And Finnis is not prepared to renounce appeals to "common morality."[17]

3. Adultery

Many moralists have also asserted the following nontrivial principle as absolute:

> (A) One ought never to commit adultery.

Consider, however, the following cases:

(C1) Abraham lives in a society in which it is customary for a man to have more than one wife. He marries Sarah, and when she proves barren, Hagar.
(C2) Bertha lives in a society in which it is customary for a woman to have more than one husband. She marries Sam, and when he grows old, Henry.
(C3) Charles lives in a society in which marriage is monogamous, but in which men who are faithful to their wives (but not women who are faithful to their husbands) are looked down upon, even by their wives, as insufficiently macho. He marries Mary, and has affairs with Jane and Jill. (I use the word *affair* to describe an informal relationship, without regard to the marital status of the parties.)
(C4) Deborah lives in a society in which marriage is monogamous, but in which both married men and married women who fail to have extramarital affairs are looked down upon, even by their spouses, as prudes. She marries Martin, and has affairs with John and Philip.
(C5) Edward and Frieda live in a society in which serial polygamy is customary—in which marriage, though exclusive, is understood by all concerned to be dissoluble. They get married, and thereafter abstain from sexual relations with others. But, after their marriage breaks down and they are legally divorced, Edward marries Linda, and Frieda marries Carlo.
(C6) In the same society, George and Hilde get married and then divorced, after which they marry Susan and John. But they have sexual relations with their new partners before their divorces are final.
(C7) Isaac and Justine are living together in an informal relationship, understood by both of them to be exclusive so long as it lasts. But Isaac has an affair with Roberta.
(C8) Karl and Leonard are also living in such a relationship—homosexual marriages not being legally recognized in their society. Karl has an affair with Joseph. (To vary the case, suppose that such marriages have received legal recognition.)
(C9) Martina and Nancy likewise have a homosexual "marriage." But Martina has an affair with Kingsley, whom she subsequently marries.
(C10) Oliver and Paula are both Roman Catholics, and understand their marriage as indissoluble. (To vary the case suppose that only Paula is a Catholic.) But Oliver leaves both the Church and Paula, and marries Dorothy in a civil or Protestant ceremony. Until his marriage to Dorothy, Paula regards Oliver as still her husband, but afterward feels free to marry William in a civil ceremony (and does so).

(C11) Quentin and Rita also are Catholics. After their marriage fails, Quentin dishonestly obtains an annulment and remarries Lucy in the Church. Rita then marries Richard.
(C12) Steven and Tina are in the same situation as Oliver and Paula. But, instead of marrying Walter, Tina lives with him without socially recognized marriage of any sort.
(C13) Umberto and Victoria are divorced, and Victoria marries Jonathan. During her marriage to Jonathan, Victoria has an affair with Umberto.[18]

I am not concerned here with the question of whether the behavior of Abraham and the rest is right or wrong by some other standard, but whether it constitutes adultery. Many people who hold *A* also hold

(F*) One ought never to have sexual intercourse outside marriage—what is in the other principal sense called "fornication."

But I here leave open the question both of the truth of *F**, and of whether *A* includes or entails it. Likewise, in cases *C8* and *C9,* I am not concerned with moral objections to homosexual practices as such.

If an act is reprehensible in precisely the way, and precisely for the reasons, adultery is (or believed to be by those who hold *A*), then it is adultery. (Those who reject *A* should probably say, as Oscar Wilde said of blasphemy, that *adultery* is not one of their words.) Still, there is a difference between saying action-kind *X* is wrong for the same sort of reasons as action-kind *Y,* and saying, straight out, that *X* is a subset of *Y.* There are forms of betrayal that are wrong for some of the reasons adultery is, without being themselves adulterous.

To the extent that the judgment "Abraham is (or is not) guilty of adultery" rests on an independent judgment of his act, *A* has become an unenlightening moral absolute, one that should be perhaps spelled out as follows:

(A*) One ought never, by one's sexual conduct, breach the obligations of (true) marriage.

*A** is an example of the uninformative moral principle that one always ought to do what the legitimate requirements of legitimate relationships demand.

A couple, one or both of whom has a divorced spouse still living, can have intentions that are in the fullest sense marital, e.g., to procreate and rear a child as an expression of their mutual love. If he were casuistically minded, D. H. Lawrence could have argued that Mellors and Lady Chatterly were not adulterers. Sir Clifford's failure to relate his will appropriately to the goods at stake in marriage, he might have argued, invalidated his supposed marriage to Lady Chatterly, whereas she and Mellors related their wills to these goods in at least a relatively appropriate way. There may be no couples who fully embody an appropriate understanding of the ends of their relationship: the marriage of the Virgin Mary and St. Joseph is traditionally regarded as celibate.

For these reasons, Finnis moves too quickly when he writes,

> Where, as in most cases of adultery, there is no doubt that the one party, if married, is not married to the other, then the Lord's precept applies exceptionlessly, whatever the other circumstances.[19]

The question whether a person relates his will appropriately to the relevant human goods, and the question whether his conduct is morally appropriate, cannot be distinguished in practice. In fact, Finnis has turned *A* into the following spurious absolute:

> (A**) One should never engage in sexual behavior that relates one's will to the goods at stake in sexual intercourse in an inappropriate way.

4. Conclusion

It nonetheless seems possible to formulate some standards that are absolute if any standards are.

> (G) It is wrong to kill people by reason of their ancestry (genocide).
> (R) It is wrong to engage in sexual activity with a person without his or her consent (rape).
> (T) It is wrong to torture a person.[20]

Despite the ambiguities about consent that sometimes afflict *R,* and the blurry line between torture and beating someone up or threatening him that afflicts *T,* it seems that these propositions are both true and exceptionless. (I leave it to the reader to find possible ambiguities in the rule against genocide.) Only an a priori conviction that all moral rules have exceptions can lend credence to the possibility of sometimes justifying their breach. Yet those who are committed to finding exceptions to all moral rules will no doubt be able to develop plausible exceptions even to *G, R,* and *T.*

THE CONCEPT OF THE SACRED

The cultural Left is correct in asserting the diversity and complexity of human life. Each marriage, for example, is unique, because each person, and each history of interaction between two or more people, is unique. Yet those who celebrate chaos themselves underestimate human complexity. For it is arbitrary for the votaries of openness to close themselves to one important human desire alone, among the galaxy of human desires—the desire to overcome the many threats, both internal and external, to an ordered life.

Moral absolutes have a motivational dimension that responds to the threat of moral chaos in a way that makes terms like *sacred* natural. A virtuous person will not merely abstain from murder, rape or torture, but will have an entrenched aversion to such acts that will, sometimes at least, prevent him from performing them even when they might appear to be justified. As Stuart Hampshire has observed, such actions involve

> a sense of disgrace, of outrage, of horror, of baseness, of brutality, and, most important, a sense that a barrier, assumed to be firm and almost [?] insurmountable, has been knocked over, and a feeling that if this horrible, or outrageous, or squalid, or brutal, action is possible, then anything is possible and nothing is forbidden, and all restraints are threatened.[21]

Sacred is not just a strong word for good.[22] In its traditional meaning, it has the double sense of "holy" and "accursed." (A man can be struck down for laying profane hands on the ark of the Lord.) Hence, if we say that human life is sacred, we mean two things. First, human beings are valuable in themselves, and their destruction for that reason an evil. Second, infringements on this good are not only bad in themselves, but threaten systematically to undermine the entire set of moral restraints that distinguish tolerable human social life from barbarism.[23]

Kai Nielsen writes:

> The general moral principles surrounding bans on killing innocent people are strong and play such a crucial role in the ever floundering effort to humanize the savage mind—savage as a primitive and savage again as in contemporary industrial society—that it is of the utmost social utility, it can be argued, that such bans on killing not be called into question in any practical manner by consequentialist reasoning.
>
> However, in arguing in this way, the moral conservative has plainly shifted his ground, and he himself is arguing on consequentialist

> grounds that we must treat certain nonconsequentialist principles as absolute (as principles which can never, *in fact,* from a reasonable moral point of view, be overridden, for it would be just too disastrous to do so).[24]

To invoke consequentialist considerations to justify the acceptance of a moral rule need not, however, mean accepting the contention that it admits of consequentialist overriders, as opposed to consequentialist applications in ambiguous cases. On the contrary, the consequentialist argument for accepting a moral rule is also an argument for resisting consequentialist exceptions to it.

Some writers argue: if we regard God or Society as the author of the moral law, each of us may have to follow its requirements, even when they mean accepting less than the best consequences overall. But if I view myself as the author of the moral law, I have no reason not to set aside a rule when it conflicts with my obligation to promote the overall good. As Conrad D. Johnson has put it, "to stand under external authority implies that the competence to make . . . fundamental revisions belongs to someone *else* (God, an elite, or the majority through the social conventions they create)."[25] Hence consequentialism is the most appropriate morality for a secular, pluralistic society. But this argument proves too much. Unless my morality includes some sense of external constraint, I have no reason not to revise it when it conflicts with my interests or even my present inclinations. I therefore have no reason to prefer altruistic consequentialism to some form of moral minimalism—whether nihilistic, egoistic, or extreme libertarian.[26]

THE SEARCH FOR ABSOLUTES CONTINUED

Strongly entrenched moral rules are necessary for a workable morality, and thus also for tolerable social life. The relevant causal claims are, however, easy to make but hard to sustain, even in retrospect. There may be people who, starting with the use of conventional playing cards, have made a shipwreck of their lives. But even in such cases it does not follow that the decision to play cards was the decisive wrong turning; that may have come later or earlier. Society has the ability to absorb remarkable amounts of misbehavior, though sometimes this misbehavior reaches a point—call it a "Watergate point"—at which it is necessary to uphold or abandon challenged standards. Such points are unpredictable in advance; deciding when they have arisen is one of the most delicate tasks of prudential judgment. Finally, the decomposition of social orders, though always risky, is not bad without qualification, for some social orders are unjust beyond the limits of tolerance.

Nonetheless, social disasters do occur, and at least some examples of them are uncontroversial, at least in retrospect. The path to disaster is paved by a multitude of individual and collective decisions, some of which at least are well-intentioned. The hope that social disaster will lead to a better social order cannot form the foundation for prudent action. Donald Evans is therefore irresponsible when he holds that "the history of allegedly revealed and allegedly exceptionless rules seems to me to be a history of empirical error and moral evil."[27] Rigorous moralists, even those who in the final reckoning are unduly so, are like a canary in a mine; they warn others of dangers that will prove lethal unless action is taken.

Moral absolutes are to be sought in those areas, several of which are considered below, that are centrally important for human beings in society, where powers capable of doing both great good and great ill are at work. A pagan would speak of the gods, whose favor lavishes benefits on human beings but whose wrath is very terrible. In a modern philosophical context we can speak of a convergence of deontological and consequentialist considerations. To talk about the consequences of a moral code is to talk about the consequences of an entire way of life.

> 1. The first of these is the domain of human life and its protection. The goods of human life require living human beings to sustain them, and a license to kill leaves few if any moral constraints toward the victims intact. Moreover, the use of violence invites retaliatory and preemptive violence. Even when the objects of violence are too weak to defend themselves or to retaliate, and are lacking in powerful protectors, the public lesson that the weak exist at the sufferance of the strong has immeasurable costs.
>
> 2. A second area in which we might find moral absolutes is that of honesty and deceit. Communication is centrally important in human life; imagine yourself in a society where no one speaks your language, and in which you are unable to learn a single word of the language others speak. If we could never trust another person to tell the truth, where it differed from what it was advantageous for him to say, or to keep a promise when so doing entailed any cost, cooperation among human beings would be impossible.
>
> 3. The rules of all societies are in flux, but there are also background understandings that contain (they never abolish) political and social conflicts, and when they collapse lead to civil war. The line between civil disobedience and terrorism distinguishes those who remain in dialogue with their fellow citizens from those who have

withdrawn from the constitutional process in bitterness and despair. To the understandings that shape civil life—which may or may not be expressed in a written constitution—the members of a functioning society accord a certain sacredness. Thus Americans regard their constitutional order as sacred, even though they hold themselves at liberty to dispute its meaning.

4. The fourth arena for absolutes includes that long and complex process by which generation succeeds generation, ranging from the sexual maturity of the parents to the sexual and social maturity of the offspring—in other words, the whole contested area of marriage, sex, child bearing, child rearing, and family life.[28] The most extreme bad consequence possible here, that the human race should cease to reproduce itself and thus die out, seems unlikely. But the other evils chaos in this area produces are evident enough: disease, bitterness between the sexes and the generations, abuse and neglect of both the old and of the young, and the exploitation of persons who are economically, emotionally, and physically vulnerable. Hence the sexual and reproductive aspect of human life requires firm, possibly even exceptionless, rules to sustain it.[29]

5. Finally, adults are able to take part in deliberations concerning the rules of social life, and if these interests are neglected can make their displeasure felt. Infants, fetuses, and small children, however, must rely on the rest of us to represent their interests. Strict moral rules constraining what may be done to them are therefore appropriate.

Moralists need to learn to respect the differing qualities of the moral terrain, as agriculturists need to learn to respect the differing qualities of the soil, some parts of which are in greater need than others of what Wendell Berry calls "kindly use." Each of us owes our existence and attributes to facts outside our control, which exemplify universal human conditions in idiosyncratic ways (all of us die, but each of us dies a different death). It is hard to reason clearly about the domain of "birth, copulation, and death," though to abandon all attempts at moral rationality, here or elsewhere, would be extremely dangerous.

In practice, moral reasoning begins with a set of fairly simple rules, of the Ten Commandments variety. We then encounter situations that make these rules seem too simple, so they are modified and adapted in various ways, leading to a far more complex set of rules and principles. But then we encounter a "check"—a realization that, if we continue to loosen our moral rules, chaos is a likely result. We return to a position of greater moral simplicity, though not necessarily the precise place where we started.

VIRTUAL ABSOLUTES

The existence of moral absolutes is a postulate—an assumption made, as a matter of rational faith, in view of the endless complexity of human situations and our need to find a sure compass in our dealings with them. For unless we are able to say to some line of practical reasoning, "thus far you shall go and no further," we shall be lost in endless perplexity.

Virtual absolutes are rules having three features: (1) they are stated, in moral education (and self-education), as exceptionless; (2) those proposing the rules have not admitted any exceptions so far—or else have included any exceptions they have come to recognize in their formulation of the rules; and (3) when someone raises the possibility of an exception, a heavy burden of proof rests with him. Many moralists have converged on such absolutes. For example, I.M. Crombie writes:

> I cannot dispute that in principle even a definite action rule may on some occasion enjoin the wrong action, but I can nevertheless decide that I will uphold certain of such rules without qualification on the grounds that it is better to do so.[30]

Finnis, on the other hand, rejects virtual absolutes as insufficient to the demands of the Catholic Tradition.[31] At this point the argument moves into moral theology (in the Catholic world it centers on the 1993 encyclical *Veritatis Splendor*), but I do not now pursue it there. My conclusion is that virtual absolutes are possible, but that absolutes in the strict sense cannot be shown to exist or not to exist by philosophical argument alone.

Part IV

Religion, Politics, and Society

Chapter 13

The Basis of Community

Not every moral position taken by an individual or minority is deserving even of respect. For an individual to take a respect-worthy stand against the dominant forces of his society, he requires a cultural tradition that both honors such conduct and supplies the standards to which the dissident can appeal—standards which themselves will always be contested. Morality either has a source transcending both social usage and individual idiosyncrasies, or it rests (in however complex and mystified a way) on power relations.

Moreover, if we believed that the world was, at the deepest level, hostile or indifferent to our moral concerns, our moral commitments would not at once disappear, but would be subject to progressive undermining upon reflection. The simplest way of completing morality is by means of supernatural sanction: good people will be rewarded, and bad people punished, either in this life or the next. But it is hard to see how someone who did not feel guilty already could believe that he would be punished, here or elsewhere. Appeal to post mortem sanctions also neglects both the virtuous person's commitment to virtue, and the pressures by which society establishes conformity to its moral codes.

Natural law ethics makes best sense in terms of a worldview for which God has created us in His image, capable of knowing what is good and right. Thus moral standards are indications of the sort of life we were intended to live—the so-called "maker's instructions" view. Revelation may clarify moral requirements, but even atheists, who do not cease to have been created in the image of God, are able to know the rudiments of the natural law. On the other hand, divine command ethics requires a natural law supplement. For we need criteria for discovering what God's will requires of us, and revelation fails, for example, directly to address technologies not in use at the time the revelation took place.

Many expounders of the natural law tradition have believed that they could establish the existence of God (and some of His attributes) by arguments accessible to all reasonable persons, so that the contemporary understanding of the line between religion and secular thought does not exist for them. It is necessary, however, before engaging in the more ordinary forms of apologetics, to confront those for whom religion is "bosh," or some other folk version of the logical positivists' *cognitively meaningless.*[1] Showing how religion is involved in a way of life will take us part of the way toward an answer.

ON WAYS OF LIFE

Goods, virtues, duties, and rights all find their place within a way of life. By a *way of life* I mean a set of interconnected and inherited practices, and of complex goods achieved through these practices, all converging on what is called the *common good,* in whose promotion each adherent of a way of life has a role to play.

I use the word *practice* in Alasdair MacIntyre's sense, to refer to a form of activity having a standard of excellence internal to itself. Examples are adjudication, basketball, friendship, medicine, romantic love, and the religious life. There are also epistemic practices, by which we conduct inquiry and validate our results. ("Practices" such as torture and astrology are degenerate forms of proper practices—in these cases, the administration of justice and psychological analysis.) Adherents of a way of life value not only its constituent practices and the goods they realize, but the survival and flourishing of their way of life itself. Our ways of life provide us, among other things, with the sense that some views are morally repugnant, so that any principle that implies them is to be rejected; without such a sense, it is always possible to "outsmart" an opponent and accept conclusions such as, judicial murder is legitimate.

I distinguish a way of life from what is called a *lifestyle.* A lifestyle is an adaptation of an individual or group to its temperament and circumstances, which unlike a way of life lacks either a normative structure transmitted from generation to generation, or the energy characteristic of great founders. The transformation of ways of life into lifestyles is called *decadence.* Decadence occurs when the participants in a way of life cease to be willing or able to sustain the complex goods internal to it, and read its constituent practices as means to satisfactions equally attainable by other and less strenuous sorts of behavior.

All ways of life are now under attack, and their defense is frequently left to those who, for some reason, are not full participants in them. (Frodo in *Lord of the Rings* may be taken as an exemplar of this sort of person.) The defense of any way of life must include the defense of the very idea of a way of life (as the defense of any truth must include the defense of the idea of truth). Conversely, the defense of the idea of a way of life must, in practice, mean the defense of some concrete way of life (as the defense of the idea of truth must include the defense of some particular truths).

Threats to our ways of life proceed along five mutually reinforcing routes. One source of threat is the outlook engendered by a market economy, for which everything is for sale—even human beings, their body parts, and their sexual and reproductive capacities. Likewise both dissent[2] and tradition[3] turn into commodities. Moreover, the large and widening gap between rich and poor generated by the market has debilitating cultural implications. This doctrine was not invented by the modern Left, nor does it presuppose economic determinism, laws of history, or the idea that religion is nothing more than the opium of the people.[4]

A second source of threat understands equality, not as requiring a fair chance to achieve excellence, but as requiring "defining deviancy down," as Daniel Patrick Moynihan has put it. To hold that children are relatively better off in a relatively traditional family is insensitive to single mothers; to teach students to write clearly is to denigrate their culture.

A third source of threat derives from America's Puritan heritage. The Puritan clergy felt a call from God to lead His people to the Promised Land whether they so willed or no. Now the heirs of the Puritans have turned their zeal against their own heritage, in a way impervious to majority sentiment, political prudence, and moral reason.

A fourth source of threat is the search, admirable in itself, for a least common denominator for humanity. Unless somehow checked by arguments that take our higher aspirations seriously, this attempt degrades all the forms of human life to a quest for consumer satisfactions. Hence the culture of "McWorld" produces, by way of reaction, a bloody tribalism informed by a desire for cultural survival.[5]

A fifth source of threat is cultural fatigue.[6] The struggle to maintain the standards of excellence internal to practices, in an environment in which standards of all sorts are being systematically assaulted, can become just too wearisome.

To deal with issues that arise in the resulting debates,[7] we need something intermediate between moral minimalism and the particular conceptions of the good embedded in our cultural and religious traditions. Natural law attempts the needed task in three ways. First, the natural law tradition is itself embedded in a way of life (and its particular requirements come to us only in that form). Second, a need for a heritage shows every sign of being founded in human nature, as much as a need for food or sex. Third, central to ways of life is a shared prereflective perception of what is natural and what not, which may end up being supported or undermined by philosophical reflection on human nature.

THE COMMON GOOD

Our society lacks an effective sense of the common good, and collective decisions are determined by political power including media hype. For example, a great deal more federal money per patient is spent on AIDS research than on Alzheimer's disease, coronary heart disease, and both prostate and breast cancer.[8] (Preventive medicine is even more neglected.) The absence of a common good means the progressive division into smaller and smaller factions. Thus assertions of the social responsibilities of ownership turn into an invitation to the war of each against all waged through the mediation of the state.[9] Partly as a result of such difficulties, the Left-Right continuum of political thought has been obsolescent since at least 1989.[10]

Insofar as reliance on "the common good of the universe"—God—invites a slide from the law of God to the demands of organized society, and is accompanied by a polemic against "personalism," it suggests totalitarian implications, even when its defenders hasten to disavow them.[11] Insofar as it relies on a supernatural common good to compensate for social injustice, it admits that the problem of the common good for *human* society is insoluble, and that opium-of-the-people religion for that reason our only recourse.

The common good is neither the good of the majority nor the aggregate of individual goods, but a good in which each member of the society somehow participates.[12] Prior to the question of consent to governmental authority is the definition of the community concerning whose government we deliberate. Fortune or Providence has placed a group of people (now the entire human race) in a situation where cooperation is necessary to survival. They must deliberate concerning the terms and ends of their association, as well as the course they are pursuing together. The resulting dialogue is a shared, complex good in its own right: it is a form of interaction its participants value both for itself and insofar as it helps them maintain social peace and cooperation. The common good is best understood, in the first instance, as a shared search for the common good, and the common bad as the breakdown of this search into factionalism on the Yugoslav model. At the end of the day, the common good is whatever shared ends emerge from this search; their content is a matter of historical contingency.

Liberals take as their primary concern the defense of the right of the individual to break relations with others. One liberal strategy is to invoke a conception of public reason to silence the expression of communal principles, even when these are true and reasonably held. The principal exponent of this doctrine, John Rawls, has since backed down so far as to deprive his position of much interest.[13] Nonetheless, he has signed a "philosophers' brief" invoking the concept of public reason to veto the legal and political expression of objections to assisted suicide.[14] The argument that such a "right" would endanger the seriously ill is well within the scope of public reason even on understandings narrower than that of Rawls.[15]

Michael J. Sandel has cut to the root of the entire Rawlsian strategy: to the extent that there is a reasonable plurality of moral and religious views, there is also a reasonable plurality of views concerning political justice. And to the extent that some views of political justice are more reasonable than others, the same is true of larger moral and religious understandings. Thus if Rawls is prepared to argue against libertarians, he should also be prepared to argue against those whose views on moral issues differ from his own.[16] On what principles such arguments are to proceed is a more difficult question.[17]

Communitarians, when they attempt to strengthen social bonds, discover that liberal individualism is part of the communal tradition they are trying to sustain. E.M. Forster's question, Should I betray my friend or betray my country? arises in countless contexts.[18] Everything depends on the size and shape of the communities on which we propose to rely, and on the way conflicts among the demands of rival communities are to be adjudicated. Secession is back on the theoretical and practical agenda.[19]

NATURAL LAW AS LAW

I therefore ask how moral requirements founded in our nature can be translated into principles governing social life. One way of putting this question is whether the natural law is, properly speaking, law (or how it can become so). Natural law has flourished best when consensus about moral and political questions was supported by extraphilosophical forces—whether the culture of the ancient *polis* or the dogmas of the Christian faith. Thus one way of translating natural law concepts into working laws is appeal to the historically given practice of a certain society. Another way of embodying natural law is by placing it within a religious tradition embodying claims richer than could be maintained by natural reason alone. In the first view writers of constitutions, legislators, judges, citizens, and private people whose activity generates normative customs are the vehicles by which the natural law enters into the practice of a community; in the second view, we understand the requirements of duty as divine commands, and look to Scripture, tradition, and current Church teaching for moral guidance.

All traditions contain more than one strand, and any institution for preserving, transmitting, and applying a tradition will sometimes produce controversial results. Americans have relied on the judiciary to specify the requirements of natural law, but many of those who believe in an unwritten constitution through which the natural law enters legal and political discourse also dislike the uses to which this idea has been put by contemporary judges.[20] Yet judicial activism cannot be identified with decisions ultra vires, for at least some examples of judicial assertiveness (*Brown v. Board of Education,* for example) are approved even by most conservative jurists.[21] On the other hand, those contemporary jurist who push most vigorously for judicial enactment of their agendas tend also to reject the natural law jurisprudence (and the underlying natural law ethics) in terms of which judicial activism makes best sense.

We here enter the perplexing world of American conservatism, which includes everyone from technocratic optimists to "traditionalists" hostile to formative figures of the American political tradition such as Jefferson and Lincoln.[22] It is not surprising that some jurists react violently to constitutional doctrines such as the following:

> We are not an assimilative, homogeneous society, but a facilitative, pluralistic one, in which we must be willing to abide someone else's unfamiliar or even repellent practice because the same tolerant impulse protects our own idiosyncrasies.[23]

Yet the proper response is surely not to deny the American individualist tradition, but to point out that stable family structures are required for the sake of vulnerable people such as children. To the extent that the questions are those of substantive social and political philosophy, they need to be discussed as such rather than as points of jurisprudence.

The second route from natural law to working laws is theological. Russell Hittinger (interpreting John Paul II) shifts the issue from the epistemological question—how the requirements of natural law are to be known—to the definitional and ontological questions: what is natural law in itself, and what is its place in the economy of divine laws (including those of the Old and New Testaments)?[24] When the issue is posed in this way, any theist must agree that the natural law owes its existence to God, and that human reason only discovers its requirements and does not create them. This proposition, however, leaves aside the question, to what extent an atheist can know the requirements of the natural law.

Believers are entitled to speak of God's law (and to insist that His law is infinitely more important than anything human authority may ordain). But within the study of jurisprudence, natural law is either one of the prelegal sources of law; or else it belongs to law in a broader sense, on which judges and legislators can and should draw in fashioning law in the narrow sense. Ontology does not resolve the issue of what focus of linguistic usage is to be taken as primary. The practical issue is to what extent moral reasoning can proceed independently of revelation and the commentaries supplied by Church authority.

RELIGION AND SOCIETY

Honest natural law does not depend on distinctively Christian doctrines, nor does it rely on contemporary theological authority such as that of the Pope. Nonetheless, the cultural background in which a philosopher works is not theologically innocent. At least at most times and most places, religion and politics (and in fact the whole social structure in which politics operates) have been intimately connected.[25] Though we cannot predict what sort of religious life, if any, future generations are going to lead, the historical evidence suggests that, for good or ill, religion will continue to be a force in social life. When one religious outlook loses its grip on the collective mind, others take its place. From its beginnings in 1962, when liberal Protestantism was showing signs of acute decline, the Students for a Democratic Society (SDS) shared many features with the utopian religious movements common throughout American history.[26]

Thus the argument for civil religion remains sound.[27] Good faith adherence to the rules of society cannot be established on self-interested grounds alone. The police cannot be everywhere (and we would not wish them to be); moreover, the police themselves need to be policed. Nor does philosophical argument alone supply sufficient support for social bonds—at least if we take consent as our core legitimizing concept.[28] Hence we cannot neglect the symbols with which allegiance to the institutions of society is established. Nor is American civil religion without content: it includes a belief that human slavery violates something sacred—a belief that provides a shared premise for discussions both of racial issues and of other issues such as abortion and surrogacy.[29] Still, civil religion subordinates our spiritual freedom to doctrines proposed, not as true, but as socially and politically convenient. Moreover, American civil religion is in tension with our church-state doctrine, a tension of which American Jews and other religious minorities are specially aware.[30]

What is required is the embodiment of the natural law in a set of social norms reflecting a shared understanding of the common good. God could play at least three roles in this embodiment. He is a Creator Who establishes the boundary conditions of our search for the common good, He is a common Creator in Whose name we can look for a common human nature (and hence also for a common good among human beings sharing that nature). He is a source of the help we need in avoiding merely partisan conceptions of the good and right.

A world in which everything were up for bargain would be intolerable, as would a world in which everything were a matter of sacred law. As a first approximation, active invocation of distinctly religious perspective belongs not to the day-to-day working of our system, but to those situations when ordinary measures fail, and politically active people realize that the fate of their society is out of their hands.[31] But people disagree about the relative importance of political issues, and not just about their resolution. The deepest issue here is, to what extent it is possible to bridge human differences, and among these, most importantly, differences of outlook.

Conclusion: Natural Law Versus Calvinism

Natural law needs to be defended against three sets of opponents: those who deny the existence of a common human nature, those who deny that human nature is evaluatively relevant, and those who maintain that human nature as we find it is so corrupt that it cannot form a sound basis for ethical reflection. Against postmodernists, who deny a common human nature, I argue that we cannot escape all limitations of our nature: we cannot become able to fly by redescribing ourselves as weightless. Against positivists, who invoke the fact-value dichotomy, I argue that our understandings of human nature are themselves value-laden: we need to find not a place for values in a world of facts, but a place for facts in a world of values.[1]

The most challenging critique of natural law ethics thus comes from the Calvinist claim that human nature is totally depraved. (Whether Calvin himself was in my sense a Calvinist is a complex question:[2] the Reformation tended to become darker in its doctrines as it became more systematic.) I understand Calvinists as holding the following propositions:

1. There is truth.
2. Certain propositions are self-evidently true, even though not everyone holds them.
3. Those who doubt or deny these self-evident truths are not limited to those who, by any "neutral" criterion, are pathological or immature.
4. There is no way of arguing with those who doubt or deny self-evident truths. As Karl Barth is reputed to have said, "Belief cannot argue with unbelief; it can only preach to it."[3]

5. Hence disputes between those who accept, and those who deny, supposed self-evident truths are irresolvable.

6. The difference between those who hold the truth and those who deny it is not one of lesser or greater intellect or education, but of an unaccountable mixture of heredity, environment, and other circumstances—in theological language, some people have received grace and others have not.

7. To make sense of the claim, that we must be something radically different from what we find ourselves to be even in our best moments, requires a Source of moral requirements both far more powerful and far wiser than ourselves.[4]

Calvinists argue as follows. All thought, whether about morals or anything else, is governed by normative principles concerning whose source and validity it is possible to inquire.[5] Norms resting on human convention have conditional validity only. All unconditionally valid norms can be traced to God, both in a metaphysical and an epistemological sense. Normative requirements derive from God as all else does, and the only way we can discern normative requirements is by appeal to faith in the fullest sense of the word (not a mere philosophical theism).

Calvinists hold a nonrelativistic conception of truth and a highly relativistic conception of justification. There are issues concerning which reasoning makes no sense, because all people are spiritually or morally blind by nature, and some people remain so. Such spiritual blindness is not a person's fault in the sense that he could have chosen otherwise, but it is a fault *in him* of a sort that warrants blame and perhaps even punishment. Nor can those who escape spiritual blindness claim any credit for doing so. If no accommodation is possible between acceptance of God's will and our desire to be at least part authors of our own lives—if there is, in other words, "a stark contrast between loyalty to autonomy and loyalty to God's fixed moral code"—then political and cultural warfare is likely to be perpetual, and to strain if not destroy whatever institutional barriers may be set against it.[6]

One reason for the persuasiveness of the Calvinist outlook lies in the fact that the oppressed, or those who deem themselves such, become oppressors with disheartening rapidity. In this aspect, Calvinism is a generalization of the deepest critique of political liberalism. As the Nazi jurist Carl Schmitt observed on behalf of a leading thinker of the counter-enlightenment,

> Liberalism, with its contradictions and compromises, existed for Donaso Cortés only in the short interval period in which it is possible

> to answer the question "Christ or Barrabas?" with a proposal to adjourn or appoint a commission of investigation.[7]

It understands public issues in terms of "the government of the mind": every society, whatever its official protestations, has an established religion that it enforces against dissenters.[8] When this religion is called into question, in the words of Sir James Fitzjames Stephen, "Force, in the widest sense of the term [including propaganda], must decide the question"[9]—a doctrine not made more soothing by the claim that we are unable to act otherwise.[10]

Responses to such views must proceed on a number of fronts:

1. *Philosophical.* The Calvinist denial of neutral epistemic principles is not free of ambiguity, and a more careful formulation might bring Calvinists and adherents of natural law closer together.[11] Yet we must reject the claim that, as John Kekes puts it, "the vices . . . motivate people *just as much as* the virtues."[12] If it were true, rational ethics would be impossible, for one might rationally prefer what Kekes considers vices to what he considers virtues, and even create a system of ethics on that basis. A person weary of a constricted life of virtue could with equal justification adopt principles authorizing the pursuit of lawless gratification: apart from some external source of help he might as well make peace with his vices.[13]

2. *Personal.* Moral judgments about specific actions or sorts of acts are very much like the judgments about rival versions of the same historical event, and about the character of historical actors. Neither historical nor moral arguments need be algorithmic to be persuasive. In view of the disarray that has overtaken the profession of history, this conclusion is not reassuring, but the difficulty has nothing to do with any metaphysical chasm between fact and value.[14] An agent in perplexity can take advice, but must take responsibility for choosing his adviser; he can pray for guidance, but must take responsibility for discerning the leadings of God from those of Satan. Each of us has entrenched interests, associations, and habits of life, which might be disrupted by our concluding, for example, that a vegetarian diet was morally mandatory. It is not possible to distinguish nature from grace—or natural reason from general revelation—by inspection.

3. *Political.* Contemporary political discussion suffers from the confusion that has overtaken the traditional Left-Right spectrum. Cultural issues cannot be dismissed as irrelevant distractions from real politics (though sometimes they are): how important a given issue is requires case-by-case judgment. It is impossible to find an Archimedean point to defend principles of political justice (including principles of tolerance). But it is equally impossible to find such a point from which to reject as hypocritical aspirations toward fairness to political adversaries. The struggle against the frame of mind that subordinates all other

questions to those of ideological allegiance, and has no place for a morality transcending political or religious conflict, remains as important as ever.[15] The foundational political task is to affirm the common nature of all human beings.

4. *Theological.* Even under the most benign political system, however, there will be permanent minorities (and possibly frustrated majorities). Groups faced with a hostile or uncomprehending world have, at various times and places, sought accommodation, common ground for cooperation, conversion of the infidel, separation, persuasion on points of special importance, and conquest.[16] Adherents of natural law face many of the same difficulties as do religiously informed moralists and political actors in the face of a public culture of disbelief.

St. Augustine is the central figure for the discourse of the Christian community, at least in the West, as it addresses the problem of arguing with outsiders. Augustine explains resistance to Christian orthodoxy as owing, not to poor reasoning, but to "most pernicious ill will" (Bk. VI, Pref.; see also Bk. II, chap. 1)[17]—a move that seems to leave no room for discussion. Yet he also constantly appeals to standards of piety and decency available to human beings as such (e.g., Bk. II, chap. 26; Bk. IV, chap. 12; Bk. VI, chaps. 2, 6, 8), and to solidarity among all human beings (Bk. IV, chap. 3; Bk. V, chap. 17).

Augustine repeatedly appeals to the unwillingness of the Roman pagans to pursue their vices consistently, as in his discussion of indecent spectacles offered to the gods (e.g., Bk. II, chap. 15 and Bk. VI, chap. 6). He argues in good stoic fashion that it is no more acceptable to make the virtues slaves of glory than it is to make them slaves of pleasure (Bk. V, chap. 20). His picture of pagan Rome as the domain of "lustful cruelty and cruel lust,"[18] and his maxim, Take away justice and what are kingdoms but great robber bands (Bk. IV, chap. 4) are both Roman in origin.[19]

Augustine attributes the duration and extension of the Roman Empire to the will of God (Bk. V, Pref., chap. 21).[20] He regards its achievements as deserving of human praise (Bk. V, chap. 15): these include the scholarship of the pagan theologian Varro (Bk. VI, chap. 2) and the frankness of the philosopher Seneca (Bk. VI, chap. 10). He argues that Christianity can preserve the best of the Roman tradition better than Rome itself was able to do (e.g., Bk. II, chaps. 18–19, 29 [quoting Vergil]. We may call Augustine's way of reasoning "ad hoc apologetics," but there is enough in common between Rome and other civilizations to make some of his arguments of universal relevance. His strongest argument is that although we all desire peace, the city of man is unable to provide it. On pagan premises, the gods themselves are at war (Bk. II, chap. 25; Bk. III, chap. 9), and the temple of Quiet is relegated to a place outside the city gates (Bk. IV, chap. 16). Moreover, fraud as much as force is an instrument of war: Machiavelli praises, but Augustine condemns as demonic, the element of deceit in Roman religion (Bk. IV, 31–32; Bk. VI, 4).[21]

For Augustine, the hallmark of sin is a rejection of the peace and harmony, both among people and within each person, which the love of God alone can bring. He does not deny that human beings are naturally capable of moral insight or moral behavior, but argues that the pagan worldview undermines that capacity, and disables its adherents from pursuing their moral insights. Yet a critic will respond that Augustine's version of Christian orthodoxy also undermines morality. For his doctrine of hell supposes a permanent, even if one-sided, war between God and some of His creatures, and hence moral conflict extending all the way down. If, at the end of things, "there will be not no death, but everlasting death" (Bk. XXI, chap. 3; cf. Bk. VI, chap. 12), as he chillingly puts it, then his argument against paganism would seem to fail.

Appendix: Hell

St. Augustine's doctrine of hell supposes a permanent, though one-sided, war between God and some of His creatures, and hence that moral conflict extends all the way down. If, at the end of things, "there will be not no death, but everlasting death," as he chillingly puts it, then his argument against paganism fails. For how can a creature exist forever in incurable alienation from the ground of its being, without the intervention of a perverse miracle? On the other hand, doctrines of universal salvation threaten the freedom of God (Who cannot be bound to offer endless chances), and of human beings (who might be perverse enough to refuse them).

In my review of theological[1] discussions pertinent to this issue, I limit myself to the Western Christian tradition, for which Augustine is a reference point.[2] A *strong doctrine* of hell holds that some (and perhaps most) men and women reject, or are rejected by, God, with painful consequences eternally prolonged—a doctrine regarded in some circles as a test of theological virility. Adherents of a strong doctrine cite such texts as Matthew 25:46, which speaks of "everlasting punishment." *Conditionalism* or *annihilationism* holds that those who are not saved cease to be: Matthew 13:40 (on the burning of the tares) suggests such a view. Finally, *universalism* holds that all people will be saved; one of its proof-texts is Revelation 8:17 ("and God shall wipe all tears from their eyes"). For it is surely a cause of sorrow to a virtuous person that a single soul should be damned, even deservedly.

THE PROBLEM

The precise question is whether Christianity and natural morality are mutually supporting (as many Christians and adherents of the natural law tradition have thought) or mutually undermining.[3] David Wells's response to mitigated doctrines of hell—that "expressions of moral horror . . . need to be heard, but then set aside so that we can concentrate more clearly on the biblical data"—is irrelevant here.[4] Likewise irrelevant are the suggestions that God feels the pains of a rejected lover,[5] or and that He would be somehow frustrated or discredited if some of us were lost.[6] It suffices that the damnation of some souls would mean the frustration of the plan of salvation He has in fact adopted. Nor is the difficulty resolved by saying that, as C.S. Lewis puts it, "the doors of hell are locked on the *inside*."[7] Nor does it help to say that God makes the rules, or that we as creatures are in no position to judge His decrees. And appeal to original sin to warrant eternal damnation merely makes matters worse.

A logically adequate resolution is the view of Reformed theologian Herman Hoeksema, that the nonelect are subject to "the sovereign hatred of God."[8] It is not possible directly to refute the proposition that God stands so far above ordinary morality that behavior that would be profoundly evil if undertaken by a human being is still consistent with His Supreme Goodness (which we would then call "metaphysical" rather than "moral"). But it is hard to see how we could rationally accept a revelation coming from such a source: the credentials of the most bizarre and destructive cult would be as good as those of Christianity. (Heidegger may have believed something of the sort.) This consideration would not trouble a hard-core Calvinist, for whom natural reason is hopelessly corrupt, but other theists find such a solution intolerable. Roman Catholic teaching, for example, denies the doctrine of predestination to eternal death.[9]

My colleague Gary Culpepper has suggested that the existence of hell need not entail the existence of permanent moral conflict, since the damned might, without repenting, recognize both the wickedness of their previous lives and the justice of their punishment. Peter Geach expresses a contrary view:

> Perforce [the damned] will accept God's power, but being wicked they will not submit to his justice; it will seem to them frightfully unfair—they will be like the brutal greedy prisoner who was dragged from the dock screaming 'Je demande la justice!'"[10]

The issue here is whether the ways in which intellect and will interact in all the human beings we know, especially when questions of morals are at issue, are suspended for the damned—whether God has given the damned extraordinary clarity of moral consciousness in order to complete their punishment. As things now stand, recognition that one is wrong is the first step toward change, and a settled disposition to evil precludes such recognition.

CONDITIONALISM

Strong doctrines of hell characteristically presuppose an understanding of the soul as naturally immortal, though presumably one that falls short of placing its annihilation beyond God's power. But, as Jonathan Kvanvig points out, the doctrine that God conserves all things implies that there is no difference between His actively destroying the damned, and merely letting them die.[11] Conditionalist doctrines, by equating damnation with the destruction of the soul, assert that some people are endlessly cut off from God's mercy, but deny that they continue to exist in perpetual enmity to God and His chosen ones. Conditionalists point out that "eternal (or everlasting) fire" is a paradoxical expression, since it is of the nature of fire as we know it to destroy that on which it feeds. Though conditionalism "substitut[es] metaphysical capital punishment for metaphysical life imprisonment," it at least avoids the suggestion of permanent cosmic war.[12]

Concerning the state of the damned, Lewis adopts a position very close to conditionalism:

> If soul can be destroyed, must there not be a state of *having been* a human soul? And is it not that, perhaps, the state which is equally well described as torment, deprivation, and privation? . . . Consignment to the destroying fire is usually treated as the end of the story. That the lost soul is eternally fixed in its diabolical attitude we cannot doubt: but whether this eternal fixity implies endless duration—or duration at all—we cannot say.[13]

Geach suggests two possible resolutions of the problem of hell, one of which is broadly conditionalist: "the realization, from [the Last Judgment] onwards, of two alternate futures for the world into which saved and damned alike rise again," and "an unending series of miseries . . . fitted into a finite time stretch" after which the damned will no longer exist.[14] The first of these solves the problem of endless warfare only for the alternate future inhabited by the saved, and I doubt the intelligibility of the second (but freely admit the weakness of intuitions of intelligibility in this context). In any event, Geach's second view approximates that of the Evangelical Clark Pinnock, "Fire, Then Nothing."[15] To the extent that they differ, Geach is arguably Manichaean, insofar as he finds it necessary to assert an infinity of evil.

Kvanvig holds that "hell is an afterlife journey toward annihilation."

> The intent of God in forming the mechanism of hell is for people to come to see their options clearly enough that they see the overwhelming desirability of eternal life over eternal death; because that may not be possible without violating their freedom, the secondary goal of ridding them of irrationality and instability in their conception of and desire for things is pursued. If the mechanism accomplishes this goal, annihilation results; if not, the process can go on eternally.

In either case, "those in hell are there because of their determination to avoid the company of the redeemed and the God who redeems."[16]

The issue remains, why, if God sees that some creature is irrevocably determined to reject Him, the creature's journey toward annihilation should be slowed in any way. The question is different from that of euthanasia, in that there is no prospect of spiritual betterment by the sufferer, and no scope for casuistry distinguishing between foresight and intention, or between killing and letting die. Thus conditionalist doctrines of hell raise the issue of whether a good God would interfere with a creature's decision not to be.[17]

Both in this book and in my earlier work on the ethics of homicide I have expressed broadly secular objections to the concept of rational suicide.[18] Most theists have severe objections to suicide in this life, and it is not clear why they should change their position when considering the life to come. A sense of the radical incommensurability of death with other possibilities is very near the core of a Jewish or Christian or any outlook critical of technocratic rationality, and should not be abandoned when contemplating post mortem euthanasia. To be sure, we might sometimes decline to interfere with a would-be suicide, on the grounds that the only available means—forcefeeding, for example—are too invasive under the circumstances. But such considerations have dubious application outside this life.

The fact that hell is usually thought of as penal now comes to the rescue of the conditionalist. Respect for the freedom of the damned prevents God from dragooning them into Heaven, but does not require Him to maintain them in permanent rebellion. Most of the objections to capital punishment exacted by human beings—our fallibility and the injustice (remediable or not) of our institutions—do not apply to God. Jerry L. Wallis suggests (following C.S. Lewis), that "the distorted pleasures of hell are sufficient from the standpoint of the damned to make life in hell preferable to extinction."[19] But it still does not follow that God either would or should preserve them to enjoy their perversity.

Many defenders of hell hold that "the misery of hell is not so much a penalty imposed by God to make the sinner pay for his sin, as the necessary outcome of leading a sinful life."[20] If so, the distinction between suicide and capital punishment as models for conditionalist doctrines evaporates. Both models would converge in the Platonic notion of death as cure for an evil soul.[21] The powerful objections to our using such ideas in our penal system do not apply to God. The disintegration of the self, which is the hallmark of moral evil, leads spontaneously to a state of affairs in which the sinner no longer exists as a person. Even offenses against justice such as embezzlement require hypocrisy and destroy the social relations essential to our existence as people. A conditionalist God merely lets the choices of the damned take their natural course. If all sins are constructively suicide, then the sinner's journey toward annihilation is his own doing rather than God's.[22] God would be saying to the sinner, "*Thy* will be done."[23]

HOPEFUL UNIVERSALISM

"Contingent" or "hopeful" universalists (Kvanvig and Wallis's terms, respectively) hold that hell is, for all we know, empty, even of Judas. Strictly, contingent universalism refers to a state of affairs that might have been otherwise, and of which it is presumed we cannot be certain, whereas hopeful universalism refers to the condition of our knowledge. Whether a contingent universalist is convinced or merely hopeful depends on how much confidence he places in probable inferences concerning the dispositions of a mysterious God—since it would strain credulity to hold that the truth of universalism was *plainly* revealed.

Necessary universalism, in Kvanvig's view, requires either that Christ's work be superfluous, or that there be no possible world in which it did not take place (or failed), and also that there be no possible world in which people are free to choose hell.[24] I doubt that any theologian worth reading is a necessary universalist in this sense, for it is contingent that God became incarnate in Christ for our salvation. Kvanvig objects to contingent universalism: "If it would be wrong to send someone to hell, it makes no difference to the inconsistency between God's sending someone to hell in the actual world or in some other possible worlds."[25] But ethics is world bound, so that there are possible worlds (assuming that talk of such worlds makes sense) in which radically different moral principles obtain, and even possible worlds (Calvinist ones, perhaps) in which ethics is metaphysically undermined. If hopeful universalists are right, however, we can hope, and act on the hope, that endless cosmic war is not our law.

John Colwell formulates hopeful universalism on behalf of Karl Barth:

> Barth, while refusing to accept universalism as an *a priori* necessity for God, presumptively limiting God's freedom, refuses with equal emphasis to reject universal salvation as a possibility for God, presumptively limiting God's grace.[26]

On the Catholic side, Hans Urs von Balthasar sums up his conclusions as follows: "Certainty cannot be attained, but hope may be justified,"[27] and perhaps is required.[28] That the universalism of such writers is a matter of hope rather than certainty is not a source of difficulty, since, or at least so I would maintain, all religious belief is hope-driven (or perhaps I should say driven by the need for hope).

Conditionalism and hopeful universalism are, though steeply contrasting doctrines, consistent with each other. Universalism might be true for human beings, and conditionalism for demons—who, without souls to feed on, dwindle away.[29] Or universalism might be true in fact, and conditionalism express what would have been if God or human beings had chosen otherwise. The choice among philosophically admissible hypotheses must be left to the theologian, though philosophy may also influence the choice among theologically admissible doctrines. It is, for example, easier for a Catholic than a Protestant to accept hopeful universalism, since the doctrine of purgatory answers the question of what God might do about flawed people who die without visible improvement.[30] Yet a strong doctrine of grace might widen our understanding of how God could overcome the sinful will of creatures and bring them to salvation.

The mysteries of time and eternity, on which all eschatological questions turn, must be left unresolved here. Suffice it to say that we cannot assume God's perspective, as doctrines of predestination invite us to do, and that grace and choice cannot be distinguished by inspection. Nor ought we think of grace as a scarce commodity.[31]

Notes

Introduction: The Need for Natural Law

1. The literature is immense, but I have specially benefited from *Natural Law Theory,* ed. Robert P. George (Oxford: Clarendon Press, 1992); and, on the theological side, from *A Preserving Grace,* ed. Michael Cromartie (Grand Rapids, Mich.: William B. Eerdmans, 1997). A provocative attempt to apply the natural law tradition to jurisprudential issues is George, *Making Men Moral* (Oxford: Clarendon, 1992). A chapter of intellectual and cultural history crucial to the development of natural law thought is surveyed by C.S. Lewis, *English Literature in the Sixteenth Century, Excluding Drama* (Oxford: Clarendon Press, 1954), Introduction.

2. See, in contrast, Russell Hittinger, "Natural Law and Catholic Moral Theology," *A Preserving Grace,* chap. 1.

3. See especially *Anti-Theory in Ethics and Moral Conservatism,* ed. Stanley G. Clarke and Evan Simpson (Albany, N.Y.: SUNY, 1989)—an anthology to which I am much indebted.

4. See Jeffrey Stout, "Truth, Natural Law, and Ethical Theory," *Natural Law Theory,* chap. 4; see especially the comparison he draws between himself and Hittinger at p. 102 n.47. Further backing for Stout's argument may be found in his *Ethics after Babel* (Boston: Beacon Press, 1988)—an honorable attempt to accept Richard Rorty's central contentions while avoiding his irresponsibility.

5. Joseph Boyle, "Natural Law and the Ethics of Tradition," *Natural Law Theory,* pp. 17–18, citing Alan Donagan, *The Theory of Morality* (Chicago: University of Chicago Press, 1977), pp. 16–17.

6. Hittinger points out that neither the United Nations nor the Roman Catholic Church, both of which make large claims about natural rights and virtues, attempt to make natural law claims justiciable within their courts. "Natural Law and Virtue," *Natural Law Theory,* ed. Robert P. George, p. 66 n.4.

7. The point is well made from the positivist side by Neil MacCormack, "Natural Law and the Separation of Law and Morals," ibid., chap. 5, responding to John Finnis, *Natural Law and Natural Rights* (Oxford: Clarendon Press, 1980).

8. All these "concessions" in fact represent the views of St. Thomas Aquinas. See *Summa Theologiae,* Ia IIae, Q. 90, a. 3 (need for institutional authority), a. 4 (need for promulgation); Q. 95, a. 2 (limited derivation of human law from the natural law); Q. 96, a. 3 (limits on legal enforcement of morals).

9. I mean *tao* in the Confucian (not the Taoist) sense: "the total normative sociopolitical order with its networks of proper familial and proper sociopolitical roles, statuses, and ranks, as well as to the 'objective' prescriptions of proper behavior—ritual, ceremonial, and ethical—that govern the relationship among those roles. On the other side, it emphatically and also embraces the 'inner' moral life of the living individual. . . . There is also one use of the term *tao* in the expression the 'Tao of heaven,' where it seems to refer to Heaven's way in the nonhuman universe as well, as well, perhaps, to all those aspects of Heaven in history over which men exercise no control." Benjamin I. Schwartz, *The World of Thought in Ancient China* (Cambridge, Mass.: Harvard University Press, 1985), pp. 62–‑63. See also James T. Bretske, S.J., "The Tao of Confucian Virtue Ethics," *International Philosophical Quarterly* 25, no. 1 (March 1995), esp. pp. 34–38, where he links *tao* to the politically important concept of *t'ien ming* (the mandate of heaven).

10. As Panurang Vaman Kane puts it, "*Dharma* is one of those Sanskrit words that defy all attempts at an exact rendering in English or any other tongue." *History of Dharmasastra,* vol. 1, pt. 1, rev. and enlarged ed. (Poona: Bhandakahr Oriental Research Institute, 1968), p. 1. But it can be understood as the law of the cosmos—embodied, in a way which Burke would find sympathetic, both in a social organization and an understanding of the stages of life. See John M. Koller, *Oriental Philosophies* (New York: Charles Scribner's Sons, 1970), pp. 41–51

Chapter 1: What Can Philosophy Do?

1. For a good discussion, see W.T. Jones, *A History of Western Philosophy,* vol. 5, 2nd ed. (San Diego: Harcourt Brace Jovanovich, 1980), chap. 9, esp. pp. 328–31. Jacques Derrida strongly rejects a theistic reading of this position, thereby asserting authorial privileges to which he is by his own showing not entitled; see his "Deconstruction and the Other" in *Contemporary Approaches to Philosophy,* ed. Paul Moser and Dwayne Mulder (New York: Macmillan, 1994), p. 368.

2. Sir Robert Birely, K.C.M.G., *The Real Meaning of Academic Freedom* (London: World University Service, 1972).

3. See Hadley Arkes, *First Things* (Princeton: Princeton University Press, 1986), Introduction. But Arkes puts his position on a different ground when he appeals to "the restoration of our own, best tradition" (p. 8) to support his arguments.

4. See Larry D. Bouchard, "A Note on the Nuer," *Hastings Center Report* 26, no. 1 (January-February 1996), pp. 15–16.

5. This is the one case where Finnis argues successfully, in *Natural Law and Natural Rights* (Oxford: Clarendon Press, 1980), that a basic good from which he proceeds is, in fact, indubitably good. For more detail, see his "Scepticism, Self-Refutation, and the Good of Truth," *Law, Morality, and Society,* ed. P.M.S. Hacker and J. Raz (Oxford: Clarendon Press, 1977), chap. 14.

6. Patrick Lee, "Is Thomas's Natural Law Theory Naturalist?" *American Catholic Philosophical Quarterly* 71, no. 4 (autumn 1997), p. 584, weakens the concept of self-evidence so much as to both draw its antidialogical sting and sharply reduce its philosophical interest.

7. Joseph Boyle neglects this distinction. See his "Natural Law and the Ethics of Tradition," in *Natural Law Theory,* ed. Robert P. George (Oxford: Clarendon Press, 1992), p. 28.

8. "Truth, Natural Law, and Ethical Theory," *Natural Law Theory,* ed. George, p. 82. He borrows the phrase from Richard Rorty, who for the most part neglects it in his philosophy.

9. I take this expression from Brian Barry, *Justice as Impartiality* (Oxford: Clarendon Press, 1995), p. 89, who takes it from Amy Gutman and Dennis Thompson. For a more detailed refutation of the principle of preclusion, see Barry, sec. 14, though Barry does not follow out his arguments consistently.

10. Jacques Maritain, for example, writes, "Objects, all objects, murmur this being; they utter it to the intellect, but not all intellects, only to those capable of hearing." *Preface to Metaphysics* (New York: Sheed and Ward, 1948), p. 44. Of the needed sort of intuition, he tells us, "Kant never had it" (p. 48); for my part, I am uncertain whether I have had it. (Many Thomists share my skepticism on this point.)

11. *Mind and World* (Cambridge, Mass.: Harvard University Press, 1994), p. 50. This objection was made by Pawel Ozdowski in correspondence.

Chapter 2: The Epistemological Issues (1)

1. On the larger ethical and social importance of epistemological issues, see Thomas A. Spragens Jr., *The Irony of Liberal Reason* (Chicago: University of Chicago Press, 1981). We should be wary, however, of attributing a single epistemic stance to either liberalism or modernity.

2. Taylor, *Philosophical Arguments* (Cambridge, Mass.: Harvard University Press, 1995), p. viii.

3. Plantinga, *Warrant: The Current Debate* (New York: Oxford University Press, 1993), p. v.

4. See Lakatos's "Falsification and the Methodology of Research Programmes" in his collection with Alan Musgrave, *Criticism and the Growth of Knowledge* (Cambridge: Cambridge University Press 1972), pp. 90–196.

5. Foundationalism comes in a number of varieties, not all of which rely on the premise that one's basic beliefs *could not* be false. See Susan Haack, *Evidence and Inquiry* (Oxford: Blackwell, 1993), chap. 1. Since such distinctions pertain mostly to empirical knowledge, I shall not explore them in detail here.

6. Likewise, Plantinga, *Warrant: The Current Debate,* p. 3.

7. See Josef Seifert, *Back to "Things in Themselves"* (New York: Routledge and Kegan Paul, 1987), and, more accessibly, Olaf Tollefsen, *Foundationalism Defended* (Bethesda, Md.: College Press, 1995).

8. Paul Moser, arguing in defense of skepticism about things in themselves, articulates what he calls "the conceptual taking requirement," namely that "your minimally understanding the question of what *X* is requires that you take certain distinguishing features or considerations as at least partly constituting what it is to be an *X*." *Philosophy After Objec-*

tivity (New York: Oxford University Press, 1993), p. 27. The conceptual taking requirement is at least plausible, but to claim to *know* that it is true, Moser must be prepared to make assertions about the nature of understanding, as it is in itself, that his own argument undermines.

9. Gilbert Harman defends this principle in *Change of View* (Cambridge, Mass.: Bradford Books, 1986), chap. 4 and pp. 46–47. He points out that it applies only to beliefs in the full sense, not to working hypotheses.

10. Matthias Steup, in his invaluable survey of analytic epistemology, *An Introduction to Contemporary Epistemology* (Upper Saddle River, N.J.: Prentice-Hall, 1996), defines *defeat* as follows: "*d* defeats *e* as evidence for *p* if and only if *e* is evidence for believing that *p*, but *e* in conjunction with *d* is not evidence for believing that *p*" (p. 39). This definition includes cases in which *d* undermines *e*'s evidentiary force, as well as those where it is evidence for *-p*.

11. See Plantinga, *Warrant: The Current Debate,* chaps. 4–7; and *Warrant and Proper Function* (New York: Oxford University Press, 1993), chap. 10. Parenthetical references in this excursus are to *Warrant: The Current Debate.*

12. Steup, pp. 17–18. Clause (i) is redundant given clause (iv), since *-p* defeats *p;* but it is included here for the sake of clarity.

13. I am here siding with "analytical pluralism" against "analytical monism"; see ibid., pp. 36–38.

14. I owe this expression to Nicholas P. Wolterstorff, "Practices of Inquiry and Entitlements to Believe," delivered at an epistemology conference at Wheaton College, fall 1995.

15. See Ian Hacking, *Representing and Intending* (Cambridge: Cambridge University Press, 1983), esp. chaps. 13, 16, on "the creation of the phenomena."

16. C.A.J. Coady, *Testimony* (Oxford: Clarendon Press, 1992), pp. 99–100.

17. For detailed argument, see ibid., esp. chap. 4. Coady's book is replete with examples of how predispositions affect the evaluation of testimony, such as Hume's refusal to accept the testimony of "fifty bare-arsed highlanders" concerning the authenticity of Ossian's epics (p. 193).

18. The principle of the inarticulate background is owed largely to Charles Taylor; see especially his "Two Theories of Modernity," *Hastings Center Report* 23, no. 2 (March-April, 1995).

19. Haack, *Evidence and Inquiry,* p. 19. Haack's account is limited to empirical beliefs: she notices the question of religious experience (though not, so far as I can see, of moral experience), but only to set it aside (p. 214).

20. Ibid., chap. 10. She calls this the question of "ratification."

21. This sentence is directed against Plantinga; see his *Warrant and Proper Function.* I am also responding to a paper entitled "Naturalism Defeated," which he delivered at Brown University in April 1996.

22. See Nancey Murphy, *Theology in the Age of Scientific Reasoning* (Ithaca, N.Y.: Cornell University Press, 1990).

Chapter 3: The Epistemological Issues (2)

1. Primary sources for this debate are Gadamer, *Truth and Method,* trans. and ed. Garret Barden and John Cumming (New York: Seabury, 1975); more briefly, "On the Scope

and Function of Hermeneutical Reflection," trans. G.B. Hess and R.E. Palmer, *Continuum* 8 (1970), pp. 70–95; and more briefly still, "Hermeneutics and Social Science," *Cultural Hermeneutics* 2 (1975), sec. III; and Habermas, "The Hermeneutic Claim to Universality," in Joseph Bleicher, *Contemporary Hermeneutics* (London: Routledge and Kegan Paul, 1980), Reading III. The most valuable secondary sources are Matthew Foster, *Gadamer and Practical Philosophy* (Atlanta, Ga.: Scholars Press, 1991), chap. 4; and Thomas McCarthy, *The Critical Theory of Jürgen Habermas* (Cambridge, Mass.: MIT Press, 1978), pp. 187–93.

2. Gadamer, "On the Scope and Function of Hermeneutical Reflection," p. 78.

3. "Questions and Counter-Questions," in *Habermas and Modernity,* ed. Richard Bernstein (Cambridge, Mass.: MIT, 1985), p. 216. See also his *Legitimation Crisis,* trans. Thomas McCarthy (Boston: Beacon Press, 1975), p. xxv, where he speaks of "the application of the Marxian theory of crisis to the altered reality of 'advanced capitalism.'"

4. See Habermas, *Theory and Practice,* trans. John Viertel (Boston: Beacon Press, 1974), chap. 7.

5. "Ideology, Social Science, and Revolution," *Comparative Politics* 5 (1975), p. 322.

6. See Heinrich's book, *The Unity of Reason,* ed. Richard Velkey, trans. Jeffrey Edwards et al. (Cambridge, Mass.: Harvard University Press, 1992), esp. the Introduction and chaps. 1, 4.

7. For a range of views on this issue, see Susan Haack, advisory ed., "Feminist Epistemology: For and Against," *Monist* 77, no. 4 (October 1994).

8. Mao Tse-tung lucidly sums up some key themes in *Four Essays on Philosophy* (Peking: Foreign Languages Press, 1968). I use the transliteration of Chinese names used in this edition.

9. The argument here was suggested by B.J. Diggins, *The Promise of Pragmatism* (Chicago: University of Chicago Press, 1994).

10. Hittinger, "Natural Law and Catholic Moral Theology," in *A Preserving Grace,* ed. Michael Cromartie (Grand Rapids, Mich.: Ethics and Public Policy Center, 1997), p. 16.

11. *Aeterni Patris* (1879). Reprinted in Victor B. Brezik, C.S.B., ed., *One Hundred Years of Thomism* (Houston, Texas: Center for Thomistic Studies, University of Houston, 1981), p. 181.

12. Consider, e.g., the following statements: "The philosophers of old who lacked the gift of faith, yet were esteemed so wise, fell into many appalling errors" (*One Hundred Years of Thomism*, p. 182), and "It pleased the struggling innovators to philosophize without any respect for faith, the power of inventing in accordance with his own pleasure and bent being asked and given in turn by each one" (p. 191). Yet the following quotation favors Descartes over Aristotle: "Therefore in this let us also follow the Angelic Doctor, who never gave himself to reading or writing without first begging the blessing of God" (pp. 195–96).

13. Consider, e.g., the position of Étienne Gilson, as summarized in Armand A. Maurer, C.S.B., "The Legacy of Étienne Gilson," ibid., pp. 34–38, 41–43; and that of Jacques Maritain, as summarized in Donald A. Gallagher, "The Legacy of Jacques Maritain, Christian Philosopher," ibid., pp. 45–59.

14. See Henry Johnstone Jr., *Philosophy and Argument* (N.p.: Pennsylvania State University Press, 1959), esp. chaps. 4–7. Oddly, Johnstone himself appears to be a relativist; he defends what he calls "the relativity of truth to argument in philosophy" (p. 57).

15. When Charles Ryder (in *Brideshead Revisited*) reproves Lord Brideshead ("Bridey") for referring to his sister Lady Julia as living in sin, Brideshead responds: "I was merely stating a fact well known to her."

16. This example is owed to Gilbert Harman.

17. The question—much debated among Thomists—whether we apprehend the human good by theoretical or practical reason—admits of no easy answer. On this debate, see Patrick Lee, "Is Thomas's Natural Law Theory Naturalist?" *American Catholic Philosophical Quarterly* 71, no. 4 (autumn 1997), pp. 567–87. On the one hand, our understanding of the human good both has practical implications, and is developed through our capacities as desiring, valuing beings. On the other hand, our various understandings of what it is to be a human being, and what is good for a human being, express a picture of what human beings are and can be.

18. I have found Matthias Steup, *An Introduction to Contemporary Epistemology* (Upper Saddle River, N.J.: Prentice-Hall, 1996), chap. 3, useful in framing this paragraph.

19. Hence the writer conceded too much to Michael Tooley in his *Ethics of Homicide* (Ithaca, N.Y.: Cornell University Press, 1978; Notre Dame: University of Notre Dame Press, 1990), e.g., pp. 95–96.

20. Harman, *Change in View* (Cambridge, Mass.: Bradford Books, 1986), p. 7.

Chapter 4: The Quest for the Self (1)

1. Hume, *A Treatise of Human Nature,* ed. L.A. Selby-Bigge (Oxford: Clarendon, 1896), Bk. I, pt. 4, sec. 6.

2. Rorty, "Putnam and the Relativist Menace," *Journal of Philosophy* 90, no. 9 (September 1993), p. 451.

3. Rorty, *Contingency, Irony, and Solidarity* (Cambridge: Cambridge University Press, 1989), pp. 194–95 n.6.

4. Merton, *New Seeds of Contemplation* (New York: New Directions, 1961), pp. 34–35, 279, 295.

5. Rorty, *Consequences of Pragmatism* (Minneapolis: University of Minnesota Press, 1982), p. xliv.

6. I have found Lynne Rudder Baker, *Saving Belief: A Critique of Physicalism* (Princeton: Princeton University Press, 1987) especially valuable here.

7. Michael Wreen, in correspondence.

8. Donald Davidson's "anomalous monism" is probably an example of this approach. See his *Essays on Actions and Events* (Oxford: Clarendon Press, 1980), essay 11; and "Thinking Causes," in *Mental Causation,* ed. John Heil and Alfred Mehle (Oxford: Clarendon Press, 1993), chap. 1.

9. According to Terence E. Horgan in *The Cambridge Dictionary of Philosophy,* ed. Robert Audi (Cambridge: Cambridge University Press, 1995), "Properties of type *A* are supervenient on properties of type *B* if and only if two objects cannot differ with respect to their *A*-properties without also differing with respect to their *B*-properties." According to O.R. Jones in *The Oxford Companion to Philosophy,* ed. Ted Honderich (Oxford: Oxford University Press, 1995), "One set of properties is supervenient on a second set when they are so related that there could not be a difference in the first without there being a difference in the second, though there could be a difference in the second without there being a difference in the first." The first definition, though not the second, allows for mutual

supervenience, whereby differences in either physical properties of the brain or mental properties of the person require differences in properties of the other sort.

10. The best-defined form of naturalism limits reality to what can be investigated for the purposes of technical manipulation; for a frank statement, see Sidney Hook, "Naturalism and First Principles," *Philosophy of Religion,* ed. Steven M. Cahn (New York: Harper and Row, 1970), pp. 335–60.

11. Searle, *The Construction of Social Reality* (New York: The Free Press, 1995); *The Rediscovery of the Mind* (Cambridge, Mass.: Bradford/MIT, 1992).

12. The most important text is Meditation VI, trans. in *The Philosophical Writing of Descartes,* ed. John Cottingham, Robert Stoothoff, and Dugald Murdoch, vol. 2 (Cambridge: Cambridge University Press, 1984), pp. 60–61. For commentary, see Margaret Wilson, "Descartes on the Origin of Sensation," *Philosophical Topics* 19, no. 1 (spring 1991), pp. 293–323. I am indebted to Celia Wolf-Devine for these references.

13. For an attempt to eke as much ethics out of Descartes as possible see Vance Morgan, *Foundations of Cartesian Ethics* (New Jersey: Humanities Press, 1994).

14. See Michael Tooley, *Abortion and Infanticide* (Oxford: Oxford University Press, 1988).

15. Or so I interpret his difficult doctrine of the active intellect as "separable, impassible, unmixed . . . immortal, and eternal." *On the Soul,* Bekker 430a 17, 23. Trans. J.A. Smith in *The Basic Works of Aristotle,* ed. Richard McKeon (New York: Random House, 1941).

16. On the position of *soul* in religious as opposed to philosophical discourse, see Carol Zalezki, *The Life of the World to Come* (Oxford: Oxford University Press, 1996).

Chapter 5: The Quest for the Self (2)

1. *Nicomachean Ethics,* Bekker 1139b4. Trans. W.D. Ross in *The Basic Works of Aristotle,* ed. Richard McKeon (New York: Random House, 1941), p. 1024. Terence Irwin translates: "either understanding combined with desire or desire combined with thought." In *Classics of Western Philosophy,* 3rd edition, ed. Steven M. Cahn (Indianapolis, Ind.: Hackett, 1990), p. 269.

2. Daniel Westberg, *Right Practical Reason* (Oxford: Clarendon Press, 1994), pt. III, esp. pp. 160–164.

3. See William J. Courtenay, *Capacity and Volition* (Bergamo, Italy: Pierluigi Lubrina Editore, 1990), esp. chap. 4.

4. "Volition," in *The Cambridge Dictionary of Philosophy,* ed. Robert Audi (Cambridge: Cambridge University Press, 1995), p. 843. See also G.N.A. Vesey, "Volition," in *Encyclopedia of Philosophy,* ed. Paul Edwards (New York: Macmillan & the Free Press, 1972), vol. 8, pp. 259–60.

5. Michael Walzer is in danger of this result. "We can pick out from our moral commitments those which make it possible to march vicariously with the people of Prague." *Thick and Thin* (Notre Dame, Ind.: University of Notre Dame Press, 1994), pp. 9–10.

6. Ryle, *The Concept of Mind* (New York: Barnes and Noble, 1949), chap. 3; quotation, p. 62.

7. *Weakwilled* is not an entirely apt expression, for it begs some deep philosophical questions, as well as ignoring the fact that, as J.L. Austin points out, "we often succumb to temptation with calm and even with finesse." *Philosophical Papers* (Oxford: Clarendon

Press, 1961), p. 146. But *weakness of will* is better than *incontinence,* which inevitably suggests, if not bed wetting, at least the temptations of bodily appetite rather than those of anger or an overscrupluous conscience.

8. This solution is owing to Thomas Reid; see the discussion in Knud Haakonssen, *Natural Law and Moral Philosophy* (Cambridge: Cambridge University Press, 1996), p. 190.

9. Michael Wreen, in correspondence.

10. See St. Augustine, *The City of God,* Bk. XII, chaps. 6–7.

11. Robert C. Roberts, "Will Power and the Virtues," *Philosophical Review* (April 1984), pp. 227–247; revised version reprinted in *Vice and Virtue in Everyday Life,* 3rd edition, ed. Christina Sommers and Fred Sommers (Fort Worth, Tex.: Harcourt Brace Jovanovich, 1985), pp. 266–87 (not in the 4th edition). The quotation is from Sommers and Sommers, p. 287.

12. *Nicomachean Ethics,* Bekker 1147a23.

13. *Summa Theologiae,* Ia IIae, q. 77, a. 2, ad 4 (vol. 2, p. 528). Cited with approval by Donald Davidson, *Essays on Actions and Events* (Oxford: Clarendon Press, 1980), p. 33.

14. See the discussion in Westberg, pp. 204–13.

15. Davidson, *Essays on Actions and Events,* p. 36.

16. Ibid., p. 42.

17. *City of God,* Bk. XIV, chap. 24, discussed in Arthur Danto, *Analytic Philosophy of Action* (Cambridge: Cambridge University Press, 1973), chap. 5.

18. For an indispensable study, see E.R. Dodds, *The Greeks and the Irrational* (Berkeley and Los Angeles: University of California Press, 1966).

19. For the denial of evil in New Age doctrine, see Ernest Holmes, *The Science of Mind,* 50th anniversary edition (New York: G.P. Putnam's Sons, 1988), p. 39.

20. A good account of this debate may be found in Alan Donagan, *Choice* (London: Routledge and Kegan Paul, 1987), chap. 1, sec. B.

21. I thus endorse the way Joseph Boyle, Germain Grisez, and Olaf Tollefsen define the issue in their *Free Choice* (Notre Dame, Ind.: University of Notre Dame Press, 1976), as well as the essentials of their solution.

22. Roger Scruton makes this point well in his *Sexual Desire* (New York: Free Press, 1986).

23. Foucault, *The Order of Things* (New York: Pantheon, 1970), p. 318. My interpretation follows Allesandro Pizzorno, "Foucault and the Liberal View of the Individual," in *Michel Foucault, Philosopher,* trans. Timothy Fuller (New York: Routledge, 1992), pt. 3, chap. 6.

24. See Richard Wasserstom, "On Racism and Sexism," in *Philosophy and Social Issues* (Notre Dame, Ind.: University of Notre Dame Press, 1980).

25. See Mary Midgeley and Judith Hughes, *Women's Choices* (New York: St. Martin's Press, 1983), esp. chap. 7 ("Biology, Mere and Otherwise").

26. Roberto Unger's "superliberalism" seems to embody this idea; see *The Critical Legal Studies Movement* (Cambridge, Mass.: Harvard University Press, 1986), esp. p. 41. He advocates a special branch of government with the purpose of coercively imposing this program in *False Necessity* (New York: Cambridge University Press, 1987), p. 453.

27. Walzer, *Thick and Thin;* quotations from pp. 85, 96, 104, 92.

Chapter 6: The Testimony of History and Cultural Anthropology

1. For detailed defense of this proposition, see especially Alasdair MacIntyre, *Three Rival Versions of Moral Enquiry* (Notre Dame, Ind.: University of Notre Dame Press, 1990); and Jeffrey Stout, *Ethics After Babel* (Boston: Beacon Press, 1988).

2. See Olaf Tollefsen, *Foundationalism Defended,* ed. Christopher Tollefsen (Bethesda, Md.: Cambridge Press, 1995), pt. I, chap. 3.

3. The assertion that "man is always free to choose new descriptions (for among other things, himself)" (*Philosophy and the Mirror of Nature* [Princeton: Princeton University Press, 1979], p. 362 n.8) is central to Rorty's philosophy.

4. See Devlin's *The Enforcement of Morals* (London: Oxford University Press, 1965). As Jeffrey Stout reminds us, "Where sacrilege and sodomy fail to offend, necrophilia, bestiality, and cannibalism often succeed." (*After Babel,* p. 146.)

5. See, for example, Michael Walzer, "Political Action," *Philosophy & Public Affairs* 2 (1972), pp. 160–80.

6. Scruton, "Godless Conservatism," *Wall Street Journal,* 5 April 1996.

7. Scruton observes, "The religious instinct is too vast and deep a force to be conjured from the depths without at the same time endangering a host of precious achievements" (ibid.).

8. See Peter L. Berger and Thomas Luckmann, *The Social Construction of Reality* (Garden City, N.Y.: Doubleday, 1967). Berger has since become a (neo)conservative—quite consistently, in my view.

9. This interpretation is suggested by the following passage from Michel Foucault, "Nietzsche, Genealogy, History," in *Contemporary Approaches to Philosophy,* ed. Paul Moser and Dwayne Mulder (New York: Macmillan, 1994), pp. 352–53. "The pursuit of origin . . . is an attempt to capture the exact essence of things, their purest possibilities, their *carefully protected* possibilities[;] . . . this search assumes the existence of immobile forms that precede the external world of accident and succession. . . . However, if the genealogist refuses to extend his faith to metaphysics, if he listens to history, he finds that there is 'something altogether different' behind things; not a timeless essential secret, but the secret that they have no essence or that their essence was *fabricated* in piecemeal fashion from alien forms. . . . What is found at the beginning of things is not the inviolable identity of their origin; it is the dissension of other things. It is disparity." Emphasis mine. I am indebted to Mark Schoening for this reference.

10. I have seen (at Providence College) the phrase "students of diversity," by which I suppose is meant students of color.

11. I make this argument at greater length in my book *Human Diversity and the Culture Wars* (Westport, Conn.: Praeger, 1996).

12. See, for example, Charles E. Curran, *Tradition and Transition in Moral Theology* (Notre Dame, Ind.: University of Notre Dame Press, 1979), chap. 3.

13. See David D. Gilmore, *Manhood in the Making: Cultural Concepts of Masculinity* (New Haven: Yale University Press, 1990).

14. See Clifford Geertz, *After the Fact* (Cambridge, Mass.: Harvard University Press, 1995).

15. See Freeman, *Margaret Mead and Samoa* (Cambridge, Mass.: Harvard University Press, 1983).

16. For details see *Cosmogony and Ethical Order,* ed. Robert Lovin and Frank E. Reynolds (Chicago: University of Chicago Press, 1985). See especially Lee H. Yearley, "Freud as Creator and Critic of Cosmogonies and their Ethics" (chap. 15); Arthur W.H. Adkins, "Ethics and the Breakdown of the Cosmogony of Ancient Greece" (chap. 11); and Yearley, "A Confucian Crisis" (chap. 12).

17. More precisely, according to the Purana tradition, *Kaliyuga,* or the age of sin, began in 3012 B.C. Vettam Mani, *Purana Encyclopedia* (Delhi: Motilil Bansarsides, 1975), p. 374.

18. See Bilihari Kaukisan, "Asian versus 'Universal' Human Rights," and Aryeh Neier, "Asia's Unacceptable Standard," *Responsive Community* 7, no. 3 (summer 1997), pp. 9–30. Kaukisan invokes "the diversity of cultural traditions, political structures, and levels of development" to restrain universalistic human rights claims (p. 11), but acknowledges that the West has a right to protest "genocide, murder, torture or slavery" (p. 19).

19. Quoted in Lawrence James, *The Rise and Fall of the British Empire* (New York: St. Martin's Press, 1996), p. 602.

Chapter 7: The Testimony of Biology and Physics

1. Mann, *The Magic Mountain,* trans. H.T. Lowe-Porter (New York: Knopf, 1963), pp. 496–97. In italics.

2. Kliever, "Preface," to her collection *Dax's Case* (Dallas: Southern Methodist University Press, 1989). For a more common sort of case, see Leslie Goerner, "Do You Understand about DNR?" *Commonweal* 126, no. 20 (21 November 1997), pp. 20–22.

3. See Paul Lauritzen, "Ethics and Experience: The Case of the Curious Response," *Hastings Center Report* 26 (January-February, 1996), pp. 6–14. For a dissenting view, see Stanley Johansen, "On Why We Should not Agree with Dax," *Dax's Case,* pp. 169–86.

4. Childress and Campbell, "Who Is a Doctor to Decide Whether a Person Lives or Dies?" *Dax's Case,* pp. 23–41.

5. "Dealing with a Catastrophe," *Dax's Case,* p. 142.

6. "Ethics and Experience," p. 13.

7. On the evolutionary importance of vivid examples, see Robert Nisbet and Lee Ross, *Human Inference: Strategies and Shortcomings in Social Judgment* (Englewood Cliffs, N.J.: Prentice-Hall, 1980), p. 60.

8. *A Pilgrim at Tinker Creek,* excerpted in *The Annie Dillard Reader* (New York: Harper Perennial, 1995), pp. 279–424; quotation, p. 382.

9. Isaac Watts, "Calvary," in Hugh McGraw et al., *The Sacred Harp* (N.p.: The Sacred Harp Publishing Co., 1991), p. 300.

10. Most strikingly in *Death in Venice,* where pederasty is presented as infused with the death wish, and in *The Magic Mountain,* where the same role is played by the impulse to lie down in the snow and die. *Buddenbrooks* develops the same themes in the life of a family.

11. See Nisbet and Ross, pp. 19–21, 24–26, 185.

12. Suggested by Leszek Kolakowski, *Religion* (New York: Oxford University Press, 1982), and further pursued in my *Relativism, Nihilism, and God* (Notre Dame, Ind.: University of Notre Dame Press, 1989), chap. 6.

Chapter 8: Goods

1. I here speak of male sexual pleasure; I do not presume to speak about the female variety.

2. Brandt, *Theory of the Good and Right* (Oxford: Clarendon, 1979).

3. I here adapt John Finnis, *Fundamentals of Ethics* (Washington, D.C.: Georgetown University Press, 1983), chap. 2, sec. 7; and *Natural Law and Natural Rights* (Oxford: Clarendon Press, 1980), chaps. 3–4. A valuable theological discussion can be found in Servais Pinkaers, O.P., *The Sources of Christian Ethics,* 3rd edition, trans. Sr. Mary Thomas Noble, O.P. (Washington, D.C.: Catholic University of America Press, 1995), chap. 17.

4. I here follow Joseph Raz, *The Morality of Freedom* (Oxford: Clarendon Press, 1986).

5. As Karol Wojtyla put it before becoming Pope John Paul II, "Sexual attraction makes obvious the fact that the attributes of the two sexes are complementary, so that a man and a woman complete each other." *Love and Responsibility,* trans. H.T. Willetts (New York: Farrar Straus & Giroux, 1981). See also the rich discussion in Roger Scruton, *Sexual Desire* (New York: Free Press, 1986).

6. Jerzy Kozinski, *Steps* (New York: Bantam, 1969), p. 23.

7. This would appear to be the implication of Sartre's philosophy, which is followed by Thomas Nagel, "Sexual Perversion," *Journal of Philosophy* 66 (1969), reprinted, e.g., in James Rachels, *Moral Problems* (New York: Harper and Row, 1971), pp. 69–83.

8. George, *Making Men Moral* (Oxford: Clarendon Press, 1993), esp. pp. 173–82; quotation, pp. 179–80. For a further account of practical reasonableness, see Finnis, *Natural Law and Natural Rights,* sec. IV.2 para. F; sec. V.1.

9. A recent example is David M. Smolin, Review of Michael J. Perry, *Love and Power, Iowa Law Review* 76 (1991), p. 1087, citing St. Augustine, *City of God,* Bk. XIV, chap. 13 (who does not in fact go so far).

10. Garvey, *What are Freedoms For?* (Cambridge, Mass.: Harvard University Press, 1996), esp. chaps. 2–4. George sketches a more systematic "pluralistic perfectionist" account of civil liberties (*Making Men Moral,* chap. 7).

11. George, *Making Men Moral,* p. 223. George's argument extends St. Thomas Aquinas's arguments for tolerating Jewish, though not Islamic or pagan, forms of religion in a "sacral" Christian political community. See ibid., p. 33ff., discussing *Summa Theologiae,* IIa IIae, q. 10, a. 11.

12. George, *Making Men Moral,* chap. 1, sec. IV. Christopher Wolfe criticizes George for insufficient reverence toward Aristotle and Aquinas in his review, *Political Science Reviewer* 25 (1996), p. 402 n.15.

13. If there is an afterlife, we do not in the strict sense die. This seems to be an oversimplification of a Christian understanding of death, but I do not pursue this issue here.

14. Garvey, *What are Freedoms For?,* p. 66.

Chapter 9: Virtues

1. This revolution is reflected in Christina Sommers and Fred Sommers, eds., *Vice & Virtue in Everyday Life,* 3rd edition. (Fort Worth, Tex.: Harcourt Brace, 1985); the most important materials are also in the 4th edition (1997). For the parallel development in

moral theology, see Servais Pinkaers, O.P., *The Sources of Christian Ethics,* 3rd edition, trans. Sr. Thomas Mary Noble, O.P. (Washington, D.C.: Catholic University Press, 1995), esp. chaps. 1 and 2. Joseph J. Kovta Jr., *The Christian Case for Virtue Ethics* (Washington, D.C.: Georgetown University Press, 1996), chap. 2, provides a good summary of neo-Aristotelian virtue ethics on the way toward making his case.

2. Samuel D. Scheffler, in his collection *Consequentialism and its Critics* (Oxford: Oxford University Press, 1988), p. 1.

3. Tolkien, *The Lord of the Rings* (Boston: Houghton Mifflin Company, 1987), p. 69.

4. I derive the concept of a moral journey from Stanley Hauerwas and Charles Pinches, *Christians Among the Virtues* (Notre Dame, Ind.: University of Notre Dame Press, 1997).

5. But even Machiavelli drew the line somewhere. In a passage that gives difficulty to interpreters, he wrote: "One cannot call it virtue to kill one's fellow citizens, betray one's friends, to be without faith, without mercy, without religion; these modes can enable one to acquire empire, but not glory." *The Prince,* chap. 8. Trans. and ed. Harvey Mansfield (Chicago: University of Chicago Press, 1985), p. 35.

6. As John Casey argues in his *Pagan Virtue* (Oxford: Clarendon, 1990).

7. See Christina Sommers, "Where Have All the Good Deeds Gone?" ibid., 3rd edition, pp. 653–57. Not in the 4th edition.

8. For a useful discussion of this conflict, see George Sher and William Bennett, "Moral Education and Indoctrination," *Journal of Philosophy,* November 1982, pp. 665–77; reprinted in Sommers and Sommers, 3rd edition, pp. 582–97; 4th edition, pp. 611–25.

9. For an example, see Lawrence Kohlberg, "The Child as a Moral Philosopher," Sommers and Sommers, 3rd edition, pp. 567–68; 4th edition, pp. 596–97. To be sure, the son of a college professor may not be entirely typical.

10. "The Child as a Moral Philosopher," Sommers and Sommers, 3rd edition, p. 575; 4th edition, p. 604 (section heading).

11. The protests have been led by Carol Gilligan, *In a Different Voice* (Cambridge, Mass.: Harvard University Press, 1982), excerpted in Sommers and Sommers, 3rd edition, pp. 508–612; 4th edition, pp. 626–40.

12. "Other Voices, Other Rooms?" Sommers and Sommers, eds., 3rd edition, p. 616; 4th edition, p. 644.

13. One aspect of this tension is explored in detail in Celia Wolf-Devine, "Abortion and the Feminine Voice," *Public Affairs Quarterly* 3 (July 1984), pp. 81–97.

14. See Brian Barry, *Justice as Impartiality* (Oxford: Clarendon Press, 1995), p. 253, citing Edward C. Banfield, *The Moral Basis of a Backward Society* (New York: Free Press, 1958).

15. Key classical texts are Aristotle, *Nicomachean Ethics,* VI; and St. Thomas Aquinas, *Summa Theologiae,* IIa IIae QQ. 47–51. Modern writers include Joseph Pieper, *The Four Cardinal Virtues* (Notre Dame, Ind.: University of Notre Dame Press, 1966); Stanley Hauerwas, *Vision and Virtue* (Notre Dame, Ind.: Fides, 1974); David Wiggins, "Deliberation and Practical Reason," *Practical Reason,* 3rd ed. Joseph Raz (Oxford: Oxford University Press, 1978); Martha Craven Nussbaum, "Finely Aware and Richly Responsible," *Anti-Theory in Ethics and Moral Conservatism,* ed. Stanley G. Clarke and Evan Simpson (Albany, N.Y.: SUNY Press, 1989); Hilary Putnam, *Realism with a Human Face* (Cambridge, Mass.: Harvard University Press, 1990); Daniel Mark Nelson, *The Priority of Prudence* (University Park, Penn.: Pennsylvania State University Press, 1992);

Joseph Dunne, *Back to the Rough Ground* (Notre Dame, Ind.: University of Notre Dame Press, 1993); and Daniel Westberg, *Right Practical Reason* (Oxford: Clarendon Press, 1994). Texts with a political spin include Ronald Beiner, *Political Judgment* (Chicago: University of Chicago Press, 1983); Allessandro Ferraro, "On Phronesis," *Praxis International* 7, no. 3/4 (winter 1987/8); and Peter J. Steinberger, *The Concept of Political Judgment* (Chicago: University of Chicago Press, 1993).

16. See W.D. Falk, *Ought, Reason, and Morality,* ed. Kurt Baier (Ithaca, N.Y.: Cornell University Press, 1986), pp. 204–9.

17. See Henry Sidgwick, *The Methods of Ethics* (New York: Dover, 1966), pp. 327–28.

18. See Vincent E. Starzinger, *Middlingness* (Charlottesville, Va.: University Press of Virginia, 1965), esp. pp. 144–53.

19. Some data are collected in Beiner, *Political Judgment,* chap. 6, especially his discussion of the controversy surrounding Hannah Arendt's *Eichmann in Jerusalem.*

20. "Finely Aware and Richly Responsible," p. 116. Recently, however, Nussbaum has abandoned her contextual approach when faced with religious practices she finds repellent. See her "Religion and Women's Human Rights," in *Religion and Contemporary Liberalism,* ed. Paul J. Weithman (Notre Dame, Ind.: University of Notre Dame Press, 1997), pp. 93–137.

21. Compare *Nicomachean Ethics,* Bekker 1140b, with *Gorgias,* Stephanus 515d.

22. *On Liberty,* chap. 4. In *Classics of Western Philosophy,* 3rd edition, ed. Stephen M. Cahn (Indianapolis, Ind.: Hackett, 1990), p. 1153.

23. Robert P. George's strongest arguments in *Making Men Moral* (Oxford: Clarendon Press, 1993) appeal to this notion.

24. This paragraph is directed at a paper on "Virtue Ethics," delivered by James Griffin at Boston University in September 1997.

Chapter 10: Duties

1. Recent proportionalist writers include Charles Curran, *Tradition and Transition in Moral Theology* (Notre Dame, Ind.: University of Notre Dame Press, 1979); Garth Hallett, *Christian Moral Reasoning* (Notre Dame, Ind.: University of Notre Dame Press, 1985); Bernard Hoose, *Proportionalism* (Washington, D.C.: Georgetown University Press, 1987) and Richard A. McCormick, S.J., in his collection with Paul Ramsey, *Doing Evil to Achieve Good* (Chicago: Loyola University Press, 1978).

2. See D.H. Hodgson, *The Consequences of Utilitarianism* (Oxford: Clarendon Press, 1967).

3. Howatch, *Absolute Truths* (New York: Knopf, 1994).

4. I here take the risk of treating Finnis and Grisez, in view of their many collaborative efforts, as for the most part interchangeable. Throughout the chapter, I cite their key writings as follows: FE = Finnis, *Fundamentals of Ethics* (Washington, D.C.: Georgetown University Press, 1980); LMS = Finnis, "Law, Morality, and 'Sexual Orientation,'"] *Notre Dame Journal of Law, Ethics, and Public Policy* 9 (1995); MA = Finnis, *Moral Absolutes* (Washington, D.C.: Catholic University of America Press, 1991); THV = John Ford, S.J. et al. *The Teaching of Humanae Vitae* (San Francisco: Ignatius, 1988); WLJ = Grisez, *The Way of the Lord Jesus,* vol. 1 (Chicago: Franciscan Herald Press, 1983); vol. 2 (Quincy, Ill.: Franciscan Press, 1993).

5. Joseph Boyle has also contributed to the development of the new natural law theory, particularly in the realm of sexual morals; see Ronald Lawler, O.F.M.Cap., Joseph Boyle, and William E. May, *Catholic Sexual Ethics* (Huntington, Ind.: Our Sunday Visitor Press, 1985). For an attempt to apply their theory to jurisprudential questions, see Robert P. George, *Making Men Moral* (Oxford: Clarendon Press, 1993). For a differently focused critique of the school, see Russell Hittinger, *The New Natural Law Theory* (Notre Dame, Ind.: University of Notre Dame Press, 1988).

6. The reference is to St. Thomas Aquinas, *Summa Theologiae,* Ia IIae, q. 18, a. 5, ad 3.

7. He is here responding to Grisez, "Towards a Consistent Natural Law Ethics of Killing," *American Journal of Jurisprudence* 10 (1970), 67–70.

8. For an example of a fundamental option theory, see Bernard Häring, *Free and Faithful in Christ,* vol. 1 (New York: Seabury, 1978), pp. 211–5, 396–410. For detailed discussion of Finnis and Grisez's views on fundamental option, see Richard A. McCormick, S.J., *The Critical Calling* (Washington, D.C.: Georgetown University Press, 1989), pp. 183–88.

9. "Beyond the Encyclical," *The Tablet,* 8 January 1994.

10. In discussing theological method he states without qualification, "One should never believe professional theologians" (WLJ 2:43)—with the exception, of course, of Grisez and his associates. (The subsequent explanation is not quite so sweeping.)

11. Grisez, *Abortion* (New York: Corpus, 1970), p. 346.

12. George, *Making Men Moral,* pp. 36, vii.

13. For a defense of the use of consequentialist arguments by religious writers, see Basil Mitchell, *Law, Morality, and Religion in a Secular Society* (London: Oxford University Press, 1970), pp. 114ff.

14. I have in mind the formulation ascribed to Aquinas in Alan Donagan, *The Theory of Morality* (Chicago: University of Chicago Press, 1977), p. 61: *"Act so that fundamental human goods, whether in your own person or that of another, are promoted in every way possible, and under no circumstances violated."*

15. See Elie Wiesel, *Night,* trans. Stella Rodway (New York: Bantam, 1989), p. 28.

16. Kant seems to adopt this solution in his *Lectures on Ethics,* trans. Louis Infield (New York: Harper and Row, 1963), esp. p. 227, at least if the deceiver does not infringe on "the rights of humanity" (as Jews who deceive concentration camp guards surely do not). For a sympathetic presentation of Kant's more usual rigorism, see Roger J. Sullivan, *Immanuel Kant's Moral Theory* (Cambridge: Cambridge University Press, 1989), pp. 170–77.

17. The approach here supersedes that taken in my *Ethics of Homicide* (Ithaca, N.Y.: Cornell University Press, 1978), sec. 26, and the Preface to the paperback edition (Notre Dame, Ind.: University of Notre Dame Press, 1990), pp. 8–12.

18. Philosophical doctrines expressing and supporting this intuition are examined in David Novak, *Suicide and Morality* (New York: Scholars' Studies Press, 1975). For a recent concise statement, see his "Suicide Is Not a Private Choice," *First Things* no. 75 (August/September 1997), 31–43.

19. *More Poems,* no. XXVI, "I Counsel You Beware." Found in *Complete Poems,* Centennial edition (New York: Holt, Rinehart, and Winston, 1959), p. 185.

20. See the discussion in Novak, *Suicide and Morality,* pp. 86–89. In a related vein, G.K. Chesterton writes, "The suicide insults everything on earth by not stealing it. He

defiles every flower by refusing to live for its sake." *Orthodoxy* (New York: John Lane, 1909), p. 132.

21. Wreen, "Importune Death a While," *Public Affairs Quarterly* 10, no. 2 (April 1996), p. 159.

22. I am here indebted to Novak's rendering of one of St. Thomas's arguments, *Suicide and Morality,* pp. 59–67.

23. St. Thomas Aquinas at least is circumspect in his defense of a duty of obedience, even to a religious superior. See *Summa Theologiae,* IIa IIae, q. 104, a. 5, esp. ad 3.

24. Donagan, *The Theory of Morality,* pp. 77–79.

25. St. Thomas Aquinas, *Summa Theologiae,* II IIae, q. 64, a. 5, ad 2. (Madrid: Biblioteca de Autores Christianos, 1952), vol. 3, p. 439. See the discussion in Novak, *Suicide and Morality,* pp. 67–69.

26. Compare Sartre on "My Own Death" (*Being and Nothingness,* Pt. IV, chap. 3, sec. E), as well as St. Augustine on suicide to avoid rape, or afterward (*City of God,* Bk. I, chaps. 16–28).

27. So St. Augustine: "The virtue, by which one rightly lives, commands the parts of the body from its seat in the soul by a holy will. While such a will remains unshaken and steadfast, whatever anyone else does with the body or in the body that a person can not avoid without sin on his own part, no blame attaches to the one who suffers it." (*City of God,* Bk. I, chap. 16.) See also Bk. I, chap. 18, for a strongly drawn distinction between the condition of the body and that of the soul.

28. See Novak, *Suicide and Morality,* pp. 97–103.

29. See my *Ethics of Homicide,* sec. 1, and the application of the conclusions reached there to abortion at pp. 89–90. On self-murder, see Wreen, "Importune Death a While," p. 158.

30. Novak, *Suicide and Morality,* p. 127.

31. Previously proposed in my articles, "The Moral Basis of Vegetarianism," *Philosophy,* October 1978; "Birth, Copulation, and Death," *New Scholasticism,* summer 1985.

32. Schopenhauer denied this proposition, advising self-starvation and celibacy, and some people at the fringes of the ecology movement agree, though they prefer nonreproductive sex, suicide, and the propagation of airborne diseases.

33. A full-page advertisement for the movie *Gattaca* puts the issue pointedly: "Children made to order." It concludes, "From where we sit, the human race could use a little improving." *New York Times,* 12 September 1997. I am indebted to Eleanore Devine for this reference.

34. *Love and Responsibility,* trans. H.T. Willetts (New York: Farrar Straus & Giroux, 1981), p. 60.

35. Insofar as is it is theological concept, *love* lies outside the scope of the present inquiry; cf. ibid., pp. 28–31.

36. Donagan, *The Theory of Morality,* p. 107.

37. Wittgenstein might assert a superior claim, but he found it very difficult to discuss concrete moral issues of any sort.

38. Plato, *Laws,* Bk. I, Stephanus 636c, trans. A.E. Taylor in *Collected Dialogues,* ed. Edith Hamilton and Huntington Cairns (New York: Bollingen Foundation, 1963), p. 1237.

39. Similar argumentation may be found in Robert P. George and Gerard V. Bradley, "Marriage and the Liberal Imagination," *Georgetown Law Journal* 84 (December 1995), pp. 301ff; and in WLJ 2: chap. 9, sec. F, esp. para. 3 (e).

40. George and Bradley, "Marriage and the Liberal Imagination," p. 301 n.4.

41. Cf. ibid., p. 313, responding to Stephen Macedo.

42. Thus the new natural lawyers cannot comfortably maintain the moral relevance of remarks such as the following: "We easily recognize the mating of animals we know to be sterile as mating, and not as failed attempts to mate. . . . By contrast, where a male mounts a female but, for whatever reason, does not manage to achieve vaginal penetration, what we have is precisely a failed attempt to mate." Ibid., pp. 313–14 and n.38.

43. Ibid., pp. 301 n.1, 305 n.19.

44. On this issue Mary Midgeley shows her usual common sense in "The End of Anthropocentrism," *Philosophy and the Natural Environment,* ed. Robin Attfield and Andrew Bolsey (Cambridge: Cambridge University Press, 1994), pp. 103–112.

45. Aspinall, "Man's Place in Nature," in *Animals' Rights—A Symposium,* ed. David Peterson and Richard D. Ryder (London: Centaur, 1979), p. 20.

46. See J. Baird Callicot, "Animal Liberation: A Triangular Affair," *Environmental Ethics* 2, no. 4 (winter 1980), pp. 311–38, reprinted in *People, Penguins, and Plastic Trees,* ed. Donald VanDeVeer and Christine Peirce (Belmont, Calif.: Wadsworth, 1986) pp. 184–203, which considers the views of Aldo Leopold. The quotation is from Donald VanDeVeer and Christine Peirce, p. 198.

47. See *Radical Environmentalism,* ed. Peter List (Belmont, Calif.: Wadsworth, 1993).

Chapter 11: Rights

1. For a critical examination of this feature of our public speech, see Mary Ann Glendon, *Rights Talk* (New York: Free Press, 1991). Alasdair MacIntyre maintains "there are no [natural or human] rights, and belief in them is one with belief in witches and unicorns." *After Virtue,* rev. edition (Notre Dame, Ind.: University of Notre Dame Press, 1984), p. 69. Likewise, Ronald Beiner argues that "we have nothing to lose with the supersession of the vocabulary of rights." *What's the Matter with Liberalism?* (Berkeley and Los Angeles: University of California Press, 1992), p. 93.

2. See Strauss, *Introduction to Political Philosophy* (Detroit: Wayne State University Press, 1989), pp. 270–7. John Finnis, *Natural Law and Natural Rights* (Oxford: Clarendon Press, 1980), p. 221, nonetheless proposes to retain the idea of natural rights, while Ernest L. Fortin, "The New Rights Theory and the Natural Law," *Review of Politics* 44 (1982), 592, is more skeptical.

3. Fortin, "The New Rights Theory and the Natural Law," pp. 594–5, 591.

4. "A human being *(homo)* is not subject to the political community in all that he is or has." St. Thomas Aquinas, *Summa Theologiae,* Ia IIae, Q. 21, a. 4, ad 3; (Madrid: Biblioteca de Autores Christianos, 1952), vol. 2, p. 163. "Any private person can be compared with the whole community as a part to a whole. And therefore if a human being is dangerous to the community and destructive of it because of some sin, he is laudably and healthily killed, in order to protect the common good." IIa IIae, q. 64, a. 2; vol. 3, p. 436.

5. The issue was squarely posed in a dialogue between Roman Catholics and Evangelicals, when Deal Hudson used the word *imperfectly,* whereas David Coffin used *wickedly,* when speaking of the use of the human mind in the fallen order. See *A Preserving Grace,* ed. Michael Cromartie (Grand Rapids, Mich: Eerdmans, 1997), p. 87.

6. George makes this point forcefully in ibid., p. 166.

7. In the eighteenth century, this issue was posed by the Calvinist John Witherspoon; see Knud Haakonssen, *Natural Law and Moral Philosophy* (Cambridge: Cambridge University Press, 1996), sec. 10.6.

8. For two very different theologies of rights, see Charles Villa-Vicencio, *A Theology of Reconstruction* (Cambridge: Cambridge University Press, 1992); and John Warwick Montgomery, *Human Rights and Human Dignity* (Grand Rapids, Mich.: Zondervan, 1986). Montgomery cites Evangelical theologians who reject the concept of rights altogether (p. 19).

9. For details see Ian Shapiro, *The Evolution of Rights in Liberal Theory* (Cambridge: Cambridge University Press, 1986). For the claim that rights-talk is tied to a distinctively capitalist form of individualism, see C.B. Macpherson, *The Political Theory of Possessive Individualism* (Oxford: Oxford University Press, 1962). Many defenders of capitalism would agree.

10. This issue was posed at a conference on "Ernest Fortin and the Revival of Christian Political Philosophy," held at Boston College on 25 October 1997.

11. For a reaffirmation of the language of human rights in circles that might be disposed to be hostile to it, see The Ramsey Colloquium, "On Human Rights," with commentary by Mary Ann Glendon and Elliott Abrams, *First Things* no. 82 (April 1998), pp. 18–30.

12. George in *A Preserving Grace,* ed. Michael Cromartie, p. 162.

13. I am here indebted to a conversation with Nicholas Ingham, O.P.

14. Nagel, *Equality and Partiality* (New York: Oxford University Press, 1991), pp. 143–44. But his discussion of sexual freedom issues (ibid., pp. 145–47) neglects the interests of parents in transmitting a way of life.

15. As Baruch Brody does; see his "The Problem of Exceptions in Medical Ethics," *Doing Evil to Achieve Good,* ed. Richard A. MacCormack, S.J., and Paul Ramsey (Chicago: Loyola University Press, 1978), chap. 2.

16. I am indebted to Jeremy Waldron, *Private Property* (Oxford: Clarendon Press, 1988), chap. 3, for help in clarifying the relationship between rights and interests.

17. My argument here is indebted to Lloyd L. Weinreb, "Natural Law and Rights," in *Natural Law Theory,* ed. Robert P. George (Oxford: Clarendon Press, 1992), chap. 10. See also the classical statement in T.H. Green, *Lectures on the Principles of Political Obligation,* ed. Paul Harris and John Morrow (Cambridge: Cambridge University Press, 1986), secs. 26–31, pp. 26–29.

18. I draw this implication in detail in my *Ethics of Homicide* (Ithaca, N.Y.: Cornell University Press, 1978) (Notre Dame, Ind.: University of Notre Dame Press, 1990), sec. 12, modified in the Preface to the paperback edition, p. 4. For further discussion see my *Human Diversity and the Culture Wars* (Westport, Conn.: Praeger, 1996), chap. 10; "'Conservative' Views of Abortion," *Advances in Bioethics* 2 (1997), pp. 183–202; and "Homicide, Criminal vs. Justifiable," *Encyclopedia of Applied Ethics* (San Diego: Academic Press, 1998), vol. 2, pp. 587–95.

19. To assert a moral consensus that leaves out Mother Teresa is nothing less than arrogance; for her views on abortion, see her Nobel Prize acceptance speech, reprinted in Katharyn Spink, *Mother Teresa* (New York: HarperSanFrancisco, 1997), p. 297.

20. For more detailed discussion of the conventionalist principle, see my *Human Diversity,* p. 125; and "'Conservative' Views of Abortion," pp. 189–90.

21. These questions are well posed, though hardly resolved, by Michael Walzer, *On Toleration* (New Haven: Yale University Press, 1997), especially his discussion of gender issues.

22. These are by no means new; they are affirmed (though without use of the word *right*) in Daniel 13, also called the History of Susanna.

23. In 1482, Pope Sixtus VI unsuccessfully affirmed process rights against the Spanish Inquisition; see the bull cited in Henry Kamen, *The Spanish Inquisition* (London: Weidenfeld and Nicholson, 1997), p. 49.

24. The Vatican has recently revised its procedures for dealing with suspect theologians in order to make for a more "transparent" process. Defense representatives will still be excluded from "urgent" cases, however—which may undermine the whole effort. *Washington Post,* 6 September 1997.

25. Cardinal Newman asks bluntly, "What have excommunication and interdict to do with Infallibility?" *Letter to the Duke of Norfolk,* in Newman and Gladstone, *The Vatican Decrees* (Notre Dame, Ind.: University of Notre Dame Press, 1962), p. 135.

26. In Walter M. Abbot, S.J., ed., *The Documents of Vatican II* (New York: America Press, 1966), p. 678 n.5.

27. Kenneth R. Craycraft Jr., "Religion as Moral Duty and Civic Right," in *Catholicism, Liberalism, and Communitarianism,* ed. Kenneth L. Grasso, Gerard V. Bradley, and Robert P. Hunt (Lanham, Md.: Rowman and Littlefield, 1995), p. 79 n.65.

28. The examples are owing to Waldron, "A Right to Do Wrong," *Ethics* 92 (October 1981), p. 21. My argument is also indebted to Waldron.

29. For example, Richard E. Flathman has argued that the right to abortion includes a right to demand an abortion from a physician who believes that abortion is wrong. "The Theory of Rights and the Practice of Abortion," American Political Science Association, Washington, D.C., 4 September 1977, as cited by Hadley Arkes, *First Things* (Princeton: Princeton University Press, 1986), pp. 202–3.

30. George, *Making Men Moral* (Oxford: Clarendon Press, 1993), p. 115.

31. Abraham Lincoln's denial of a right to do wrong involved slavery. Cited in Arkes, p. 24; and in George, *Making Men Moral,* pp. 110–11.

32. A disturbingly large number of people's views on abortion seem to imply a right to commit murder; see the poll cited in George, *Making Men Moral,* p. 112 n.5.

33. Edward Johnson, "Life, Death, and Animals," in *Animal Rights and Human Obligations,* 2nd edition, ed. Tom Regan and Peter Singer (Englewood Cliffs, N.J.: Prentice-Hall, 1989), pp. 142, 148. The reference is to my *Ethics of Homicide,* p. 49.

Chapter 12: The Question of Absolutes

1. A useful, though sometimes philosophically maladroit, account of these conflicts is James Davison Hunter, *Culture Wars* (N.p.: Basic Books, 1991).

2. Margolis, *The Truth About Relativism* (Oxford: Basil Blackwell, 1991), pp. xiv, 7.

3. Finnis, *Moral Absolutes* (Washington, D.C.: Catholic University of America Press, 1991), p. 7. *Rape,* in contrast, appears only once in his index (and the same is true of *genocide*), and *torture* not at all.

4. See my article, "The Conscious Acceptance of Guilt in the Necessary Murder," *Ethics* 89, no. 3 (April 1978), pp. 221–39.

5. McDowell, "Virtue and Reason," in *Anti-Theory in Ethics and Moral Conservatism,* ed. Stanley G. Clarke and Evan Simpson (Albany, N.Y.: SUNY Press, 1989), p. 93.

6. This sentence is directed against Martha Craven Nussbaum, "'Finely Aware and Richly Responsible,'" *Anti-Theory in Ethics and Moral Conservatism,* chap. 5.

7. Aristotle, *Nicomachean Ethics,* 1107a9–17. Interpretations of this passage are discussed by Finnis, *Moral Absolutes,* chap. 2, sec. 1. Adultery for Aristotle is not adultery in the Christian or post-Christian sense, however. A married man who has intercourse with an unmarried woman is not, in Aristotle's sense, guilty of adultery.

8. See, for example Annette Baier, "Doing Without Moral Theory," *Anti-Theory in Ethics and Moral Conservatism,* chap. 1.

9. Plato, *Crito,* 49b, trans. Hugh Treddenick, *Collected Dialogues,* ed. Edith Hamilton and Huntington Cairns (New York: Pantheon, 1961), p. 34.

10. Nagel, "War and Massacre," *War and Moral Responsibility,* ed. Marshall Cohen, Thomas Nagel, and Thomas Scanlon (Princeton: Princeton University Press, 1974), pp. 12–13.

11. On this issue, see David Malament, "Selective Conscientious Objection and the *Gillette* Decision," ibid., pp. 159–80.

12. Paul VI, *Humanae Vitae* (1968), sec. 14. Trans. in *The Papal Encyclicals, 1958–1981,* ed. Claudia Carlen, I.H.M. (N.p.: Consortium, 1981), p. 227.

13. I here tighten up Donald Evans, "Love, Situations, and Rules," *Norm and Context in Christian Ethics,* ed. Gene H. Outka and Paul Ramsey (New York: Charles Scribners' Sons, 1968), pp. 401–12.

14. See *Summa Theologiae,* Ia IIae, q. 100, a. 6, ad 3. I follow Patrick Lee's interpretation, "The Permanence of the Ten Commandments," *Theological Studies* 42 (September 1981), pp. 422–43; quotation, p. 433.

15. See Naomi Wolf, "Our Bodies, Our Souls," in *Vice and Virtue in Everyday Life,* 4th edition, ed. Christina Sommers and Fred Sommers (Fort Worth, Tex.: Harcourt Brace, 1997), pp. 843–60.

16. Finnis, *Moral Absolutes,* pp. 72, 38–39.

17. See Finnis's book with Germain Grisez and Joseph Boyle, *Nuclear Deterrence, Morality, and Realism* (Oxford: Clarendon Press, 1987), esp. chap. 4.

18. See Evelyn Waugh, *Men at Arms* (Boston: Little, Brown, 1952), chap. 13. These cases were formulated before President Clinton made sexual casuistry notorious.

19. Finnis, *Moral Absolutes,* p. 8.

20. But Alan Donagan, *The Theory of Morality* (Chicago: University of Chicago Press, 1977), p. 188, argues that torture would sometimes be legitimate, unless prohibited by positive law.

21. Hampshire, "Absolutism and the Good Life," in *Absolutism and its Consequentialist Critics,* ed. Joram Graf Haber (Lanham, Md.: Rowman and Littlefield, 1994), p. 121. My argument owes a great deal to Hampshire.

22. I am here agreeing in part and disagreeing in part with Jenny Teichman, "Is Anything Sacred?" *Providence: Studies in Western Civilization* 2 (fall 1993), 27–34. I am grateful to Leonard Hindsley, O.P. for letting me see a copy of this article before publication. See also Teichman's articles, "What Is Sacred?" *New Criterion,* November 1993, pp. 8–15; and "The False Philosophy of Peter Singer," *New Criterion,* April 1993, pp. 25–30.

23. Richard Stith has persuasively argued that the language of respect and reverence is to be preferred to that of value when discussing life issues. For a recent statement of his

views, see "On Death and Dworkin," *Maryland Law Review* 56, no. 2 (1997), 289–383, esp. pp. 310–28, 347–58. Hence I depart from my book *The Ethics of Homicide* (Ithaca, N.Y.: Cornell University Press, 1978) (Notre Dame, Ind.: University of Notre Dame Press, 1990), p. 206; but see p. 209.

24. Kai Nielsen, "Against Moral Conservatism," *Absolutism and its Consequentialist Critics,* p. 172.

25. Johnson, "The Authority of the Moral Agent," in *Consequentialism and its Critics,* ed. Samuel D. Scheffler (Oxford: Oxford University Press, 1988), p. 270. I do not ascribe the argument in the text to Johnson.

26. On minimalism and its relationship to the extremism implied by consequentialism, see Shelly Kagan, *The Limits of Morality* (Oxford: Clarendon Press, 1989), pp. 5–6, 386–90.

27. Evans, "Love, Situations, and Rules," p. 413.

28. For detailed discussion, see my anthology with Celia Wolf-Devine, *Sex and Gender* (Belmont, Calif.: Wadsworth, forthcoming 2000).

29. For one possible way of developing this line of thought, see Christopher Derrick, *Sex and Sacredness* (San Francisco: Ignatius, 1982).

30. Crombie, "Moral Principles," *Christian Ethics and Contemporary Philosophy,* ed. Ian T. Ramsey (New York: Macmillan, 1966), p. 258.

31. Finnis, *Moral Absolutes,* p. 5.

Chapter 13: The Basis of Community

1. Philosophers still say of expresions that are not utter gibberish that they lack clear sense. Such remarks themselves stand in need of elucidation: they are best understood as challenges to the speaker to say more fully what he means. Even so, it is not clear what constitutes a sufficient answer to such challenges, or when such challenges are appropriate. (I am here indebted to discussions with Hilary Putnam and Michael Wreen.)

2. See Thomas Frank, *The Conquest of Cool* (Chicago: University of Chicago Press, 1997). Note the blunt statement quoted at p. 122: "When the new generation buys they want it for now. They are not interested in how long it will last."

3. See Michael Kamen, "History Is our Heritage," in *Historical Literacy*, ed. Paul Gangnon et al. (Boston: Houghton Mifflin, 1991), chap. 7; and Robert Hewison, *The Heritage Industry* (London: Methuen, 1987), which also examines the political manipulation of the concept of heritage.

4. See Plato, *Republic,* Stephanus 422e–23a, 551d; Aristotle, *Politics,* Bk. IV, chap. 11. I am also indebted to conversations with Patrick Walker.

5. See Benjamin Barber, *Jihad vs. McWorld* (New York: Times Books, 1995).

6. I owe this phrase to Beth Soll.

7. The key figure in debates about distinguishing development from decadence is Cardinal Newman. I found Owen Chadwick, *From Bossuet to Newman,* 2nd edition (Cambridge: Cambridge University Press, 1987), particularly helpful in understanding Newman's thought and the problems it raises.

8. *Chronicle of Higher Education,* 18 April 1997. I am indebted to Thomas Feeley, C.S.C., for this reference.

9. This is John Gray's analysis of our condition; see his *Post-liberalism* (New York: Routledge, 1993), p. 4.

10. In reaching this conclusion, I join Christopher Lasch (*The True and Only Heaven* [New York: Norton, 1991], chap. 1) and Eugene Genovese (see *The Southern Tradition* [Cambridge, Mass.: Harvard University Press, 1994]); for a short statement, see "Eugene Rivers' Challenge: A Response," www.polisci.mit.edu/BostonReview/BR 19.5/eugene-rivers.html, reproduced from the *Boston Review.*

11. See Charles De Konick, *De la primauté, du bien commun: contre les personalistes* (Québec: Éditions de l'Université Laval, 1943), reviewed by Yves Simon, *Review of Politics* 6 (1944), pp. 530–33. This book engendered a bitter controversy, in which the pertinent social and political issues are somewhat masked. See I. Th. Eschmann, "In Defense of Jacques Maritain," *The Modern Schoolman* 22, no 4 (May 1945), pp. 183–208; and De Konick, "In Defense of Saint Thomas," *Laval Théologique et Philosophique* 1, no. 2 (1945), pp. 8–109. De Konick disavows the alleged totalitarian implications of his views "In Defense of St. Thomas," sec. XI, as well as at the very beginning of *De la primauté,* (p. 1). See also his invocation of the "private law of the Holy Ghost ("In Defense of St. Thomas," sec. XII).

12. St. Thomas Aquinas's conception of the common good is studied in historical context by Thomas Gilby, *The Political Thought of St. Thomas Aquinas* (Chicago: University of Chicago Press, 1958), chap. 7, sec. 5.

13. Compare the original text of *Political Liberalism* (New York: Columbia University Press, 1994), with the Preface to the paperback edition (1996). See also "The Idea of Public Reason Revisited," *University of Chicago Law Review* 64, no. 3 (summer 1997), pp. 765–802. I am indebted to Dermot Luddy for discussions of recent developments in Rawls's philosophy.

14. Published as "Assisted Suicide: The Philosophers' Brief," *New York Review of Books,* 27 March 1997; for discussion see Michael J. Sandel, "The Hard Questions: Last Rights," *New Republic,* 14 April 1997, p. 27. Rawls has since acknowledged, in an interview, that there are a variety of arguments against a right to assisted suicide admissible within public reason; see Bernard G. Prusak, "Politics, Religion, and the Common Good," *Commonweal* 125, no. 16 (Sept. 25, 1998), p. 14.

15. See the classic argument by Yale Kamisar, "Euthanasia Legislation: Some Non-Religious Objections," in *Euthanasia and the Right to Death*, ed. A.B. Downing (Los Angeles: Nash, 1970); and the up-to-date discussion by Herbert Hendin, "Physician-Assisted Suicide: What Next?" *Responsive Community* 7, no. 4 (fall, 1997), pp. 21–34.

16. Sandel, *Liberalism and the Limits of Justice,* 2nd edition (Cambridge: Cambridge University Press, 1998), pp. 184–218.

17. Sandel says that he believes that the Roman Catholic position on abortion can be refuted (ibid., p. 198), but he does not say how. On homosexuality, Sandel takes a liberal position, and excludes without discussion appeals to the Bible either as a source of divinely revealed truth or as a founding document of our civilization (ibid., pp. 208–9).

18. Alasdair MacIntyre argues that "in an Aristotelian perspective anyone who can formulate such a contrast has no country." *After Virtue,* rev. edition (Notre Dame, Ind.: University of Notre Dame Press, 1984), p. 156. But there were conflicts of loyalty even in the ancient *polis,* as the case of Antigone shows.

19. For contemporary discussions, see Allen Buchanan, *Secession* (Boulder, Colo.: Westview, 1991); *Secession, State & Liberty,* ed. David Gordon (New Brunswick: Transaction, 1998); and Michael Walzer, *Thick and Thin* (Notre Dame, Ind.: University of Notre Dame Press, 1994).

20. See Russell Hittinger, "Natural Law in the Positive Laws," *Review of Politics* 55, no. 1 (winter, 1993), pp. 5–34; and the same author's Introduction to Russell Kirk, *Rights and Duties,* ed. Mitchell S. Muncy (Dallas: Spence, 1997), esp. pp. xxi–xxviii.

21. This sentence is directed against Hittinger, "Natural Law in the Positive Laws," p. 13 and n.19. I am not sure that he would agree with *Brown,* however, in view of his hesitations about the Fourteenth Amendment (Introduction, p. xxx). The more usual conservative position is represented by Robert Bork, who defends the result though not the opinion in *Brown;* see *The Tempting of America* (New York: Free Press, 1990), pp. 74–84.

22. A good short guide to the world of American conservatism is Peter Augustine Lawler, "In Search of American Conservatism," *Gravitas* (spring 1996), pp. 31–35. I am indebted to Mark Henrie for this reference.

23. Justice Brennan dissenting in *Michael H. v. Gerald D.* (1989).

24. Hittinger, "Natural Law as 'Law,'" *American Journal of Jurisprudence* (1994), pp. 1–32.

25. Peter L. Berger, *The Sacred Canopy* (Garden City, N.Y.: Doubleday Anchor, 1969), esp. chaps. 1–2, provides a sketch of the role of religion in the construction and maintenance of social reality, and discusses the possible theological ramifications of his account in App. II. Yet Berger accepts the liberal Protestant metanarrative of the dwindling importance of religion; see ibid., chap. 5. For a critique of this metanarrative, see John Milbank, *Theology and Social Theory* (Oxford: Basil Blackwell, 1991), pp. 92–98.

26. Todd Gitlin's perceptive book, *The Sixties* (Toronto: Bantam, 1987), makes this fact evident on every page. He describes People's Park (Berkeley, 1968) as "one tantalizing trace of a good society, . . . the practical negation of American death, . . . a redemption worth fighting for" (p. 355).

27. See Jean-Jacques Rousseau, *The Social Contract,* trans. and ed. Maurice Cranston (Baltimore: Penguin, 1968), Bk. IV, chap. 8, "The Civil Religion." For a contemporary statement, see Robert Bellah, *The Broken Covenant* (New York: Seabury Crossroad, 1975).

28. One contemporary jurisprudent observes summarily: "Recent work in political philosophy has made it apparent that, notwithstanding the standard lore of American government, all citizens do not consent to be governed by the laws of the United States." Steven J. Burton, *Judging in Good Faith* (Cambridge: Cambridge University Press, 1992), pp. 217–18. He cites an impressive list of authorities for this proposition (p. 215 n.24). Alexander Bickel, on the other hand, took consent seriously, though in a rather ill-defined form. See *The Morality of Consent* (New Haven: Yale University Press, 1975), esp. chap. 1. A complete discussion of this issue would have to take into account the view that agreement to participate in a shared enterprise generates a (not exactly moral) obligation to observe its norms, even when this agreement does not meet the requirements of the standard liberal conception of consent. See Margaret Gilbert, *Living Together* (Lanham, Md.: Rowman and Littlefield, 1996), esp. chap. 15.

29. This sentence is directed against Michael Walzer, particularly his paper "Drawing the Line: Religion and Politics," delivered at the Legal Theory Workshop, Yale Law School, 2 April 1998. See also his *On Toleration* (New Haven: Yale University Press, 1997), pp. 76–80.

30. A range of Jewish positions is included in *American Jews & the Separationist Faith,* ed. David G. Dalin (Washington, D.C.: Ethics & Public Policy Center, 1993). The political role of Buddhists, Hindus, and Moslems remains to be defined.

31. So it was, for example, with Abraham Lincoln. See David Herbert Donald, *Lincoln* (New York: Simon and Schuster, 1995).

Conclusion: Natural Law Versus Calvinism

1. As Hilary Putnam puts it. *Realism with a Human Face,* ed. James Conant (Cambridge, Mass.: Harvard University Press, 1990), chap. 10.

2. Consider the following quotation: "Indeed [St. Paul] shows that ignorance is uselessly presented as an excuse by some gentiles, since they prove by their own deeds that they have some rule of righteousness; for no nation has so abandoned everything human as to discard all laws. . . . All have some conceptions of justice and rectitude which are naturally inborn in the hearts of men." Commentary on Romans 2:14–15, quoted by Susan E. Schreiner, "Calvin's Use of Natural Law," in *A Preserving Grace,* ed. Michael Cromartie (Grand Rapids, Mich.: William B. Eerdmans, 1997), p. 56.

3. Despite extensive research, I have been unable to verify this quotation, and have come to suspect that it is apocryphal. But the sentiment pervades Barth's writings; see for example his *Anselm: Fides Quaerens Intellectum,* trans. Ian W. Robertson (N.p.: Pickwick Press, 1975), esp. chap. 1, where he writes: "The aim of theology cannot be to lead men to faith, nor to confirm them in the faith, nor even to deliver their faith from doubt" (p. 17).

4. Herman Dooyeweerd writes: "By the fall of man, human thought . . . has become the 'carnal mind' (Colos. II:18), for it does not exist apart from its apostate religious root. And thought includes the logical function." *A New Critique of Theoretical Thought,* trans. David H. Freeman and William S. Young (Amsterdam: Uitgeverij H.J. Paris, 1953), vol. 1, p. 100. In a more moderate vein, Emil Brunner, who, although invoking "preserving grace" to sustain a natural theology, nonetheless writes: "Only the Christian, *i.e.,* the man who stands within the revelation of Christ, has the true natural knowledge of God." "Nature and Grace" in Barth and Brunner, *Natural Theology,* trans. Peter Fraeknel (London: Geoffrey Bles, 1946), p. 27.

5. Though she goes too far when she suggests that epistemology is a branch of ethics, Linda Zagzebski has persuasively argued that the two fields are close allies at all levels. See her "Virtue in Ethics and Epistemology," *American Catholic Philosophical Quarterly* 71 Supp. (1997), pp. 1–17.

6. For a contemporary example, see David M. Smolin's Review of Michael J. Perry, *Love and Power, Iowa Law Review* 76 (1991). For background, see Bradley J. Longfield, *The Presbyterian Conflict* (New York: Oxford University Press, 1991), esp. chap. 2 on J. Gresham Machen. Stanley Fish suggests a secular analogue of Calvinism; see his "Mission Impossible: Settling the Just Bounds Between Church and State," *Columbia Law Review* 97, no. 8 (December 1997), pp. 2225–2333; also his controversy with Richard John Neuhaus, "Why We Can/Can't Get Along," *First Things* no. 60 (February 1996), pp. 18–40. Disguised epistemological Calvinism appears in the Roman Catholic world under the name of integralism, as manifested in the Oath Against Modernism, for example. See Gabriel Daly, O.S.A., *Transcendence and Immanence: A Study in Catholic Modernism and Integralism* (Oxford: Clarendon Press, 1980) and Marvin R. O'Connell, *Critics on Trial: An Introduction to the Catholic Modernist Crisis* (Washington, D.C.: Catholic University of America, 1994). Russell Hittinger suggests a contemporary version of integralism in his essay, "Natural Law and Catholic Moral Theology," *A Preserving Grace,* chap. 1. The integralist outlook has also garnered Protestant support; see Stanley Hauerwas, *In*

Good Company (Notre Dame, Ind.: University of Notre Dame Press, 1995), especially the essay "The Importance of Being Catholic: Unsolicited Advice from a Protestant Bystander."

7. Schmitt, *Political Theology: Four Chapters on the Theory of Sovereignty,* ed. and trans. George Schwab (Cambridge, Mass.: MIT Press, 1983), p. 62. See also his *The Concept of the Political,* ed. and trans. George Schwab (New Brunswick: Rutgers, 1976). For an account of Schmitt's views and influence see Mark Lilla, "The Enemy of Liberalism," *New York Review of Books,* 15 May 1997, pp. 38–44.

8. See Phillip E. Johnson, *Reason in the Balance: The Case Against NATURALISM in Science, Law, and Education* (Downers Grove, Ill.: InterVarsity Press, 1995); quotation, p. 104; see also his chap. 2 on "The Established Religious Philosophy of America." For a more moderate view, see Nicholas P. Wolterstorff, "Why We Should Reject What Liberalism Tells Us," in *Religion and Contemporary Liberalism,* ed. Paul J. Weithman (Notre Dame, Ind.: University of Notre Dame Press, 1997), pp. 162–81.

9. *Liberty, Equality, Fraternity,* ed. R.J. White (Cambridge: Cambridge University Press, 1967), p. 165.

10. The claim of inevitability is traditional. Thus the Athenians in the *Melian Dialogues:* "Our opinion of the gods and our knowledge of men lead us to conclude that it is a general and necessary law of nature to rule whenever one can." Thucydides, *The Peloponesian War,* Bk. V, sec. 105; trans. Rex Warner, ed. M.I. Finley (Harmondsworth: Penguin, 1972), p. 404.

11. For an argument to this effect concerning religious knowledge, see John Greco, "Catholics vs. Calvinists on Religious Knowledge," *American Catholic Philosophical Quarterly* 71, no. 1 (winter 1997), pp. 13–34.

12. Kekes, *Against Liberalism* (Ithaca, N.Y.: Cornell University Press, 1997), p. 202; emphasis mine.

13. The linkage between Calvinism and libertinism has been most engagingly explored in the aftermath of the Jansenist movement. In the Abbé Prévost's *Manon Lescaut,* a young man entangled with a mercenary woman remarks: "Ah, yes, duty says I should practice what I preach, but am I capable of any action at all? Think of the help I should need to make me forget Manon's charms? . . . I do not know what I am, and I am not at all sure what I ought to be, but I am experiencing all too clearly the truth of what the Jansenists say." Second edition, trans. Leonard Tancock, ed. Jean Sgard (London: Penguin, 1991), p. 68.

14. See Peter Novick, *That Noble Dream* (Cambridge: Cambridge University Press, 1988), who points out that doubts about historical objectivity followed on the inability of historians to agree.

15. On "secular" versions of this outlook, see Tony Judt, *Past Imperfect* (Berkeley and Los Angeles: University of California Press, 1992), esp. chaps. 4, 9, 11, 12. Note Sartre's outburst: "An anti-Communist is a dog, I don't change my views on this, I never shall." *Situations,* vol. 4 (Paris, 1961), pp. 248–49, quoted at p. 180.

16. The discussion of the role of natural law in *A Preserving Grace* ends up turning on strategic questions of this sort. *Religion and Contemporary Liberalism* contains an up-to-date discussion of the resulting philosophical and political issues.

17. Parenthetical references are to the *City of God.*

18. The phrase is used to describe abortion in *De Nuptiis et Concupiscentia,* Bk. I, chap. 15. Quoted in Germain Grisez, *Abortion* (New York: Corpus, 1970), p. 145.

19. See Cicero, *On the Republic,* Bk. III, chap. 14, sec. 24; and chap. 31, sec. 43.

20. For three very different contemporary renderings of Augustine's political concepts, see Ernest L. Fortin, Introduction to Augustine, *Political Writings,* trans. Michael W. Tkacz and Douglas Kries, ed. Ernest L. Fortin and Douglas Kries (Indianapolis, Ind.: Hackett, 1994); R.A. Markus, *Saeculum* (Cambridge: Cambridge University Press, 1970); and John Milbank, *Theology and Social Theory* (Oxford: Basil Blackwell, 1991). I have also benefited from the older discussion by John Neville Figgis, *The Political Aspects of S. Augustine's 'City of God'* (Gloucester, Mass.: Peter Smith, 1963 [orig.: 1921]), esp. chaps. 4–5.

21. For Machiavelli on religion, see *Discourses,* Bk. I, chaps. 11–15; Bk. II, chap. 2.

Appendix: Hell

1. For valuable historical studies, see D.P. Walker, *The Decline of Hell* (London: Routledge and Kegan Paul, 1964); and Geoffrey Rowell, *Hell and the Victorians* (Oxford: Clarendon, 1974).

2. The detailed views on hell attributed to St. Thomas Aquinas in the *Supplementum,* edited by a disciple from an immature work, may not reflect the Angelic Doctor's mature mind. See the Editor's note in the *Summa Theologica (= Summa Theologiae),* trans. Dominican Fathers (New York: Benziger Brothers, 1948), vol. 3, p. 2573. *The Catechism of the Catholic Church* (Liguori, Mo.: Liguori Publications, 1994) asserts the existence and eternity of hell, but not the everlasting suffering of named or anonymous persons: it observes that "the chief punishment of hell is eternal separation from God," but for the rest takes refuge in the paradoxical expression "eternal fire." Para. 1035.

3. In contrast with the approach taken here, two recent book-length philosophical discussions of hell view it as a specially difficult case for the problem of evil; see Jonathan Kvanvig, *The Problem of Hell* (New York: Oxford University Press, 1993); and Jerry L. Wallis, *Hell* (Notre Dame, Ind.: University of Notre Dame Press, 1992), especially the Introductions to both books.

4. Wells, "Eternal Punishment," *Christianity Today,* 20 March 1987, p. 41.

5. This sentence is prompted by Wallis, pp. 105–10.

6. This clause is prompted by Peter Geach, *Providence and Evil* (Cambridge: Cambridge University Press, 1977), pp. 124–26.

7. Lewis, *The Problem of Pain* (New York: Macmillan, 1971), p. 127. Wallis (chap. 5) provides a detailed account on how this might happen. Another statement of Lewis's views on hell, which presents a number of difficulties of interpretation, is *The Great Divorce* (New York: Macmillan, 1946), esp. chaps. 9, 13, 14.

8. Quoted in Kvanvig, p. 109.

9. *Cathechism,* para. 1037.

10. Geach, *Providence and Evil,* p. 145.

11. Kvanvig, *The Problem of Hell,* pp. 70–71.

12. The quotation is from ibid., p. 68.

13. Lewis, *The Problem of Pain,* pp. 125, 127. For discussion of this aspect of Lewis's position, see Kvanvig, pp. 120–23.

14. Geach, *Providence and Evil,* pp. 141, 149.

15. Pinnock "Fire, Then Nothing," *Christianity Today,* 20 March 1987, pp. 40–41. Such views are very popular among Evangelicals; for a review of the debates, see Tony Gray, "Destroyed For Ever," *Themelios* 21, no. 2 (1996), pp. 14–18.

16. Kvanvig, *The Problem of Hell,* pp. 152, 171, 158.

17. Kvanvig relies heavily on the concept of rational suicide in evaluating doctrines of hell (see esp. pp. 83–87, 138–44, 149–52).

18. See *The Ethics of Homicide* (Ithaca, N.Y.: Cornell University Press, 1978; Notre Dame, Ind.: University of Notre Dame Press, 1990), secs. 3, 26.

19. Wallis, *Hell,* p. 137, citing *The Problem of Pain,* p. 126.

20. Ibid., p. 150, citing Geach, p. 138.

21. Plato, *Laws,* Stephanus 957e, *Gorgias,* Stephanus 512a–b, *Republic,* Stephanus 410a.

22. In a possibly unique discussion of a concrete moral issue, Wittgenstein suggests that suicide is "the elementary sin." *Notebooks,* ed. G.H. von Wright and G.E.M. Anscombe; trans G.E.M. Anscombe (New York: Harper Torchbooks, 1969), p. 91 (entry for 10.1.17). On the theological side, Augustine argues that, since offenses to God do not injure Him, the heart of sin is self-injury (*Confessions,* Bk. III, chap. 10; Bk. IV, chap. 9), suicide being the most thoroughgoing sort of self-injury. St. Thomas Aquinas likewise holds that "God is not offended by us unless we act against our own good" (*Summa Contra Gentiles,* Bk. III, chap. 122, sec. 2).

23. As Lewis says in *The Great Divorce,* p. 69.

24. Ibid., pp. 77–78.

25. Kvanvig, *The Problem of Hell,* p. 76.

26. Colwell, *Actuality and Provisionality* (Edinburgh: Rutherford House, 1989), p. 265. For textual support for this interpretation, see Barth, *Church Dogmatics,* vol. 2, pt. 2, ed. G.W. Bromiley and T.F. Torrance, trans. G.W. Bromiley et al. (Edinburgh: T. & T. Clark, 1957), pp. 477, 484, 496.

27. Von Balthasar, *Dare We Hope "That All Men be Saved"?,* trans. David Kipp and Lothar Krauth (San Francisco: Ignatius Press, 1988), p. 187. Similar views are defended by Karl Rahner, *Theological Investigations,* vol. 4, trans. Kevyn Smith, (Baltimore: Helicon Press, 1966), pp. 338–39 and n.16.

28. On the obligation to hope for everyone's salvation, see von Balthasar, pp. 211–21; at p. 187, however, he is content to argue that such hopes are permissible.

29. According to the *Catechism of the Catholic Church,* angels are immortal, but the possibility is left open that devils have lost this quality through their fall, as did Adam and Eve; see paras. 391–93, 330, 400. See also von Balthasar, pp. 143–47.

30. Many Protestants, including C.S. Lewis and Jerry L. Wallis (p. 169 n.11), now accept the doctrine of purgatory. Wallis's doctrine is untraditional in at least one respect, however: he allows for sanctifying grace after death (e.g., pp. 92, 100).

31. Dubious economic metaphors persist in the literature, as when Jerry L. Wallis speculates about "what proportion of persons a perfectly good God would judge it tolerable to lose" (p. 103).

Selected Bibliography

Note: Listing is limited to works of relevance to more than one chapter.

OF GENERAL PHILOSOPHICAL INTEREST

Anscombe, G.E.M. *Intention,* 2nd edition. Oxford: Basil Blackwell, 1963.

Aristotle. *Basic Works*. Ed. Richard McKeon. Random House Lifelong Library. New York: Random House, 1941.

Boyle, Joseph, Germain Grisez, and Olaf Tollefsen. *Free Choice.* Notre Dame, Ind.: University of Notre Dame Press, 1976.

Devine, Philip E. *Relativism, Nihilism, and God.* Notre Dame, Ind.: University of Notre Dame Press, 1989.

Finnis, John. "Scepticism, Self-Refutation, and the Good of Truth." *Law, Morality, and Society.* Ed. P.M.S. Hacker and J. Raz. Oxford: Clarendon Press, 1977. Chap. 14.

Geertz, Clifford. *Local Knowledge.* New York: Basic Books, 1983.

Gibbard, Allan. *Wise Choices, Apt Feelings.* Cambridge, Mass.: Harvard University Press, 1990.

Gillespie, Michael Allen. *Nihilism Before Nietzsche.* Chicago: University of Chicago Press, 1995.

Johnson, Phillip E. *Reason in the Balance: The Case Against NATURALISM in Science, Law, and Education.* Downers Grove, Ill.: InterVarsity Press, 1995.

Lampert, Laurence. *Leo Strauss and Nietzsche.* Chicago: University of Chicago Press, 1996.

Margolis, Joseph. *The Truth About Relativism.* Oxford: Basil Blackwell, 1991.

McDowell, John. *Mind and World.* Cambridge, Mass.: Harvard University Press, 1994.

Nisbet, Robert and Lee Ross. *Human Inference: Strategies and Shortcomings of Social Judgment.* Ed. Walter Mischel et al. Century Psychology Series. Englewood Cliffs, N.J.: Prentice-Hall, 1980.

Plato. *Crito. Gorgias. Laws. Republic.* All in *Collected Dialogues.* Ed. Edith Hamilton and Huntington Cairns. New York: Pantheon, 1961.

Putnam, Hilary. *Realism with a Human Face.* Cambridge, Mass.: Harvard University Press, 1990.

Schwartz, Benjamin I. *The World of Thought in Ancient China.* Cambridge, Mass.: Harvard University Press, 1985.

Searle, John. *The Construction of Social Reality.* New York: The Free Press, 1995.

———. *The Rediscovery of the Mind.* Cambridge, Mass.: Bradford/MIT, 1992.

Steup, Matthias. *An Introduction to Contemporary Epistemology.* Upper Saddle River, N.J.: Prentice-Hall, 1996.

St. Thomas Aquinas. *Summa Theologiae.* Madrid: Biblioteca de Autores Christianos, 1952. I have used both the older Dominican Fathers and more recent Blackfriars translations.

Zagzebski, Linda. "Virtue in Ethics and Epistemology." *American Catholic Philosophical Quarterly* 71 Supp. (1997): 1–17.

ETHICAL THEORY

Aristotle. *Nicomachean Ethics.* Trans. and ed. Martin Ostwald. Library of Liberal Arts, Oskar Piest, founder. Indianapolis, Ind.: Bobbs-Merrill, 1962.

Arkes, Hadley. *First Things: An Inquiry Into the First Principles of Morals and Justice.* Princeton: Princeton University Press, 1986.

Barden, Garret. *After Principles.* Notre Dame, Ind.: University of Notre Dame Press, 1990.

Clarke, Stanley G. and Evan Simpson, eds., *Anti-Theory in Ethics and Moral Conservatism.* Albany, N.Y.: SUNY, 1989.

Devine, Philip E. "A Fallacious Argument against Moral Absolutes." *Argumentation* 9, no. 4 (November 1995): 611–16.

Donagan, Alan. *The Theory of Morality.* Chicago: University of Chicago Press, 1977.

Finnis, John. *Fundamentals of Ethics.* Washington, D.C.: Georgetown University Press, 1983.

———. *Moral Absolutes.* Washington, D.C.: Catholic University of America Press, 1991.

———. *Natural Law and Natural Rights.* Clarendon Law Series. Oxford: Clarendon Press, 1980.

George, Robert P., ed. *Natural Law Theory: Contemporary Essays.* Oxford: Clarendon Press, 1992.

Grisez, Germain. "The First Principle of the Practical Reason," *Natural Law Forum* 10 (1965): 168–201.

Haakonssen, Knud. *Natural Law and Moral Philosophy: From Grotius to the Scottish Enlightenment.* Cambridge: Cambridge University Press, 1996.

Haber, Joram Graf, ed. *Absolutism and Its Consequentialist Critics.* Lanham, Md.: Rowman & Littlefield, 1994.

Hittinger, Russell. *The New Natural Law Theory.* Notre Dame, Ind.: University of Notre Dame Press, 1988.

Hodgson, D.H. *The Consequences of Utilitarianism.* Oxford: Clarendon Press, 1967.

Kant, Immanuel. *Grounding for the Metaphysics of Morals.* Trans. James W. Ellington. In *Classics of Western Philosophy,* 3rd edition. Ed. Stephen A. Cahn. Indianapolis, Ind.: Hackett, 1990.

Lee, Patrick. "Is St. Thomas's Natural Law Theory Naturalist?" *American Catholic Philosophical Quarterly* 71, no. 4 (autumn 1997): 567–87.

———. "The Permanence of the Ten Commandments," *Theological Studies* 42 (September 1981).

MacIntyre, Alasdair. *After Virtue,* rev. edition. Notre Dame, Ind.: University of Notre Dame Press, 1984.

———. *Three Rival Versions of Moral Enquiry.* Notre Dame, Ind.: University of Notre Dame Press, 1990.

McCormick, Richard A., S.J., and Paul Ramsey, eds. *Doing Evil to Achieve Good.* Chicago: Loyola University Press, 1978.

Pieper, Joseph. *The Four Cardinal Virtues.* Notre Dame, Ind.: University of Notre Dame Press, 1966.

Raz, Joseph. *The Morality of Freedom.* Oxford: Clarendon Press, 1986.

Scheffler, Samuel D., ed. *Consequentialism and Its Critics.* Oxford Readings in Philosophy. Oxford: Oxford University Press, 1988.

Sommers, Christina and Fred Sommers, eds. *Vice & Virtue in Everyday Life: Introductory Readings in Ethics.* 3rd edition. San Diego: Harcourt Brace Jovanovich, 1993. 4th edition, 1997.

Stout, Jeffrey. *Ethics after Babel.* Boston: Beacon Press, 1988.

Sullivan, Denis. "Intrinsically Evil Acts: Clarifying a Confused Debate." *American Catholic Philosophical Quarterly.* 72 Supp. (1998):329–40. Appeared too late to take into account here.

Teichman, Jenny. "Is Anything Sacred?" *Providence: Studies in Western Civilization* 2 (fall 1993): 27–34.

———. "What Is Sacred?" *New Criterion.* (November 1993): 8–15.

SELECTED MORAL ISSUES

Life and Death

Cohen, Marshall, Thomas Nagel, and Thomas Scanlon, eds. *War and Moral Responsibility.* Princeton: Princeton University Press, 1974.

Devine, Philip E. *The Ethics of Homicide.* Ithaca, N.Y.: Cornell University Press, 1978; Notre Dame, Ind.: University of Notre Dame Press, 1990.

———. "Relativism, Abortion, and Tolerance." *Philosophy and Phenomenological Research* 48 (1987): 131–38.

Finnis, John, Germain Grisez, and Joseph Boyle. *Nuclear Deterrence, Morality, and Realism.* Oxford: Clarendon Press, 1987.

Grisez, Germain. *Abortion.* New York: Corpus, 1970.

Hendin, Herbert. "Physician-Assisted Suicide: What Next?" *Responsive Community* 7, no. 4 (fall 1997): 21–34.

John Paul II. *The Gospel of Life (Evangelium Vitae).* Boston: Pauline, n.d.

Kamisar, Yale. "Euthanasia Legislation: Some Non-Religious Objections." In A.B. Downing, ed. *Euthanasia and the Right to Death.* Los Angeles: Nash, 1970.

Kliever, Lonnie D., ed. *Dax's Case.* Dallas: Southern Methodist University Press, 1989.

Novak, David. "Suicide Is Not a Private Choice." *First Things* no. 75 (August/September 1997): 31–43.

Stith, Richard. "On Death and Dworkin." *Maryland Law Review* 56, no. 2 (1997): 289–383.

Uhlmann. Michael M., ed. *Last Rights? Assisted Suicide and Euthanasia Debated.* Washington, D.C.: Ethics and Public Policy Center; Grand Rapids, Mich: Wm. B. Eerdmans, 1998.

Environmental Issues

Attfield, Robin and Andrew Bosley, eds. *Philosophy and the Natural Environment.* Cambridge: Cambridge University Press, 1994.

Callicot, J. Baird. "Animal Liberation: A Triangular Affair." *Environmental Ethics* 2, no. 4 (winter 1980): 311–38. Reprinted in *People, Penguins, and Plastic Trees.* Ed. Donald VanDeVeer and Christine Peirce. Belmont, Calif.: Wadsworth, 1986: 184–203.

Devine, Philip E. "The Moral Basis of Vegetarianism." *Philosophy.* October, 1978.

List, Peter, ed., *Radical Environmentalism.* Belmont, Calif.: Wadsworth, 1993.

Regan, Tom and Peter Singer, eds., *Animal Rights and Human Obligations,* 2nd edition. Englewood Cliffs, N.J.: Prentice-Hall, 1989.

Sex

Derrick, Christopher. *Sex and Sacredness.* San Francisco: Ignatius, 1982.

Devine, Philip E. "Birth, Copulation, and Death." *New Scholasticism.* (summer 1985).

Devine, Philip E. and Celia Wolf-Devine. *Sex and Gender.* Belmont, Calif.: Wadsworth, forthcoming, 2000.

Finnis, John. "Law, Morality, and 'Sexual Orientation.'" *Notre Dame Journal of Law, Ethics, and Public Policy* 9 (1995).

Ford, John, S.J., et al. *The Teaching of Humanae Vitae.* San Francisco: Ignatius, 1988.

George, Robert P. and Gerard V. Bradley. "Marriage and the Liberal Imagination." *Georgetown Law Journal* 84 (December, 1995): 301ff.

Paul VI. *Humanae Vitae* (1968). Trans. in Claudia Carlen, I.H.M. ed., *The Papal Encyclicals, 1958–1981.* N.p.: Consortium, 1981.

Scruton, Roger. *Sexual Desire.* New York: Free Press, 1986.

Wojtyla, Karol (John Paul II). *Love and Responsibility.* Trans. H.T. Willetts New York: Farrar Straus & Giroux, 1981.

SOCIAL AND POLITICAL PHILOSOPHY

Aristotle. *The Politics.* Ed. and trans. Carnes Lord. Chicago: University of Chicago Press, 1984.

Buckle, Stephen. *Natural Law and the Theory of Property.* Oxford: Clarendon, 1991.

Devlin, Patrick. *The Enforcement of Morals.* London: Oxford University Press, 1965.

Garvey, John H. *What are Freedoms For?* Cambridge, Mass.: Harvard University Press, 1996.

George, Robert P. *Making Men Moral: Civil Liberties and Public Morality.* Oxford: Clarendon Press, 1993.

Nagel, Thomas. *Equality and Partiality.* New York: Oxford University Press, 1991.

Rawls, John. "The Idea of Public Reason Revisited." *University of Chicago Law Review* 64, no. 3 (summer, 1997): 765–802.

———. *Political Liberalism.* New York: Columbia University Press, 1993. The introduction to the paperback edition (1996) seriously modifies Rawls's theory.

———. *A Theory of Justice.* Cambridge, Mass: Harvard University Press, 1971.

Sandel, Michael J. *Liberalism and the Limits of Justice,* 2nd edition. Cambridge: Cambridge University Press, 1998. The second edition contains a decisive refutation of the later Rawls.

Shapiro, Ian. *The Evolution of Rights in Liberal Theory.* Cambridge: Cambridge University Press, 1986.

St. Thomas Aquinas. *Selected Political Writings.* Ed. A.P. D'Entrèves. Trans. J.G. Dawson. Oxford: Basil Blackwell, 1978.

Walzer, Michael. *On Toleration.* New Haven: Yale University Press, 1997.

———. *Thick and Thin.* Notre Dame, Ind.: University of Notre Dame Press, 1994.

Wolfe, Christopher and John Hittinger, eds. *Liberalism at the Crossroads.* Lanham, Md.: Rowman and Littlefield, 1994.

RELIGION

Allsopp, Michael E. and John J. O'Keefe, eds. *Veritatis Splendor: American Responses.* Kansas City: Sheed and Ward, 1995.

Barth, Karl. *Church Dogmatics.* Ed. G.W. Bromiley and T.F. Torrance. Trans. G.W. Bromiley et al. Edinburgh: T. & T. Clark, 1957.

Bellah, Robert. *The Broken Covenant.* New York: Seabury Crossroad, 1975.

Berger, Peter L. *The Sacred Canopy.* Garden City, N.Y.: Doubleday Anchor, 1969.

Braaten, Carl and Robert Jenson, eds. *The Two Cities of God: The Church's Responsibility for the Earthly City.* Grand Rapids, Mich.: Eerdmans, 1997.

Carter, Stephen L. *The Culture of Disbelief.* New York: Basic Books, 1993.

Catechism of the Catholic Church. Liguori, Mo.: Liguori Publications, 1994.

Chadwick, Owen. *From Bossuet to Newman,* 2nd edition. Cambridge: Cambridge University Press, 1987.

Clouser, Roy A. *The Myth of Religious Neutrality.* Notre Dame, Ind.: University of Notre Dame Press, 1990.

Cromartie, Michael, ed. *A Preserving Grace.* Grand Rapids, Mich.: William B. Eerdmans, 1997.

———. *No Longer Exiles.* Washington, D.C.: Ethics and Public Policy Center, 1993.

Fish, Stanley. "Mission Impossible: Settling the Just Bounds Between Church and State." *Columbia Law Review* 97, no. 8 (December, 1997): 2255–2333.

Grasso, Kenneth L., Gerard V. Bradley, and Robert P. Hunt, eds. *Catholicism, Liberalism, and Communitarianism.* Lanham, Md.: Rowman and Littlefield, 1995.

John Paul II. *Fides et Ratio. Origins* 28, no. 19 (22 October 1998): 317–347. Appeared too late to take into account in this book.

———. *Veritatis Splendor. Origins* 23, no. 18 (14 October 1993): 297–334.

Johnston, Douglas and Cynthia Sampson, eds. *Religion, The Missing Dimension of Statecraft.* Oxford: Oxford University Press, 1994.

Jurgensmeyer, Mark. *The New Cold War?* Berkeley and Los Angeles: University of California Press, 1994.

Milbank, John. *Theology and Social Theory.* Oxford: Basil Blackwell, 1990.

Murphy, Nancey. *Theology in the Age of Scientific Reasoning.* Ithaca, N.Y.: Cornell University Press, 1990.

Outka, Gene H. and Paul Ramsey, eds. *Norm and Context in Christian Ethics.* New York: Charles Scribner's Sons, 1968.

Pennock, J. Ronald and John W. Chapman, eds. "Religion, Morality, and the Law." *Nomos: Yearbook of the American Society for Political and Legal Philosophy.* Vol. 30. New York: New York University Press, 1988. Very valuable.

Pinkaers, Servais, O.P. *The Sources of Christian Ethics.* Trans. from the 3rd edition by Sr. Mary Thomas Noble, O.P. Washington, D.C.: Catholic University of America Press, 1995.

Schmitt, Carl. *Political Theology: Four Chapters on the Theory of Sovereignty.* Trans. George Schwab. Cambridge, Mass.: MIT Press, 1983.

Skillen, James W. *The Scattered Voice.* Grand Rapids: Zondervan, 1990. Discusses the varieties of ways Christians have approached political issues.

Smolin, David M. Review of Michael J. Perry, *Love and Power. Iowa Law Review* 76 (1991): 1067–104.

St. Augustine. *Confessions.* Many editions.

———. *City of God.* Many editions. Excerpted in *Political Writings.* Trans. Michael W. Tkacz and Douglas Kries. Ed. Ernest L. Fortin and Douglas Kries. Indianapolis, Ind.: Hackett, 1994.

Weithman, Paul J., ed. *Religion and Contemporary Liberalism.* Notre Dame, Ind.: University of Notre Dame Press, 1997.

Index

About the Author

PHILIP E. DEVINE is Professor of Philosophy at Providence College, where he frequently teaches in the Program on the Development of Western Civilization. He is the author of *The Ethics of Homicide* (1978), *Relativism, Nihilism and God* (1989), and *Human Diversity and the Culture Wars* (Praeger, 1996).

ISBN 0-313-30702-4
90000>
EAN
9 780313 307027
HARDCOVER BAR CODE